LESLIE STAROBIN

Ann Braude is Director of the Women's Studies in Religion Program and Senior Lecturer on American Religious History at Harvard Divinity School. She is also the author of *Radical Spirits: Spiritualism and Women's Rights in Nineteenth-Century America*, and *Women and American Religion*, and co-editor of *Root of Bitterness: Documents of the Social History of American Women* (2nd edition).

Transforming the Faiths
of Our Fathers

BL
72
.T73
2004

Transforming
the Faiths
of Our Fathers

WOMEN WHO CHANGED
AMERICAN RELIGION

Edited by

Ann Braude

MAY 1 9 2005

TRANSFORMING THE FAITHS OF OUR FATHERS
Copyright © Ann Braude, 2004.
All rights reserved. No part of this book may be used or reproduced in any
manner whatsoever without written permission except in the case of brief
quotations embodied in critical articles or reviews.

First published 2004 by
PALGRAVE MACMILLAN™
175 Fifth Avenue, New York, N.Y. 10010 and
Houndmills, Basingstoke, Hampshire, England RG21 6XS.
Companies and representatives throughout the world.

PALGRAVE MACMILLAN is the global academic imprint of the Palgrave
Macmillan division of St. Martin's Press, LLC and of Palgrave Macmillan Ltd.
Macmillan® is a registered trademark in the United States, United Kingdom
and other countries. Palgrave is a registered trademark in the European Union
and other countries.

ISBN 1–4039–6460–2 hardback

Library of Congress Cataloging-in-Publication Data
Transforming the faiths of our fathers : women who changed American
religion / edited by Ann Braude.
    p. cm.
Includes bibliographical references and index.
ISBN 1–4039–6460–2 (cloth)
    1. Women religious leaders—United States—Biography. 2. Religious
leaders—United States—Biography. 3. Feminists—United States—
Biography. I. Braude, Ann.

BL72.T73 2004
200'.92'273—dc22
                                                                    2003063525

A catalogue record for this book is available from the British Library.

Design by Letra Libre, Inc.

First edition: June 2004
10 9 8 7 6 5 4 3 2 1

Printed in the United States of America.

For my father
Marvin Braude

CONTENTS

ACKNOWLEDGMENTS

A GENEROUS GRANT FROM THE E. RHODES AND LEONA B. CARPENTER Foundation made possible both this book and the conference on which it is based. The Religion and the Feminist Movement Conference took place November 1–3, 2002, sponsored by the Women's Studies in Religion Program at Harvard Divinity School. My greatest thanks go to the women who changed American religion, both those included here and the legions who are not. I thank especially those who spoke at the conference but could not be included in the book: Mary Daly, Roberta Hestenes, Mary Hunt, Gerda Lerner, Jeanne Audrey Powers, Donna Quinn, Letty Russell, Betty Bone Schiess, and Addie Wyatt. I am also grateful to Nan Self and Viscontes C. Johnsen, as well as to the 300 participants who attended the conference. The Cloverleaf Foundation generously supported Canadian participants. A senior fellowship from the Yale Institute for the Study of American Religion enabled me to edit this volume, as well as to work on the larger research project of which it is a part.

The conceptualization of the project benefited immeasurably from conversations with Leila Ahmed, Clarissa Atkinson, Sara Evans, Carolyn de Swaarte Gifford, Emilie Townes, Judith Plaskow, Joan Martin, Mary Hunt, Elisabeth Schüssler Fiorenza, Rosemary Radford Ruether, Kathleen Sands, Ann Taves, Laurel Ulrich, and Gale Yee. At later stages Carol Hurd Green, Colleen McDannel, Jan Schipps, Eleanor Gadon, and Sue Horner made important suggestions.

I am particularly grateful to the Director's Council of the Harvard Divinity School Women's Studies in Religion Program for their encouragement, guidance, and support, especially Lynda Goldstein, Kathy Borgen, Helen La Kelly Hunt, and Letty Cottin Pogrebin. I also appreciate the personal interest in the project of the Reverend Ann B. Day, president of the Carpenter Foundation.

At Harvard Divinity School, Dean William Graham, Susan Sherwin, Tom Jenkins and Nancy Birne lent invaluable support. Natasha Goldman served as an outstanding conference organizer, and Alyson Dickson provided expert research assistance and helped in innumerable other ways, as did Monique Moultrie, Katy Attanasi, Susanna Drake, Laurene Waltman, Brenna Daugherty, and Tracy Wall. The twenty-five Harvard Divinity School students who volunteered at and before the conference helped make it both possible and worthwhile.

My husband, Andy Adler, held our family together before and during the conference, and at all the other times. This book is dedicated to my father, Marvin Braude, who was present at every minute of the conference. During his thirty-two years of public service on the Los Angeles City Council, he taught me that individuals can change the world.

INTRODUCTION

Ann Braude

A GENERATION HAS COME OF AGE THAT NEVER EXPERIENCED religion before the women's movement. If you were born after 1965, you may not remember when inclusive language was unknown, when a woman minister was a curiosity, when brides routinely vowed before God and family to "obey" their husbands. Many of this generation have never covered their heads to enter a church or seen nuns concealed from head to foot in habits. They don't remember when a woman could not read the Torah in a synagogue or when a girl could not assist the priest as an alter server in a Catholic church.

These changes, and the new world they herald, did not come about by themselves. Nor are they universal. Where new language, liturgy, ritual, and policy exist, we owe them to the actions and insights of individuals committed to expanding the practice of their faiths to incorporate the full humanity of women. Change followed concerted efforts to convince religious communities that treating women as equals with men was consistent with the will of God.

In the following pages, the women who ignited these transformations tell their stories. Their lives bear witness to watershed events that changed the practice of many religions forever. In their ordinations, excommunications, confrontations with authority, and revelations of power we see history in the making. We see ancient traditions grappling with modern values and women of faith struggling to reconcile loyalties that sometimes came into conflict.

The women who tell their stories in this book understand their efforts as part of the movement to secure equal rights for women, the movement to liberate women and men from internal and external assumptions about limits on women's abilities or potential—the movement known as feminism.

The conjunction of religion and feminism may surprise. On both the right and the left, pundits portray religion and feminism as inherently incompatible, as opposing forces in American culture. On one hand, some feminists assume that religious women are brainwashed apologists for patriarchy suffering from false consciousness. They believe allegiance to religious communities or organizations renders women incapable of authentic advocacy on women's behalf. On the other hand, religious hierarchies often discourage or prohibit women's public leadership. Some leaders assume that those who work to enhance women's status lack authentic faith. Many accounts of second-wave feminism reinforce these views by mentioning religion only when it is a source of opposition, usually to the Equal Rights Amendment or to reproductive freedoms. Meanwhile, among theological conservatives, religious feminism is often portrayed as a subversive attempt to mislead the faithful, while feminism in general is described as an agent of secularism or as destructive of religious values.

As a historian, the portrayal of religion and feminism as antithetical appears to me to be inaccurate, a misreading of America's past. When Elizabeth Cady Stanton and Lucretia Mott called the first women's rights convention in Seneca Falls in 1848, they included religion.[1] Participants were asked to consider the "social, civil, *and religious* conditions and rights of woman." Similarly, when the "second wave" of American feminism began in the 1960s, vibrant feminist movements emerged within most American religious groups. While the religious climate of the period helped ignite the discontent with women's limited options described in Betty Friedan's *The Feminine Mystique* (1963), it also nurtured strains that inspired rebellion against it.

Unlike their secular counterparts, religious feminists did not have to build women's networks from scratch. Large and well-organized church and synagogue women's groups devoured *The Feminine Mystique* when it appeared in 1963. "What kind of woman are you? Betty Friedan will help you decide," promised a 1963 invitation to a Sisterhood luncheon at Temple Emanu-el in Dallas, Texas. The book was required reading for the 175 national leaders of Methodist women whose 1963 meeting was devoted to "Women in a New Age." Those 175 used what they learned to lead the 1.2 million members of United Methodist Women. In contrast, it would be another six years before the National Organization for Women was founded to pursue the concerns raised in Friedan's book, and NOW's membership would never match that of United Methodist Women.

In 1965, a year before the founding of NOW, Church Women United sponsored a Committee on the Changing Role of Women that insisted on the need to make "a radical challenge to the Church . . . and raise the question of why the Church is not practicing what it preaches." Although not as large as women's religious organizations, the National Organization for Women also combined attention to religion and feminism. From its first year, it sponsored a Women and Religion Task Force, which worked for the ordination of women, inclusive language, and equal rights for laywomen. Like Stanton and Mott, the NOW task force viewed the right to practice one's religion in equality with men as part of the platform of women's rights.

The appearance of religiously oriented antifeminist groups has obscured the existence and impact of religious feminism in the public eye. But in today's world, in which religious values play an increasing role in public policy debates, religious feminisms are more important than ever. If these voices are ignored, then religion is abandoned to those who would use it to restrict women's possibilities. More than 90 percent of Americans profess belief in God. If feminism is in fact incompatible with religion, it can never have the far-reaching impact for which its proponents hope.

As a group, religious feminists have worked over the last forty years to lift the religious women of the ages from obscurity, to acknowledge their roles in scripture, ministry, theology, worship, teaching, and devotion. Imagining and constructing nonsexist religious models for the women and men of the future, they have critiqued the conditions that fostered women's exclusion, so that those conditions can be changed. What a dreadful irony it would be, if their own history, the story of religion's interaction with feminism, fell out of the narrative, just at the moment when the history of the second wave is being written and reified in a host of new publications.

To begin to document this history, twenty-five key figures, including the sixteen represented in this volume, came together at Harvard Divinity School to tell their stories.[2] They told those stories to an audience of three hundred women (and five men) over the course of three days. Speakers included Catholic, Protestant, Evangelical, Pentecostal, Jewish, Muslim, Mormon, Buddhist, womanist, mujerista, and goddess feminists. The audience consisted of approximately one-third religious professionals and activists on women's issues, one-third academics, and one-third students, with a healthy smattering of "other." Although the program included the best-published leading lights of religious feminism, many presenters reported that they had never been asked to tell their own stories before and that this was the first conference focusing on the history of which they have been a part.

The presence of religious professionals—denominational officials, clergy, chaplains, lay leaders—as well as feminist leaders who emerged from religious organizations ensured that conversations considered the realities of broad constituencies, both within and beyond religious contexts. A conference born out of a historian's concern to set the record straight grew into an opportunity to bridge the generations, bringing historic leaders of the 1960s and 1970s together with students born after those years, students who will lead in the next generation. The students at the conference represented twenty-three different institutions, including candidates for ordination in several denominations.

The power of personal stories drove the conference. There was not a dry eye in the house when Mormon feminist Margaret Toscano described her excommunication by a board of male elders in her local church. For many the source of her feminism was as startling as her expulsion: Toscano awoke to the God-given reality of women's equality during a sacred ceremony in the Salt Lake City Temple, when women as well as men received the "robes of the holy priesthood." Far from a rejection of her Mormon faith, her essay in this volume narrates a feminist journey rooted in the core of her tradition.

Likewise, for Azizah al-Hibri and Riffat Hassan, Muslim faith instilled consciousness of God's equal regard for men and women that served as a foundation for feminist consciousness. The experience of Muslim feminists points toward both tensions and unexpected alliances that emerge among religious feminists. Hassan and al-Hibri concurred with Evangelical speakers that feminism must be grounded in scripture to reach most women. In contrast, as Hassan's essay recounts, they eventually found themselves at odds with other non-Muslim feminists after an initial acceptance. "As long as they saw me as a deviant within the Islamic tradition, as a rebel, they were very supportive of me," she writes. "But the moment we started talking theology and they realized that I wanted to do my theological work in the context of Islam, that I wanted to work from within the faith perspective, I encountered the worst hostility I have ever encountered in my life." During a year as a women's studies research associate at Harvard Divinity School, Hassan found most in common with the other non-Christian in the group, Goddess feminist Carol P. Christ.

Some of the stories stretched back before the 1960s. Pastor Addie Wyatt described her mother bringing her to the Church of God when they joined the African American migration from rural Mississippi to Chicago in 1930.

> Women were accepted in the ministry of the Church of God in 1930 but even before then, and we had wonderful models of great theologians, preachers, evangelists, teachers, secretaries, ushers, choir members, musicians, and we thought that whatever we wanted to do in God's church was available for us to do. And we also were made to believe that God had prepared a life for us, within us, to do whatever we needed to do to make life better for ourselves and for all people.

Wyatt began her ministry at the age of eight, scouring the neighborhood for children she could bring with her to Sunday school. Only when she went to work in the stockyards of Chicago as a teenager did she experience sexism. "I never really knew that women were discriminated against," she said. "I knew that Blacks were, but I never really knew that women were taught and treated in an inferior manner until I entered the paid workforce." This revelation propelled her into the women's movement, where she served on the commission that planned the 1975 International Women's Year Conference in Houston. It also led her into the labor movement, where she became the first woman International Vice President of the Amalgamated Meat Cutters and Butcher Workers of North America.

Addie Wyatt's experience of encouragement for women within the context of a Black Pentecostal church contrasts starkly with the discouragement received by white evangelicals Roberta Hestenes and Virginia Mollenkott. In fact, Wyatt was nearly unique among conference participants in reporting no tension between her own leadership and expectations within her religious community.

Roberta Hestenes, perhaps the most prominent evangelical to openly embrace the term "feminism," described coming to faith in the context of "dispensational fundamentalism, a very conservative, patriarchal, hierarchical tradition." Raised in an alcoholic and violently abusive home, she did not believe that human beings could care about or love each other, until she joined a small Christian community on her college campus. Experiencing tension between the radical equality of the Christian message and the culture of fundamentalism, she soon found herself forced to choose between a call to Christian service and proscriptions on women's leadership. "Which is the more important thing here," she asked herself, "whether or not you are finding a way to share the love which you have experienced and discovered, or that the person who does that sharing comes wrapped in maleness?"

Pioneers from liberal denominations had just as much work on their hands. Jeanne Audrey Powers, one of the first women ordained in the United Methodist Church in 1958, became a role model and supporter to generations of women clergy, now numbering 8,000 in her denomination. For Betty Bone Schiess, one of the famous "Philadelphia eleven" irregularly ordained before women were officially accepted into the Episcopal priesthood, the struggle for equality did not end with the ordination of women. Letty Russell, one of the first Presbyterian women ordained as well as one of the first female graduates of Harvard Divinity School, described the "the gift of being a misfit." As someone both outside and within the institutional power structure, she felt able to understand "the meaning of hospitality and honoring difference from the side of a stranger." The practice of God's hospitality, she said, "means that I am constantly looking for ways to empower other outsiders in the institutions where I work and live. I always have to ask myself as I gather with a group, 'Who is missing? Who are the ones whose voice is not heard?'" That constant questioning was clearly evident in a seemingly endless series of careers committed to human liberation. Russell's career began with seventeen years in an East Harlem parish, followed by three decades on the faculty of Yale Divinity School. After her retirement, she began teaching in a new international feminist theology program.

Efforts to transform religious communities met with varying degrees of success. Canadian clergywoman Lois Wilson reached the highest levels of leadership, becoming the first woman moderator of the United Church of Canada, a president of the World Council of Churches, chancellor of a university, and eventually a member Canada's senate. Others, like Dominican sister Nadine Foley, question where, if anywhere, communities of women fit in the church, noting that technically sisters are neither clergy nor laity, so they are left out of many church rules and teachings altogether.

While many women worked against sexism within their religious communities, others became convinced that their faith tradition could not be cleansed of sexism and left it behind. Many in both groups took inspiration from the groundbreaking theological work of Mary Daly. Daly returned to Harvard Divinity School for the conference more than thirty years after she was the first woman ever to preach from the pulpit of Harvard's Memorial

Church in 1971. Daly recalled the "antisermon" she gave on that day, leading hundreds of women in a "walk-out" from patriarchal religion into the sunshine outside of Memorial Church.[3] In her introduction to Daly's talk, Mary Hunt spoke of the corporate debt of religious women to Daly's courage and creativity, even if they do not agree with her. "Many women, especially in Christian churches, saw themselves, or were seen, in relation to Mary Daly," Hunt explained. "She was somehow 'out there' and they were somewhere between here and there, working in the space she created between ecclesial institutions and the no-woman's land, better, every woman's land of 'leaving' patriarchal religions behind."

The feminist spirituality movement emerged as an alternative for those who hoped to abandon patriarchal traditions without abandoning spiritual experience and religious community. Wicca, Goddess worship, and a variety of New Age spiritualities incorporated feminism and spread it into new arenas. Carol Christ's searing account of her rejection of Christianity in favor of the Goddess draws us into the depth of thought with which many women made this momentous decision. Vicki Noble's adventures both recall the vibrant creativity of the early women's movement and document the continuing evolution of feminist spirituality.

The vantage point of these stories challenges many well-accepted assumptions about second-wave feminism. The common portrayal of the movement as affecting a relatively narrow and homogeneous group falls away. Attention to Catholic, Evangelical, Mormon, Jewish, and Muslim feminists, for example, suggests the movement's deep and broad reach into every region and sector of American life. Even attention to Protestants points away from stereotyped images, highlighting the participation of African American women such as the Methodist leader Theressa Hoover, the Episcopal priest Pauli Murray, or Presbyterians Thelma Adair and Katie Geneva Cannon, as well as Methodist minister Delores Williams, whose lyrical evocation of womanist experience is included here. Roman Catholic theologian Rosemary Ruether also chose to focus on the issue of race in her talk, questioning the notion that feminist theology began in a predominantly white context. For Latina theologian Ada María Isasi-Diaz, the perception that sexism and poverty were inextricably linked sometimes led to conflict and sometimes generated cooperation with other religious feminists.

Jewish women played central leadership roles in the secular women's movement, but were relatively slow to combine attention to religion and women's rights. Writer Letty Cottin Pogrebin, one of the founders of *Ms.* magazine, takes readers with her as she is forced out of Jewish rituals by her exclusion as a woman and then enabled to return by a feminist movement that convinced her she had a right to participate in her own tradition. Judith Plaskow further explores the particular challenges of being a full participant in a faith in which the separation of men and women has traditionally held the force of religious law. While Plaskow has worked to criticize and change such laws, Blu Greenberg articulates feminism within the context of Orthodox Jewish law.

Perhaps the story that departs most from stereotypes is that of Charlotte Bunch, a founder of the women's liberation movement who went on to become a key figure in the campaign to define women's rights as human rights under international law. She recalls women's leadership being encouraged in the Methodist Youth Movement and the YWCA while it was discouraged in the antiwar movement and other leftist groups. Many participants expressed surprise that such a prominent feminist drew inspiration from women missionaries and church groups. Readers of Hilary Clinton's memoir *Living History* will note a similar pattern in which a mature political agenda continues the goals advocated for a century by Methodist women's organizations and inculcated in Methodist youth groups.

Including religion in feminism's history opens our eyes to the movement's impact on both private and public lives. When religion is ignored, feminism can appear to be concerned exclusively with women's political and economic realities, whereas the transformation of consciousness, including religious outlooks, is surely among its most far-reaching repercussions. Including religion helps correct the traditional foci of men's history: it moves beyond approaches that privilege politics and economics as the most significant arenas of action. The dean of American women's history, Gerda Lerner, helped participants in the conference put individual stories in historical context by giving a two-millennia overview called "Religion and the Creation of Feminist Consciousness." Arguing that wrestling with biblical texts necessarily preceded the birth of feminist consciousness, she placed religious women at the center of this evolution. Her presentation made clear the price of not knowing our history, of having to claim the right to speak anew against the claim that women's silence is required by God.[4]

Once the dramatis personae of the historical drama expands to include religious women, the chronology and regional focus of feminist history begin to shift as well. Many published accounts focus on events in New York and the San Francisco Bay area, and begin to see the movement declining by the mid-1970s. This reflects the focus on one sector of the movement's avant-garde, ignoring important leaders from the Midwest, where religious affiliation was more likely to play a role in public activism than on either coast. For the historical time line, explorations of religious feminism also shift our perspective. The movement spread like groundcover, flowering in some settings long after its vibrancy had diminished elsewhere. While the demise of feminism has been reported frequently, it is only now working its way into some groups, like the Reformed Church of America, a group that is relatively conservative theologically, but has recently decided to ordain women after long debate. Orthodox Judaism, represented here by Blu Greenberg's essay, is another important example. Some of the most astonishing feminist advances there have occurred only in the last four or five years.

The stories in this volume testify to religious women's determination to stake a claim to their faith traditions, refusing to be marginalized. We watch them maintain ties to their communities of faith while transforming them from within and simultaneously participating in the struggle for women's rights in the larger world. In this way their stories may speak to younger women who see in second-wave feminism an exclusive focus on gender that obscured other forms of oppression and other aspects of identity. Whether Latina or Lutheran, Muslim or Methodist, religious feminists pursue women's rights in the context of complex communities.

Stories build bridges. "If you told me an hour ago I'd be crying over the plight of a Mormon woman I would have called you a liar," an African American Catholic told me after Margaret Toscano's presentation. While the stories here are inspiring, the struggles they recount are for the most part incomplete. The largest religious groups in the United States, the Roman Catholic Church and the Southern Baptist Convention, still do not view women as capable of filling their most important leadership roles as ordained clergy. The perspectives that support these viewpoints have gained ground during the last twenty years, since some of feminism's most spectacular victories. As these views advance, we see women once again confronted with the erasure of their history, with the claim that women have never done something, therefore they cannot do it. Restrictions on women's roles are trumpeted as part of "traditional" religious values, when, in fact, they are often neither traditional nor religious. The Southern Baptist Convention's decision to stop ordaining women in 1984, for example, reversed hundreds of years of Baptist tradition giving every congregation the right to call its own minister. Without history, claims that sexism is justified by religious teachings go unchallenged.

Many important individuals and groups were absent from the conference program. The conference lacked Native American tribal members on the program, as well as Asian Americans, Lutherans, and representatives of the YWCA, to name just a few of the significant gaps. I would have loved to have had a Unitarian Universalist tell the story of the 1977 resolution in which that denomination's General Assembly called on all its members "to examine carefully their own religious beliefs and the extent to which these beliefs influence sex-role stereotypes." I would have loved to have a member of the Greek Orthodox church explain Orthodox feminists' pursuit of the deaconate. I was grateful that most of these groups were well represented in the audience, for no one person knows the whole history that the conference began to reconstruct. No single view encompasses feminism's passage across the broad landscape of American religion, emerging with new vibrancy here just when things looked most desperate there. The speakers were given a formidable assignment: to narrate the watershed moments of some long and illustrious journeys in twenty minutes or less. They were asked to keep their accounts brief to leave time for discussion, when those in the audience who had other pieces of the story could add it. Together we began to piece together a multifaceted narrative that still needs to be told.

During discussion at the conference, many young women told their own stories, stories that both diverged from and intersected with those in this volume. While some conditions and experiences of the 1960s and 1970s seem inconceivable today, others are frustratingly familiar. Students told of struggles to combine work for women with family life, to address sexual identity, to confront internal tensions within feminism and within their religious communities. Some contrasted the speakers' experiences at a time when feminism was in the news and change seemed inevitable with the climate on their campuses today. They complained of the apathy of students who take some feminist gains for granted, yet feel powerless to push for more.

The women who tell their stories in these pages couldn't study feminist theology—as Elisabeth Schüssler Fiorenza makes abundantly clear; they had to invent it. They had to imagine the possibilities of their inclusion as full human persons in their faiths. Because of what they imagined, a new world has opened to young women who have grown up with the innovations they wrought. These writers had few women teachers, but they have many students. Their stories are important for their own sake, as examples of how individuals shape history. But they are even more important as a resource to build a new world not yet imagined. These stories connect the activists of today with the movement that shaped their world, not so that they can replicate it, but so that they can move beyond it.

The final speaker, the Dominican sister Donna Quinn, spoke for many when she called the conference "a eucharistic celebration." For her the trials and triumphs of the lives that were told bespoke transcendence and transformation. "The women's movement has been church to me," she told the conference. "I always say, out with scripture, just throw it out. What better stories than those we have been told and those we hold in our hearts, as yet unspoken." In a sort of feminist Pilgrim's Progress, sixteen women who changed American religion tell the story of the soul's journey to wholeness. These are lives of love and labor, dedicated to seeking justice.

NOTES

1. Elizabeth Cady Stanton, Susan B. Anthony, and Matilda Joslyn Gage, eds., *A History of Woman Suffrage*, vol. 1 (Rochester, N.Y.: Fowler and Wells, 1889), p. 67. Emphasis added.
2. The Religion and the Feminist Movement Conference, sponsored by the Women's Studies in Religion Program at Harvard Divinity School, took place November 1–3, 2002, supported by a generous grant from the E. Rhodes and Leona B. Carpenter Foundation.
3. Mary Daly read from her book-in-progress, *Amazon Grace*.
4. Gerda Lerner's talk, "Religion and the Creation of Feminist Consciousness," was published in the *Harvard Divinity School Bulletin* vol. 31, no. 3 (Summer 2003), 11–13.

ONE

Lois Miriam Wilson

1965 Ordained, United Church of Canada
1976 First woman moderator, United Church of Canada
1983 President, World Council of Churches

I FIRST CAME TO SEE FEMINISM AS RELEVANT TO MY OWN LIFE IN 1965
when Faith Joynson, a young girl in our church group, gave me the book
The Feminine Mystique by Betty Friedan.[1] I could hardly believe what I was

reading because it reflected so much of my own experience. My oldest daughter, Ruth, who was thirteen at the time, tells me that as I read, I would spontaneously cry out, "That's right!" I understood that feminism didn't necessarily demand that I abdicate my role as wife and mother of four, but it assumed that I had additional contributions to make to society and a unique perspective forged out of experience. This insight was consonant with my understanding of the gospel at that time. So begins my story of how religion and feminism intersect in my life and in my attempts to change the world.

Many experiences, individuals, groups, and events contributed to this epiphany. My mother was a very independent woman. She was short in stature, so she cut off the legs of any chairs in the house that were too high for her legs to reach the floor. My father prided himself in being a critical thinker and a nonconformist. He was distributing birth control information to couples he married long before that was legal. Yet later, when it came to the question of my ordination, my father underlined his favorite theme, "The home is older than the church." So I received mixed messages from my home.

A significant contribution to my preparedness of seeing religion and feminism as relevant to each other was my participation in the Student Christian Movement on university campus in the late 1940s. Unusually for that time, the national staff was a team of one man and one woman, which gave both my husband-to-be and me the model for team ministry we later practiced. We hosted a number of international visitors, the Reverend K. H. Ting, currently Anglican bishop in China, being among them. In 1947, when he asked me what I was going to do with my life, I answered, "Get married." He then repeated the question, claiming I had not answered his question. Heavens, I thought, does he mean that I have to do something else with my life besides getting married? Apparently his question paid off, because the sequel is that in 1987, on a visit to Nanjing, K. H. invited me to give a lecture on feminist theology to the candidates for ministry at that seminary.

And then there was Suzanne de Deitrich, whose life and work taught me that it was possible for women to be serious biblical scholars. I began to understand the importance of the biblical text as foundational for my life, as a few of us took our brown bag lunches at noon for study together. Having read that God so loved the world (John 3:16), we began to understand that the gospel priority was for the poor, the widows, the orphans, and the marginalized. It was an ecumenical movement in the broadest sense of that term, *oikoumene*, meaning "the whole inhabited world." International visitors provoked my lifelong interest in public policy. It was in the Student Christian Movement that I was among those who protested the internment of the Japanese Canadians by the Canadian government during World War II. It was my first glimmer that Christian faith sometimes was best expressed by resisting injustice—a lesson remembered as I grew into feminist understandings.

I decided to study theology and found myself among an all-male faculty and student body. I had my first experience of exclusion when one of the male students was invited to preach weekends at an appointment I had hoped to be given, and the word came back that they "didn't want a woman."

In 1945 I told my parents that I was thinking of becoming an ordained minister. My mother responded by posing the question as to whether a woman could combine marriage and a career short of dropping her professional life and becoming a valuable volunteer, as she had done. My father asked me what man would marry an ordained woman? But when they understood I was serious, they both swung all support behind me.

In 1950 I married a newly minted ordained minister. I returned from our honeymoon to attend the ordination of my male classmates, and when my husband, Roy, looked at me, he said, "You look as if you would rather have been ordained than marry me." I responded, "You are both ordained *and* married. Why can't I be?" We inherited the tradition of ordaining women from the Congregationalists, one of the three uniting churches that formed the United Church of Canada, but in practice, that meant single women only.

In 1928 the General Council of the United Church declared that "there was no bar in religion or reason to the ordination of women to the ministry." But there were plenty of other obstacles, not the least of which were cultural assumptions about the proper place of women. For women, it had to be a choice between ordination and marriage because of the church's policy of settling new ordinands for a two-year period wherever in Canada they were needed. In 1962 the General Council adopted only one recommendation of the Commission on Ordination. It declared that ordination would be contemplated for women only if a suitable ministry could be arranged that would not interfere "with the stability of the marriage and their position as wives, so that they would be able to fulfill the vows of ordination." My husband Roy was one of 62 men and women out of 377 delegates who insisted that their negative votes be recorded.

That same year, First United Church congregation proposed that I should pursue ordination. By that time I had four children ten and under, and no day care. I waited until the youngest was four and then set the wheels in motion. Almost all of the men I consulted counseled me against ordination. The current moderator of the day, the Reverend J. Mutchmor, asked me, "Who would wear the pants in the family? Who would have priority use of the car? Would not a husband-and-wife team constitute a power bloc in the congregation?" However, the congregation strongly supported my candidacy. I was not perceived as a woman demanding her "rights" but as one in whom the local congregation wished to invest more responsibility and spiritual leadership.

I was finally ordained in 1965, on our fifteenth wedding anniversary, and settled in team ministry as pastoral minister in the congregation then pastored by my husband, even though I insisted on part-time ministry only—which broke several well established church policies! All the people participating in the "laying on of hands" for me were men—it simply never occurred to me to ask any women. But later on I was shocked when reviewing my records to discover that my application for my ordination in 1965 had been signed Mrs. R. F. Wilson simply because no other signature occurred to me.

I ministered in team ministry with my husband for seventeen years. We covered both the private and public places of our congregation: he did the "in-house" work, and I did the "out-house" work. This meant he did most of the weddings and funerals, and I did the support of laity in the community work with refugees, the people on welfare, and women prisoners. We shared the preaching.

In the mid-1960s, I tried for months to get a male to initiate and direct a citywide program called "Town Talk" that I had learned about in Duluth, Minnesota. I felt a male, rather than I, would be better received by citizens. But having failed to locate such a male, I finally stepped in. We invited everyone and all organizations in a city of 100,00 people (Thunder Bay) to coordinate programs and identify the priorities for the future of that city. It was an invitation to look at the ethical and moral questions implicit in City Hall's agenda. It was successful beyond all expectations and launched me nationally into some prominence. It was supported and facilitated by people drawn from the ecumenical religious community and was my first significant interaction with Vatican II Roman Catholics and the public. A Catholic sister told me, "Now you know that the whole city is your parish!"

In 1969 our church building burned to the ground, and that enabled the congregation to replace it with a multipurpose building that included 450 units of housing for single people, handicapped folk, and a number of Muslim students; stores and offices that enabled us to apply the profits to keeping a lid on the rental costs of housing units; recreational space; a media center; and a church sanctuary on the second floor. Although it had no steeple, we thought it looked like what a church should be—a slice of life with a believing community at its center. It grew out of our theological understandings garnered through Town Talk and our understanding that the gospel has primarily to do with the *oikoumene*—the whole inhabited world.

My life as a congregational minister provided several events where the intersection of religion and feminism came to the fore. In 1974, when my congregation was in joint worship with a nearby Anglican congregation after we had experienced the destruction of our building by fire, a woman approached the altar rail for communion, took one look at me, and said, "I'll have mine from the other minister." At that time, there were no ordained women priests in the Canadian Anglican Communion. I must have been advancing quickly in my feminist understandings by that time, because I turned to my Anglican priest colleague and said, "She needs counseling." Some brides thought they would not be properly married if by a woman. The same held true of funerals; "Do you do funerals?" I was frequently asked, followed by a skeptical but admiring nod of the head. And after a sermon the comment might be "That was very good, my dear" in a surprised tone of voice. Or worse still, "Big things come in short packages." In a discussion with an Orthodox priest, he told me quite seriously that I could never be ordained because I couldn't grow a beard. I thanked him for that insight.

I experienced exclusion outside the church also. I was asked to give the blessing at a political party fundraising dinner. I happened to glance at the agenda in the male chairman's hand, and it read "Ask Lois Wilson to ask the blessing unless another clergyman is present"! I was barred from berthing my small sailboat at the Yacht Club because it had to be done in my husband's name, and I refused, because my husband wasn't interested in sailing—I was! Up to that point I had no idea that it was perfectly acceptable for a woman to "crew" but not to handle the tiller. I was also barred from using the main entrance to a prestigious club and had to use the "women's" side entrance.

These were familiar experiences of exclusion, but this time they fueled my passion as a feminist. They encouraged my efforts to integrate religion and feminism, both of which I now understood as having to do with birthing a community that would transform things as they are, both personal and societal.

Two women in particular contributed to my awakening consciousness. In 1976, after I had preached what I thought was a stunning sermon at prestigious Timothy Eaton United Church, Toronto, a friend, Shelley Finson, caught me and expressed dismay at my language. "I never used any four letter word," I responded. "No," she said, "but your language was all-male. You preached as though you are a man." I had to change my style of preaching, consonant with my new feminist understandings. My young friend Jane, a victim of incest, poked me in the ribs one Sunday when we were singing "This Is My Father's World." "That's the trouble," she said, "it *is* my father's world!" After I had become sensitive to the nuances of language in the 1970s, I was at a conference at which several Roman Catholic sisters were present. We had an argument about whether the word "man" meant everyone, or was only for the males. I took the latter view. To illustrate my point I asked the sisters to follow me, and I led them into a washroom clearly marked "men." I think they won't ever again give anyone that argument about "man" including everyone. And speaking of language, I fervently hope that chancellors of universities will cease making women "fellows," as I had to do for ten years as Chancellor of Lakehead University, Thunder Bay, Ontario.

My growth as a Christian feminist has not been in a straight line. I would take one step forward and then two back. The grassroots Friends of Hagar was a case in point. In 1975 there was the first gathering of Christian feminists in Saskatchewan, pulling women from the five western provinces. They were funded by the federal government's Status of Women Committee. In Ontario Shelley Finson had formed the Friends of Hagar, which at the time struck me as a grumpy group of church workers who complained about their experience in the church. All kinds of women moved in and out of this group—Jewish, pagan, Ba'hai, Christian denominations—and it served as a consciousness-raising group. Gradually groups sprung up across Canada. The numerous gatherings were always ecumenical, and theological leadership and intellectual frameworks from Rosemary Reuther and Elisabeth Schüssler Fiorenza were extraordinarily helpful. I remember feeling uncomfortable with what was transpiring, until one sensitive soul kindly advised me to absent myself if I really wasn't enjoying the group. I left, only to return a few years later when I became aware of the privileged position of my own life and the ugly scarring experiences of some other women.

I have always understood Christian faith as having to do with the world we live in and the situation of people in that world. In 1972, when our new multipurpose complex was being built, I left the church's employ for a year to work as an officer of the Ontario Human Rights Commission. After a year of it, I was delighted to return to the church's employ! I experienced the subtle racism that Canadians are so fond of, when we inevitably assure ourselves that we at least are better than our neighbors to the south. I got very tired of middle-class male managers telling me they couldn't hire any women in their company because there were no washroom facilities on premises. I learned the law can be a great teacher, as I politely but firmly insisted that they *build* a washroom and hire females. I began to see the crossover of gender issues with race as I explored the case of a Black Jamaican woman who was denied a job as nurse in a health care facility because, as the administrator explained to me, "Did you not know that black hands are colder than white hands, and our nurses have to give back rubs?"

The moderator of the United Church of Canada is its chief executive officer, and in 1980, when I was the first woman in history to have been elected, the term was two years. How did I fare in a man's world? "A little girl like you in charge of the United Church of Canada," quipped a former chancellor of Queens University. "Can you handle the job?" one of my female colleagues asked me doubtfully. I became aware that my staff had a file marked "Anonymous Letters" that they were not sharing with me. When I finally got access, it was to discover such beauties as "Can't you do anything with your hair?" and "Why don't you go home and look after your kids?" Shortly after my election was announced I was prepared to adjourn the meeting of the General Council with a feminist benediction that made my perspectives clear. It became clear to the United Church that we were on a new road.

I tried to resist the temptation to repeat male models of leadership that I knew so well. My ears rang with "We always do it this way." My challenge as a woman who had grown up in a male-dominated world but who had finally accepted the insights of feminism was to forge a creative tension that would lead the church in new directions. The key question for me was whether a woman's leadership would make any difference. Would I use my leadership to empower rather than control others? Would I cut myself a piece of the pie or try to bake a whole new cake?

A few weeks after my election I had an interesting exchange with a Roman Catholic theologian in the women's washroom at Toronto School of

Theology. "Our Protestant institutions have ordained women to ministry but have hired few women as professors at our theological colleges," I commented. "Our Catholic institutions have hired six women as professors in our seminaries, but won't ordain women to the priesthood," she responded. By way of contrast, there were women theologians in the United States already in theological schools—Mary Daly, Rosemary Reuther, and Letty Russell, to name a few. Canada did not have such leadership in our national churches or in theological schools. Our movement was very much grassroots from its beginning. The Royal Committee on the Status of Women that took place thirty years ago prompted the United Church of Canada to form a Committee on the Relationship of Men and Women in the Church and Society. But it took many years before the church began to use the language of sexism.

I traveled widely during my moderatorial years, visiting partner churches in Asia, Africa, India, and Latin America. I will never forget attending a World Day of Prayer service in Brazil where all the prayers were read by men. The reason, I was told, was that the women were all illiterate! Women of the Third World raised my consciousness by leaps and bounds—those vomiting blood in El Salvador, the Mothers of the disappeared in Argentina (the Mothers of May Square); the mothers of the pro-democracy South Korean students massacred at Kwangju in 1980; the relatives of those in Chile sent to isolated villages for six months, the village having been told previously of the coming of a sex offender in their midst; the Indian women who wanted birth control information to prevent being caught in the never-ending cycle of poverty; the South African women caught in apartheid structures; the aboriginal women in Canada consigned to poverty and destined to be victims of racism for life. I listened intently to their stories, and they converted me firmly and finally to feminism. It is always risky to listen, because you might be converted.

Why, I asked myself, were these terrible things happening to women who were in very great pain—and most of them not authored by women? I began to feel their pain in my own bones and to long for their liberation into a world of equity and justice, of inclusive community and hope. I learned from them the meaning of solidarity and interdependence, of mutuality and endurance. They never gave up their struggle for justice. Their suffering became their passion in the deep double sense of that word. They worked with their suffering. They wept. They shouted. Their Christianity was not a suffering-free faith, nor was their God a mild and apathetic being. For them the shape of life itself was cruciform. I learned from them that to stand alongside them in their suffering was to lead suffering out of its private corner into the public arena and to thereby achieve strength.

When I was in Argentina I was able to tell Juanita, one of the Mothers of May Square, of the plight of women in South Korea whose young people has received long prison terms for working with the poor. One Tuesday I gave a fish pendant to her that had been given to me by a South Korean woman. One side in Greek it said, "Jesus Christ is Lord." On the other side it said, "Set the prisoners free." On Thursday of that same week I met two other Mothers who thanked me for my gift. "But I've never met you before, I've never given you a gift," I responded. But they said to me, "You gave us a gift on Tuesday, and each of us gets to wear that pendant for two weeks." Out of their individual suffering and pain they had forged themselves into a community and had transformed their suffering and pain into purposeful and tenacious life goals. I felt their suffering so closely that it became grafted on my heart. Never again was I able to say I was not in pain. While in the West many people try to run from suffering and death, these women accepted the inevitability of personal suffering and the suffering of others, and passionately embraced and transformed it for the sake of the public good. I also learned more about the International Monetary Fund and its effects than I had ever learned at home.

Currently the listening stance becomes even more important for me. The biggest issue for Canadian churches is the residential school scandal of thirty years ago, when aboriginal children were removed from their families by government and churches for schooling, strapped for speaking their own language, and sometimes sexually abused. What is being determined through the courts is who was hurt by that system, and who profited. The churches' push for restorative justice is part of the picture of what used to be a somewhat private church matter emerging into a public issue of huge proportions.

In 1979, when I was elected for a three-year term as president of the Canadian Council of Churches (again, the first woman), I convened a meeting of identifiable women bureaucrats of various Christian denominations, funded again by the federal government's Status of Women Committee. Gradually women in the national church offices began to recognize the need to link with the women's movement. There was a growing understanding of the issues: language, employment, and pornography. Theological schools began to feel guilty about not having any female staff. The United Church began to send key women to conferences on Women in Ministry sponsored by the National Council of Churches, USA, and to make reports to the General Council. The numerous gatherings that spun off were always ecumenical, and the theological leadership provided by Reuther and Schüssler Fiorenza was extraordinarily helpful.

The Women's Inter Church Council began to take up issues of concern to women, and their work on violence against women became extremely important. The question of how one can be a Christian and a feminist simultaneously began to surface.

My election as one of the six presidents of the World Council of Churches in 1983 was a watershed event for me. I stood on the shoulders of women who preceded me, like Brigalia Bam of South Africa, who was one of the first women to staff the women's desk internationally, and Connie Parvey, who authored much of the Sheffield Report, a groundbreaking study on the role of women in the Christian religious community. The women had been able to have a motion passed to the effect that 50 percent of the presidents must be women. I shared the female "half" with Dame Nita Barrow of Barbados and Margaret Buhrig, the first laywoman to serve as director of a lay academy in Europe. It would have been hard for me to have given any productive leadership in those eight years without the support and interaction of those two great women. I was also privileged to meet with feminist theologians from the Third World—Ofelia Ortega, Aruna Gnanadason, Maria Therese Prochilo Santiso, to mention only a few. Dorothee Sölle came into my world at this time.

The first time I heard the word "strategy" associated with feminism and religion was when Barbel Potter used it to prepare us for work in that bastion of male dominance—the World Council of Churches. At the time, I was the only female "head of church" on the Central Committee. We women would gather a day before in order to get to know each other's first names. We would then examine the agenda to identify missing issues that needed to be added. In our women's caucus we also identified both the mover and seconder of any necessary addition to the agenda. We then discussed which particular agenda items needed to be addressed by women and for women, and we lined up both the mover and seconder. This was all done to enable women to get to the microphone before the patriarch of somewhere got hold of it and tied it up for the next half hour. Our plan worked beautifully, and I have used this strategy in many other groups.

The presence of a few patriarchal females reduced feminists to a distinct minority on the executive of the World Council of Churches. We created a secret hand signal that we used whenever we perceived a woman was being put down or ignored in that circle. Immediately a feminist would speak and offer support for whatever position had been taken.

In 1986 the World Council mounted a significant consultation on "Women in Church Leadership" undergirded by a helpful liberation Bible study by Cora Ferro of the Theological Seminary in Costa Rica. From her I learned to do theology by starting with women's experience, situation, and struggle. It kindled my imagination and built on the splendid work of Elisabeth Schüssler Fiorenza and her "hermeneutics of suspicion."

The World Council launched the Ecumenical Decade of Churches in Solidarity with Women in Church and Society in 1988, only to discover that the main thing uniting women around the world was the violence they experienced. Some of this was from their own male church leaders. We also found that church leaders were happy to receive small international teams on the subject of women and religion, but they were stronger on offering huge meals than sitting down for serious discussion of the issues.

In December 1989 hundreds gathered around the statue of the "Crucified Woman" in anguish on the day after the massacre of fourteen female engineering students in Montreal by a male rejected engineer-to-be. The statue is a naked woman, with arms outstretched, in the cruciform position. In it women see their own suffering, dying, and resurrection embodied in a woman's body. It has caused controversy, healing, and change. Every year on December 6, the anniversary of the Montreal massacre is remembered in Canada. And the statue continues as a meeting place for remembrance and a launching pad for the transformation of women's pain and suffering into resurrection and hope.

The World Council confirmed my engagement in interfaith exchanges with women of many religious communities. I had begun these in the mid-1970s after the expelled Ugandans came to Canada and after my trip to India, where I knew myself as a distinct minority in a sea of Muslims and Hindus. Upon returning to Canada I organized a multifaith group of feminists who met around subjects pertaining to women and bodily functions such as menstruation, intercourse, pregnancy, lactation, and menopause. We asked each other how our religious tradition had addressed these matters in our experience and critiqued these positions from a feminist perspective. Nobody missed a meeting, because we knew so little about each other and our several religious traditions.

A 1990 World Council of Churches consultation in Toronto, "Faithful Women," chaired by Diana Eck, helped me appreciate the strength of feminism in religions other than my own. More than sixty women from five continents representing a cross section of the world's religions shared our differing traditions about women's realities and perspectives. I will never forget Riffat Hassan's feminist interpretation of the Qur'an on that occasion. A subsequent 1995 consultation hosted by the Center for the Study of Religions and Society, University of Victoria, B.C., focused on "Women Changing Rituals Changing Women" within their own tradition and, again, reinforced for me the way in which so many feminists have integrated feminist perspectives with the practice of their religion.

Even as major interfaith understandings grew, such as my own church's document "Bearing Faithful Witness," which established a new relationship with the Jewish community, there was little recognition of a feminist perspective. I offered an additional chapter to the document availing myself of the splendid work done by Bernadette Brooten. I offered a critique of Christian women's approach to Judaism—the one that assumes Jesus' approach to women was like a lightning bolt, rather than being built on the insights of the progressive Jewish community of the day.

In 1990 the World Council of Churches sent me on a tour of India to meet with students and theological professors about the possibilities of the ordination of women in both the Church of South India and that of North India. I met endless numbers of male students and told them my story. Two or three women were present at some of these meetings, and they sat silently and quietly in the background.

Not all of the women in India were prepared to sit silently in the background. On that same trip I arrived at the Bombay airport ready to join in a meeting of Christian feminists in that city. When I arrived at the meeting place, I saw that there were two women sitting on the floor, planning strategy. They were so heavily engrossed in their task they never did have time to talk to me. I gathered from their conversation that there had been a huge billboard at the Bombay airport featuring a male movie star. The bubble coming from his mouth had him saying, "If rape is inevitable, lie back and enjoy it." The women had a can of black paint each and were planning to paint over the billboard under cover of darkness. "Won't you get caught?" I asked. "We hope so," they said. "We hope we get sent to jail. Think of the publicity." The rockers of the cradle had become the rockers of the boat—a great intersection of feminists and "those who have turned the world upside down," as Christians are described in the book of Acts.

I also began to receive many invitations to speak at publicly sponsored feminist events, but was clearly expected to bring the dimensions of Christian faith to my address. So I trotted off to Paris for an international consultation sponsored by the French feminist group CHOISIR on how Christian faith blocked, encouraged, or discouraged women to run for politics. I was teamed with a Roman Catholic archbishop, the chief rabbi of France, and a Muslim imam, all of whom indicated their traditions fully supported equality of women and men. I contrasted the Protestant fundamentalist position that relegates women to the home, to my feminist position that encourages women to walk on water, and was greeted with wild applause. At that time, too, I was frequently asked to address the subject of women and new dimensions of power assuming I had learned something about that in my years of church leadership. All of this forced me to dig deeply into my own tradition and my growing understanding of feminism and power.

And then, to my surprise, in 1998 I was appointed by Canada's prime minister to a four-year term in the Senate, Canada's upper chamber. Thirty-three percent of Senate membership is women, which is higher than the 20 percent of elected women in our House of Commons. But the Senate is also the one place in my experience where it was impossible to create a feminist caucus bridging party differences. There were feminist causes within a political party, but not one for the whole chamber. Much to my surprise, I discovered that my years in church leadership had been a great preparation for the Senate. I began to integrate the passions of my life into legislation—feminism, faith, development, and human rights.

I was given the opportunity to influence public policy from the inside and was asked by the government to represent Canada at the Cairo review of the Conference on Population and Development. At the original Cairo conference, Rosemary Reuther and Riffat Hassan had both for perhaps the first time publicly challenged the sexual policies of their respective religious leaders. At the review process in New York, the attempt to role back the Cairo international agreement on access to information about reproduction, abortion, and related matters was supported by an unholy combination of the Vatican and Protestant and Muslim fundamentalists. Those of us whose countries supported the Cairo agreement won the day by staying up later than the others and thereby protecting the original document and the rights of women.

I joined with splendid young feminist lawyers in supporting the inclusion of a feminist perspective in the proceedings of the International Criminal Court, as they made sure that rape was recognized as a crime against humanity, not just something that happens to women during a war. I was recruited to chair a Canadian government and nongovernmental organization partnership to implement Security Council Resolution 1325, which recommends gender equality through all United Nations machinery and encourages foreign ministers to appoint women to important international negotiating sessions, an initiative that followed the series of UN conferences on women: Mexico, Copenhagen, Nairobi, and Beijing. In 1999, as Canada's special envoy to the Sudan, I discovered at the International Partners Forum that I was the only woman among twenty-seven men! In the Senate I was in a position to monitor whether emerging legislation incorporated the United Nations Convention on the Child and the Convention for the Elimination of Discrimination Against Women.

My parting contribution to the Senate was a speech commending legislation that would accord same-sex couples the same privileges as heterosexual couples.

The tensions between feminism and my faith were never crisis events, but rather slow troublesome developments. The resources I pulled on were the ones that have supported me all my life: feminist groups and networks in my own country, women of the Third World, feminist theologians from around the world who have contributed through their writings and books to my understanding of the biblical text especially—particularly Asian and Jewish theologians. There was also the support of my husband and some few male friends, as they gradually embraced feminist perspectives.

One tension that bothered me for some time was between feminism and the traditional interpretation of the Bible. The Bible was full of stories, and in my experience feminists usually began by sharing their stories. Perhaps there was something here to explore.

On a trip to the USSR a grandmother questioned me as to whether I had taught my three-year-old granddaughter the Nicene Creed. I had to fudge that one, but she did raise for me the question of how I saw my role as grandmother in passing on the faith to generations to come. When I came home I asked my oldest daughter, mother of five, for a Bible storybook so I could read to her kids. She brought me a book that had the same old bed-sheet costumes on the biblical characters and the same old patriarchal interpretation of the stories as had been familiar to me as a child. Here once again women were portrayed as helpless victims of war or violence, dependent on men for identify or deliverance; as seductive temptresses or, worse, as obedient, passive, and compliant appendages to a male figure. One of my granddaughters asked me, "Is there anything in that Bible for girls?" My daughter persuaded me that since I was a trained theologian and a feminist, I should write the biblical stories from a feminist perspective for her children. That started me on a three-year project that enabled me to read feminist theology widely, and that is when I read or reread the books of most of the people at this conference. I had an absolute ball. I met with circles of feminists in Christian churches, later augmented by meeting with Jewish feminist theologians, and out of that was able to write two books of Bible stories for children from a feminist perspective.[2]

I wanted to find a way to reconcile my profound love and debt to the biblical record with my strong awareness of women's struggles toward wholeness and liberation. I wanted to communicate those learnings to the children and grandchildren before they got to be fifty years of age! This is all by way of saying that all of you in this room have been a generous and rich resource for me in my growing understandings of the relevance of religion to feminism. And so emerged Miriam the rebel; Orpah, who reclaimed the heritage of her mother's house rather than follow Naomi; audacious Vashti; and vulnerable Hagar. There emerged Mary the mother of Jesus whose Magnificence threatened the status quo so dangerously that the Christmas radio program planned for broadcast by theological students in Buenos Aires in 1981 was banned from the air by the military junta.

So I was able to demolish biblical stereotypes of women; to uncover and expose the role of some women in biblical texts as enablers and supporters of a patriarchal society; and to tell stories of spiritually independent women that strengthened the image of biblical and contemporary women in children's eyes.

How did I come to see sympathy between the liberation of women and the core of my faith tradition? So much of my early work in ministry had to do with the sad situation of women in Third World countries and with matters of social justice. I have been privileged to be invited to exchanges with the Association of Theologically Trained Women of India and to lead Bible study with some of the women in Cuba. In both cases, it was women in pain and poverty who recalled me to the intersection of feminism and my faith.

I understood that both my faith and my feminism had to do with community and with wholeness between human beings and with the created order. Women of the Third World reinforced this insight for me. Lee Oo Chung, a Korean theologian, for example, helped me to realize that the words so frequently translated as "healed" in the biblical stories are more properly translated as "liberated" or "freed." I had always wondered why so many of the women who encountered Jesus seemed to be in need of healing. Wasn't there an able-bodied woman among them? Why was this patriarchal bias so prominent in the text? And a close male friend asked why were so few women even mentioned in the lectionary.

In the last ten years I have finally begun to make the connections between feminism and ecology, and find that much of my energy, writing, and theological orientation are in this area. This has been greatly assisted by my aboriginal feminist friends and by the work of Sally McFague.

I have also begun to appreciate the role of imagination in both feminism and Christianity. Both propose an alternate worldview to the presumed world we take for granted—the world of disease, of death, of hopelessness, of abuse and violence, poverty and environmental degradation. The bold 1994 Re-Imagining Conference in Minneapolis kindled my imagination and brought gales of fresh air to my understanding of Christian faith. A conference at the University of Toronto in 2000 on feminist utopias did the same thing for me in terms of feminism.

It is the questions feminists and women of faith pose that move us along. We ask, "Where can I find or help create authentic human community that will affirm me in my particularity, my sexuality, my gender, my faith, my language, but bring me into life-giving and life-sustaining relationships with others quite different from myself?" "Where can I find community that demonstrates a symbiotic relationship with the earth and all its creatures?" "Where can I find or help to create an interdependent community that is just and equitable, where those on the edge and those at the center walk together?" "Can women embrace power so that it will bring about transformation of things as they are?" "Can we restore the focus of faith to the healing of divisions and brokenness in the human and nonhuman community, to the creation of healthy human relationships with each other, with the Creator, and with creation itself?" "Where, in religious terms, can I witness, or be part of such resurrection, of hope?" For me, the intersection of feminism and Christian faith offers some partial but hopeful answers to these questions.

Feminists need a different wardrobe if we intend to transform the future. We need goggles that will enable us to see the world at 180 degrees, as it really is. We will need flippers for our feet as we swim against the current. We will need to know how to practice resistance. Let our imaginations soar! Let us revise those nursery rhymes that we teach our children. Instead of "Sugar and spice and everything nice, that's what little girls are made of," try "Subversive and strong, the whole day long, that's what little girls are made of!" That, I think, is a worthy mission statement for those of us who practice the spirituality of engagement.

NOTES

1. Betty Friedan, *The Feminine Mystique* (New York: Norton, 1963).
2. Lois Miriam Wilson, *Miriam, Mary and Me (Women in the Bible)* (Kelowna, B.C.: Northstone, 1997) and *Stories Seldom Told: Biblical Stories Retold for Children and Adults* (Kelowna, B.C.: Northstone, 1997).

TWO

Letty Cottin Pogrebin

1955 Excluded from minyan for mother's kaddish
1971 Cofounder, *Ms.* magazine
1991 Author, *Deborah, Golda and Me: Being Female and Jewish
in America*

I GREW UP IN NEW YORK CITY IN THE 1940S, STEEPED IN JEWISH
practice and peoplehood. Ceremonial objects were on display throughout
our house—kiddush cups, hallah cloths, seder plates, Hanukkah menorahs,

spice boxes—the Judaica taking pride of place amidst walls of books, paintings, and testimonial plaques. My mother kept a kosher kitchen, lit candles at sundown every Friday, and cooked from *The Jewish Home Beautiful*, whose chicken soup recipe I use to this day.[1] My father knew the prayer book by heart. At home he led us in the Sabbath blessings. In synagogue he often served as the *baal koreh*, one who chants from the Torah scroll (where the Hebrew script is written without vowels or notes), an esteemed role for which he practiced in the evenings. His flat singsong was the background audio of my Judaism.

Testimonial plaques attested to my parents' service to the Jewish community. My father was the president of our synagogue, the Jamaica Jewish Center, and in due course the head of every communal organization with a branch in Queens—B'nai Brith, Anti-Defamation League, United Jewish Appeal, Zionist Organization of America, and the Jewish War Veterans. My mother was active in our temple sisterhood, National Council of Jewish Women, and Hadassah, for whom she hosted innumerable strawberry luncheons and canasta parties to raise money for Israel.

The Jewish calendar trumped the secular one in our family. We consulted it for the starting times of Sabbath and religious holidays. My mother made such a big deal of Hanukkah, the eight-day festival of lights and rededication, that it never occurred to me to envy my gentile friends their Christmas. (Eight nights of presents and crispy potato latkes didn't hurt, either.) Passover brought her extended family to our "finished basement" where my father sat at the head of a long table and conducted the seder amid a cacophony of questions and commentary from my kibitzing uncles while my mother and my aunts served. (Somehow we made it through the haggadah despite wisecracks like "Enough with the plagues; let's eat!" Or "Where is it written Jews have to take as long getting to the meal as the Hebrews did to reach the Promised Land?") On Rosh Hashanah eve, dressed in our finest clothes, we dipped our apple slices in honey and prayed for a sweet new year, then feasted on a six-course meal. More often than not, the rock pile of bakery taiglach remained untouched (like the perennial Christmas fruit cake) while my mother's homemade desserts were devoured. Though we went to services (my father's turf), what happened in synagogue was, in the end, less crucial to my sense of the sacred than the ritual meals that unfolded at my mother's table. Yet it was years before I understood how hard she worked or what she actually did to make Judaism a vibrant presence in our home.

Not surprisingly, my parents' passions became my own. I learned to read Hebrew soon after mastering Dick and Jane. *The Adventures of K'ton Ton*, about a Jewish Tom Thumb, was my favorite children's book. A Star of David hung on a slender chain around my neck. When I was nine, ear glued to the radio, I tallied the historic United Nations vote that made Israel a state. I deposited a portion of my weekly allowance in a blue and white tin whose contents were made payable to the Jewish National Fund (JNF). I belonged to Young Judea, danced the hora, collected acres of trees or, rather, JNF certificates proclaiming that a sapling or two had been planted in the nascent Jewish state in honor of my birthday, Hanukkah, or Lag B'Omer, thanks to the generosity of a friend or relative. (Convinced that an Israeli forest bore the name Letty Cottin, I was shocked to discover on my first trip to Jerusalem that my trees were anonymous.) Jewish observance was as organic to my upbringing as learning to brush my teeth or make my bed. Sabbath eve and Saturday mornings I went to shul. Every night I said the *sh'ma*, the core prayer of Jewish faith.

My father saw to it that I had a good Jewish education—for a girl—what with thrice-weekly after-school religious classes, two years at yeshiva, and three at Hebrew High School from which I graduated at fourteen. In February 1952 I was one of the first girls in the Conservative branch of Judaism to be bat mitzvah. Though the female equivalent of the ancient male coming-of-age ceremony was then considered radical, our synagogue performed bat mitzvahs in the main sanctuary (in contrast to congregations that relegated girls to the rec hall or refused to allow the ceremony at all), which is not to say we were egalitarian. The main service on Saturday mornings includes a Torah reading and women were not permitted to chant from the Torah, so bat mitzvahs always happened on Friday evenings, and girls could only read from the haftarah (selections from the Prophets). That inequity escaped my notice, as did the paucity of women in the Bible, or their complete absence on the *bimah* (speakers' platform) and the stained glass windows. In 1952 I questioned nothing and accepted everything. Yet by 1955 I had turned my back on Judaism. The return trip would take more than twenty years.

In a sense, my journey is an allegory that needed a movement to give it a name. I left organized religion because of female exclusion, male supremacy, and a host of sexist indignities and inequalities—reasons one could call feminist though my estrangement long predated organized feminism. And I returned to Judaism in a denouement that would not have been possible without the women's movement, specifically the Jewish women's movement and the chutzpah of my foremothers whose groundbreaking rituals and revolt against patriarchy blazed a trail I could follow back to my people.

This rebellion and reconnection is described in my memoir *Deborah, Golda, and Me: Being Female and Jewish in America*, a narrative in three arcs suggested by its title.[2] The "Deborah" part recounts the spiritual arc of my journey, which began when the dictates of the Jewish calendar assigned the Song of Deborah (Judges 5:1–31) as the haftarah reading for my bat mitzvah Sabbath, one of those propitious coincidences whose meaning becomes clear only in retrospect. (Or, as the rabbi in my novel, *Three Daughters*, puts it, "Coincidences are God's way of remaining anonymous."[3]) Given my subsequent adult commitment to advancing female leadership, a divine hand seems to have guided me at age thirteen to the story of Judaism's most independent woman, the prophet, judge, and military commander whose life has become a metaphor for feminists of faith.

The "Golda" in my book title refers of course to Golda Meir, the feisty Zionist organizer who rose through the ranks to become Israel's prime minister. To my generation, Golda (like Madonna, always known by her first name) was not only a consummate champion of Jewish nationhood but a rare symbol of female autonomy and power. A commanding presence on the main stage of history, she stood toe-to-toe with men like David Ben Gurion, King Abdullah of Jordan, Henry Kissinger, Richard Nixon, and Gamal Nasser while most women were tiptoeing through the minefields of femininity. Though I'd no sooner presume to equate myself with Golda than with the prophet Deborah (and though I've often critiqued Golda's blindness to both Palestinian aspirations and Jewish women's interests), she is my trope for the political aspect of my journey, the struggle to assert oneself as a Jew in secular society and as a woman in the Jewish world.

Finally, the "Me" in the book's title aspires to synthesize false dualities and resist forced choices. Whether posited as spiritual vs. political, populist/intellectual, yin/yang, or faith/feminism, such oppositional categories are not just inadequate descriptions of human reality, they are coercive, constricting strategies of social control whose objective, however hidden or nuanced, is to keep women divided within ourselves and from one another. Many of us who are both "female and Jewish in America" choose to reject either/or dichotomies. We carry what W. E. B. Dubois, in the African American context, called "double consciousness."[4] (Add ethnic, racial disability, sexual preference, or other identity sensibilities and the Jewish female consciousness may well be further expanded.) We embrace both Deborah and Golda, the agendas of Judaism and feminism, the people in our faith community and the family of women—while reserving the right to name their errors and resolve their contradictions.

In my life as a Jew, the original dichotomy, my first forced choice, was Mommy vs. Daddy. His realm was synagogue, Jewish history, text, and tradition. Hers was the aesthetic, emotional, and mystical dimension of Jewish life. My challenge was to be loyal to both when they were so different from each other.

My mother's family emigrated from Hungary in 1909, driven from their shtetl by anti-Semitic bigotry and fear for their lives. Since girls of her era received no formal education in Judaism, everything my mother knew about ritual observance she learned from her mother. An amateur artist and former designer, my mother enhanced Jewish celebrations as naturally as she embellished a simple dress with ebony buttons or a lace collar. For Purim, she made me a Queen Esther with a celery body, red pepper arms, and parsley skirt. She taught me to fashion Calder-style sculptures—David, Goliath, Daniel in the lion's den—out of my father's pipe cleaners or the wires that secured the caps of milk bottles. On Hanukkah, she painted the Macabbean revolt on the dining room mirror so that, despite the news of Hitler's atrocities reaching us daily, I might imbibe Jewish heroism along with my gefilte fish.

When I say she kept kosher, I choose, as she did, to overlook "lamb chops on paper," the strips of meat she fried in a special pan (otherwise kept in a brown paper bag under the kitchen sink), and served to me on a paper plate. Whenever this treat was sizzling on the stove, she would open the windows and fan away its aroma, a habit I never found odd enough to question just as I never wondered why, with a cabinet full of china, she presented it to me on a paper plate. The day my Irish Catholic friend brought a sandwich to lunch, called it a BLT, and insisted the "B" was not "lamb chops on paper," I stormed home in confusion.

My mother, embarrassed but unapologetic, explained that it was much more important for her to make me strong than to follow every kosher law to the letter. Jewish children were dying every day in Europe. I was skinny and prone to bronchitis. My gentile friends were sturdy and robust. The difference had to be bacon, and if pig was the secret of American good health, she would cook it, I would eat it, and God would understand. God would understand.

Her intensely personal Judaism was even more idiosyncratic for its Old World superstitions. Just because she lacked formal learning didn't mean my mother wasn't a God-fearing Jew; it meant she had to buttress her beliefs with folklore and women's intuition. According to her theology, the Devil and God were in constant struggle for our souls and since God couldn't be expected to protect our family from evil all the time, she took it on herself to decode the Devil's wily ways and foil his plans. So precise were her antidotes to his poison, I could have sworn she was on speaking terms with the Evil Eye.

For example, since it was a violation of the Second Commandment for human beings to play God, we were not permitted to anticipate the divine will. This is why we were forbidden to take pictures of a pregnant woman or buy a layette or furniture for a baby's room before it was born, or do anything that suggested we believe we could control our own fate. Couldn't talk about a vacation before we'd actually returned home from it alive (unless we said "God willing" every time we used the future tense). Had to tie a red ribbon on a bassinet to ward off the Eye (rather like marking a no-fly zone around the infant), and make sure there was bread and salt in a new home before it was safe to spend the night. Or else!

Thou Shalt Not Covet was interpreted as follows: If envy is a sin against God, it must be catnip for the Devil. Therefore I couldn't say, "I wish I had curly hair like Stacey's," or accept a compliment from someone who wished she had my green eyes. If my mother witnessed such an exchange, she would zoom in with a whispered "*kaynahurra*" (Yiddish for "no evil eye.") But since she wasn't able to monitor all my social transactions, she had to hedge her bets: When she came to kiss me good night, she would pucker her lips against my forehead and make three *thpoo-thpoo-thpoo* sounds to suck out whatever jealousy had besmirched me while she wasn't looking.

Since the world of the dead was known to be the Devil's domain, any association with death and dying could open the door to his powers. That's why children were not permitted to attend funerals, visit bereaved households, or be present in synagogue during Yizkor, the memorial service. If my mother was mending a garment while I was wearing it, I had to chew a thread because the only thing a person should be sewn into is her shroud. (Presumably, if my jaw was moving, the Devil couldn't mistake me for dead and snatch my soul.) I had to close the window blinds so the moon couldn't shine on my bed. (It should only shine on one's grave.) Also prohibited were normal adolescent exclamations like "I'm dying of curiosity!" or "This is to die for!" Such loose talk attracts the Evil Eye and a *kaynahurra* after the fact might not save me.

The day I first menstruated, I showed my mother the evidence and to my astonishment, she slapped me across the face. Flustered by her own violence, she explained that the slap had been necessary but she'd accompanied it with a Yiddish wish: "I asked God to make this the worst pain you'll ever know as a woman." (It didn't work.)

Like other unschooled women, my mother turned to superstition to impose order on the universe. It gave her some sense of control over the incomprehensible. She worked hard to beat back the Devil and sanctify her home because no other religious arena was available to her. Her Judaism was emotional, intuitive, decorative, intimate, mystical, personal. She worshipped God in relationship. Hers was the piety of the heart.

My father's Jewish life was the polar opposite—rational, community-based, institutionalized, scholarly, formalistic, authoritative—and not a little bit ego-driven. Like my mother, he was one of seven children, but rather than having to drop out of school to help support his family, sacrifices were made so that he, the firstborn boy, could finish high school, college, and law school. As a young man, he also studied Torah and Talmud, taught Hebrew school on the side, and prepared boys to become bar mitzvah at $150 each, a princely sum in the 1920s.

When it was time for my bat mitzvah, his skills were put to good use. For months, he tutored me several nights a week after dinner, sessions I cherished not just because he was a wonderful teacher but because it kept him home when he usually went out every night to a meeting. My father was a *macher* (a big man in the Jewish community), and I confess that I benefited from his status. When he was president of our synagogue, I had the run of the place. The telephone operator in the office let me wear her headphones and work the snaky cords of her switchboard. The rabbi gave me a special pat on the head at services. My mother and I sat in the first pew while my father occupied a throne-like chair on the bimah from which he prayed loudly, took his *aliyah* (the honor of reciting the blessings that bracket the Torah reading), or chanted from the Torah scroll. When not on his throne, he was circulating through the congregation, greeting people, showing them to their seats, handing out *tallesim* (prayer shawls) to the men, helping people find the right place in their prayer books. After services, he shook hands and shared jokes with his cronies from the Men's Club or made plans for the next meeting.

Though a major presence in Jewish organizational life, my father was largely absent from mine. I don't recall feeling neglected—my mother's loving attention more than made up for his disappearances—but I vividly remember that my parents' arguments centered on his not making family his priority. To be fathered by this man (and forestall their explosive battles), I discovered early on that I could earn his time by engaging him in a discussion about Israel, one of his legal cases, or a Talmudic fine point. But those months when he was preparing me for my bat mitzvah, he treated his time with me as sacrosanct. I understood that I had to chant my *haftarah* perfectly because he was so invested in my performance. I was, after all, my father's student. Where my mother's love was unconditional, my father made demands I had to stretch to meet. He was my religious and intellectual mentor, my model for public service, and first exemplar of the rewards of hard work. I wanted what both parents had to offer but sensed through their festering conflicts and ongoing tension that I had to choose between them, a choice that would have been forced upon me had my mother not died of cancer in April 1955 when I was fifteen.

One night during the *shiva* period (the first seven days of mourning that are marked at home by daily memorial services), my father began counting for a minyan, the quorum of ten Jews required for the recitation of the mourner's kaddish. In 1955 ten Jews meant ten Jewish men, and though our house was packed with visitors, only nine of them were male.

"Count me, Daddy!" I begged. Of course I knew that Jewish law barred women from the minyan, but I also knew that my father cut corners when it suited him, smoked on the Sabbath, for instance, because he refused to interpret the proscribed act of making fire as a law against flicking his Bic. "It's forbidden," he said with a scowl, and called the synagogue to have them send a tenth man. The guy who showed up could barely read Hebrew and had never met my mother. No matter. He passed the physical.

Every culture counts what it values and values what it counts, whether fourteen Stations of the Cross, eight nights of Hanukkah, or ten Jews for a *minyan*. Bereft, grieving, cut off from the fullest expression of my faith, I understood for the first time that I did not count in the minyan because I did not count as a Jew. The exclusion was an epiphany. Regardless of how much I knew, what rituals I fulfilled, or how fervent my beliefs, I was a woman and thus could never be a "real" Jew. If I didn't count in the minyan for my mother's kaddish, I decided, I would count myself out altogether. At the age of fifteen, I abandoned my father's religion—the Judaism of In and Out, Better and Lesser, patriarchs and hierarchies—and disengaged from the "We" I'd grown up with. That September I left my father's house for a dorm at Brandeis University, a Jewish-sponsored nonsectarian school where I dated mostly gentiles, closed my shades against the moon, and tried not to envy kids who had mothers.

After graduation, I moved to Greenwich Village and had virtually no contact with my faith community. I did not belong to a synagogue, communal organization, or Israeli support group. I did not keep kosher or observe the Sabbath. Seders were still family events, but Hanukkah was a solo celebration, birthday candles in a miniature menorah. Only on the High Holy Days did I enter a shul and then not as a member but a visitor who sampled a different synagogue each year, bought a ticket and sat in the "overflow service," astonished at how deeply moved I was by the religion I had rejected. My husband, raised in a secular Yiddishist family whose "faith" was Marxism, left it to me to decide whether to educate our kids religiously. I opted out, making my children the second-generation victims of the sexism that wounded their mother. Because of my estrangement, they had no Sabbath services, Hebrew school, or bar or bat mitzvahs. No synagogue except on the High Holy Days. Nothing but my mother's home-based traditions—candles and blessings, ritual meals, incantations against the Evil Eye.

Things began to change for me in 1970 when a few Jewish men in Saltaire, our mostly gentile summer community on Fire Island, decided it would it be nice to have Rosh Hashanah services on somebody's back deck and not have to schlep back to the city. (Like me, these were once-a-year-Jews who bought tickets for the synagogues they didn't belong to.) A plan was hatched. One man borrowed *mahzors* (High Holy Day prayer books) from a congregation in town. Another collected the yarmulkes people had accumulated from various weddings and bar mitzvahs. Still another went to the Lower East Side and bought a shofar. A local artist made a stained glass Star of David to decorate our makeshift bimah. The Saltaire Market, our only store, donated sacramental wine and honey cake. Someone provided flowers. Quite late in the planning process, it occurred to the organizing committee that they ought to include Hebrew prayers in the service. But who could take this on? All the men had been bar mitzvah but not one remembered his Hebrew or felt equipped to do it. For some reason—nostalgia? spiritual hunger? community responsibility? the challenge of it?—I volunteered.

This was more than thirty years ago, mind you, before there was a *Ms.* magazine, before the ordination of a single woman rabbi, before Jewish feminism was a twinkle in its founders' eyes. I became the *chazanit* (cantor) of our island congregation—forty-odd adults and children—despite the fact that none of us had ever witnessed a woman in that role. Without fully understanding my motivations, I think I did it because I knew how to do it, a standard that carried no weight in official Judaism but was all that mattered to the little band of displaced Jews that had dubbed itself B'nai Saltaire. Necessity, it turns out, is also mother of revolution.

From the liturgy that typically lasted more than four hours in my childhood synagogue, our self-appointed "rabbi" (a stockbroker by day) and I extracted a ninety-minute service that captured the essence of the holy day. He read the English portions, I chanted the Hebrew, and as I stood on that wooden deck amid the beach grass and blueberry bushes, with prayers on my lips and the sea breeze in my hair, I truly meant it when I sang "Amen."

Yom Kippur was another matter; for Kol Nidre, I felt I needed God's permission. If it was okay for me to lead this most sacred service of the year, I needed a sign. Maybe because I was raised in close proximity to the mystical, I usually get an answer to such supplications, a message I can read. This one arrived as a blazing autumn sunset, reply enough, and when the sky faded to a soft purple and I began chanting Kol Nidre, a profound feeling of harmony coursed through me, a deep, sure knowledge that what I was doing was not just okay in God's eyes but good. Good for our community of casual Jews whose association with the Days of Awe was never more intimate and participatory. Good for the Jewish people who gained from the ingathering of its strays. And, dare I say, God understood. Not just why this particular Jew had strayed but what had to happen to bring her back—a radical act of inclusion, proof positive that Judaism belongs not just to the men who make the rules but to any woman who takes the trouble to claim it.

Becoming the founding cantor of B'nai Saltaire marked my first step back to my people. For thirteen years I led the Hebrew prayers (eventually ceding my role to another woman). During that time our congregation grew so large that we had to move our services to the town's Episcopal Church whose board kindly contributes the space. Simultaneously during those years, much was happening in the Jewish world to facilitate my journey. When the Reform movement ordained Sally Preisand, America's first woman rabbi, she took the pulpit at Stephen Wise Free Synagogue, a Reform temple that happens to be around the corner from my home, and I became a member—my first communal connection in more than two decades. But thrilled as I was with the sight of a woman in robes, I missed the spirit of the Conservative liturgy. I longed for more congregational singing, felt displaced by the choir, and wished the prayer book contained as much Hebrew as the one we used at the Jamaica Jewish Center. How indelible are the religious reference points of one's childhood, how powerful the echoes.

The Jewish Theological Seminary began ordaining women in 1985. Soon afterward my friend Bella Abzug, the congresswoman known for her big hats and progressive views, convinced me to join B'nai Jeshurun, an old and established Conservative congregation on the Upper West Side that was in the process of being rejuvenated by an activist rabbi. Marshall Meyer, a protégé of the great modern philosopher Rabbi Abraham Joshua Heschel, had just returned from a quarter century in Buenos Aries where, in the shadow of Argentina's state terrorism, he built a thriving Jewish renewal movement from scratch. At B'nai Jeshurun he established an inclusive, egalitarian congregation—women, men, straight, gay, singles as well as couples, disabled people, young and old—and a Judaism that found its expression not just in prayer and study but in song, dance, and social action. I had found my spiritual home.

Nevertheless, if you'd asked me my religion at the time, I'd have said it was feminism. And I'd have been surprised had anyone pointed out the disproportionate number of Jewish women in the movement's leadership and rank-and-file or, more precisely, women who happened to be Jewish. While not denying their ethnic origins, these women neither practiced their religion nor showed any particular interest in its patriarchal sins. A few, like myself, were once observant but had left the fold in frustration or rage; most had been virtual strangers to the synagogue. I don't remember any of us acknowledging our Jewish background to one another or wondering if our libratory impulses might have originated in our upbringing or in Judaism itself, whose fundamental ethos—intolerance for injustice, empathy with the oppressed, belief in the collective—dovetailed with the feminist struggle. For the most part, we had no use for religion; our purview was the world.

But starting in the mid-1970s, I became aware of a small contingent of women whose religious affiliation was their primary identity. You might say they were Jews who happened to be feminists. Under the rubric of "Jewish feminism" or "feminist Judaism," they formed a movement within the movement, and their goal was nothing short of the eradication of male supremacy and gender inequality in Jewish life.

Marrying feminist analysis to Talmudic disputation, they challenged their brethren not just to talk the talk but to walk the walk toward justice for Jewish women. Poets and liturgists degendered God language and prayer books. Educators created nonsexist, female-inclusive Hebrew school curricula. Feminist scholars drew on the sages and sources to prove women's entitlement to wear phylacteries or tallit, to serve in the pulpit, have an aliyah, read from the Torah, and count in the minyan. Some fought for equity in Jewish academia and seminaries. Others took aim at gender bias in the allocation of community resources and demanded attention be paid to issues like homophobia, reproductive rights, or child care. Still others advocated for victims of domestic violence and sexual abuse, problems rarely acknowledged within the community because of the *shonde* (shame) factor. And happily for me, many Jewish feminists were creating new ceremonies, among them the women's seder. In 1976 Esther Broner, author of *The Women's Hagaddah*, invited me to join her and five other "Seder Sisters" in planning a feminist seder to be held on the third night of Passover.[5]

In the past, women were only allowed to clean out the cupboards, cook, and serve. Esther Broner's words in an early version of the haggadah recall, "We were told that we were brought out of Egypt from the house of bondage, but we were still our fathers' daughters, obedient wives, and servers of our children, and were not yet ourselves." At the feminist seder, we women become ourselves. We are made present in the ceremony. We introduce ourselves by our matrilineage—"I am Letty, daughter of Cyral, daughter of Jennie"—and the mere mention of our mothers and grandmothers inevitably brings tears. (Gloria Steinem always acknowledges her Jewish grandmother Pauline, a first-wave feminist.) Esther conducts the service and everyone contributes a midrash, a piece of personal testimony, a song (Bella always bellowed her favorite Yiddish melody and, since her death, we sing it in her memory). Passing around a pitcher of water and a bowl, we wash each other's hands. We recite the Plagues of Women (rape, battery, breast cancer, unequal pay . . .). We honor the nameless women in the Bible and those named but eclipsed by their husbands and sons. We ask the Four Questions of womankind. (Why do Jewish parents still want a firstborn son? Why do Jewish men prefer "shiksas"? Why do Jews hear a "kike" joke and call the ADL but hear "JAP" jokes and laugh—or tell them with impunity? Why is there so rarely a woman in the delegation of "American Jews" sent to meet with prime ministers and kings?)

Our women's seder celebrated its twenty-eighth anniversary in 2003. Replicated in many forms in hundreds of communities around the world, this new ritual reveals how much can be gleaned from Jewish tradition by those willing to mine it with the tools of feminist transformation. Other innovative rituals have likewise affirmed this epiphany and sustained women like me through the fallow years: Rosh Hodesh (first of the month) groups, a cross between a graduate seminar and a 1970s-style consciousness-raising session. Women's Purim celebrations that acknowledge both Esther and Vashti. Tashlich ceremonies in which we cast off our sins and the sins committed against us. Courses that view the sacred texts through a gender lens. The new tradition of adding Miriam's Cup to the seder table, an homage to Moses' sister, the prophet who danced the Hebrew women across the Sea of Reeds.

Miriam and Deborah and the Deborahs of my generation taught me it was possible for a woman to practice her faith without losing her dignity.

The Golda part of my journey describes a simpler trajectory, the coming of age of a political Jew. My spiritual search was a private matter, but I saw no reason to assert my ethnic identity, such as it was, in the secular world. Like many assimilated second-generation Americans, I had the luxury of forgetting my Jewishness thanks to never having experienced anti-Semitism in Jamaica, at Brandeis, or in New York City, where parking rules are suspended for Tisha b'Av, or in book and magazine publishing, where I held a number of jobs before becoming a writer. Of the five founders of *Ms.* magazine, two of us were Jews, two were Christian, and Gloria Steinem was half and half. The only time my religion came up at the office was when I was asked to translate *mishegas* or explain why Orthodox women wear wigs. Just as it made sense for a Catholic colleague to edit a piece on pro-choice nuns, it seemed only logical for me to edit "Is it Kosher to Be Feminist?" but beyond that, my being Jewish seemed irrelevant. Judaism and feminism were two separate worlds.[6]

That view was forever altered by the United Nations International Women's Decade whose opening conference, held in 1975 in Mexico City, was the venue for the passage of the infamous "Zionism Is Racism" resolution. Instead of grappling with such global problems as female infanticide, genital mutilation, illiteracy, hunger, poverty, and sexual oppression, the conference agenda was hijacked for a vituperative campaign against Israel that was fomented by women or fronted by women on behalf of their respective governments. Mexico City was my wake-up call. How could so many supposed movement colleagues forsake the agendas of international sisterhood to support chauvinist nationalist interests? Was it possible that, in working to liberate all women, I was empowering some women to destroy Israel?

Five years later, at the mid-decade conference in Copenhagen, the anti-Israel rhetoric was compounded by flagrant anti-Semitism. Delegates to the nongovernmental organization gatherings were heard shouting, "Hitler should have finished the job!" "Kill the Jews!" "The only good Jew is a dead Jew." The atmosphere was permeated by the threat of violence. American Jews and Israeli women were harassed, isolated, terrorized, traumatized. Clearly, sisterhood was not powerful enough to immunize women against the virus of religious bigotry or to trump the vicissitudes of Middle East politics. But a question began nagging me: Was anti-Semitism a by-product of the biases of the UN General Assembly, or might it also be festering beneath the surface of American feminism? After interviewing eighty Jewish women around the country, I published an article, "Anti-Semitism in the Women's Movement," in *Ms.* in 1982 that documented large and small insults, exclusions, humiliations, ostracism, and stereotyping of Jewish women in feminist contexts.[7] Academic conferences that acknowledged the experiences of women of various minority groups but not of the Jews. Women's meetings scheduled on the High Holy Days, or without regard for the sabbath needs of their observant Jewish members. Convocations that conjured Jesus' divinity before a mixed audience. Defacement of posters on the walls of women's centers advertising Jewish caucuses or speakers. JAP-bashing on campus. Defamatory references to "Jewish money," "Jewish clannishness," "Jewish hair."

The evidence of my own research persuaded me to go public as a Jew. I could no longer claim my religious identity was "irrelevant" to my life in the women's movement or anywhere else. I could no longer divide myself in half, ignoring Deborah while in Golda's territory or Golda when on Deborah's terrain. As a woman and a Jew, a writer and an activist, it was incumbent on me to behave in the world as a representative of both constituencies and to carry the interests of each group into the purview of the other. I would have to advance feminist goals in Judaism, stand up for Jews in the women's community, and integrate the several selves in my soul.

Lately I've come to think of my identity as a long, solid board, a seesaw that can tip in the direction of feminist advocacy when womankind are at risk and toward Jewish advocacy when Jews are imperiled. My board is firm, strong enough to carry double weight, and impervious to those who would split it, saw it, or sandbag it on either end.

Which reminds me of a workshop I attended years ago. Entering the room, we found a few dozen signs posted along the walls, each containing a single word: WOMAN, WIFE, DAUGHTER, MOTHER, WORKER, STU-DENT, FEMINIST, HUMANIST, SOCIALIST, CHRISTIAN, JEW, MUSLIM, AGNOSTIC, ATHEIST, AMERICAN, INTELLECTUAL, and so on. The facil-itator directed us to quickly review the signs and, without thinking too hard about it, "Go stand under the one that best describes your identity."

In 1972 I had no trouble placing myself under the word FEMINIST. Had I been given the same instruction in 1982 after my survey of anti-Semitism in the movement, I might have stood under the sign that said JEW. Today I would simply refuse to choose.

NOTES

1. Betty D. Greenburg and Althea O. Silverman, *The Jewish Home Beautiful* (New York: The Women's League of the United Synagogue of America, 1941).
2. Letty Cottin Pogrebin, *Deborah, Golda, and Me: Being Female and Jewish in America* (New York: Crown Publishers, 1991).
3. Letty Cottin Pogrebin, *Three Daughters* (New York: Farrar, Straus and Giroux, 2002).
4. W. E. B. DuBois, *The Souls of Black Folk* (Chicago: A. C. McClurg, 1903).
5. Esther M. Broner and Naomi Nimrod, *The Women's Hagaddah* (San Francisco: Harper San Francisco, 1994).
6. Audrey Gellis, Bracha Sachs, and Paula Hyman, "Is It Kosher to Be Femi-nist?" *Ms.* Magazine 3 (July 1974).
7. Letty Cottin Pogrebin, "Anti-Semitism in the Women's Movement," *Ms.* Magazine 10 (June 1982).

THREE

Azizah al-Hibri

1983 Author, *Women and Islam*
1986 Founding editor, *Hypatia: A Journal of Feminist Philosophy*
1993 Founder, Karamah: Muslim Women Lawyers for Human Rights

ASSALAMU ALAYKUM (PEACE BE WITH YOU).

My name is Azizah al-Hibri, and I am an American Muslim immigrant. I came to this country in 1966 from Beirut, Lebanon, and I would like to tell you a little bit about my journey. Like many of the people who spoke before me, I was deeply religious. I came from a leading religious family in my country. My grandfather, who was very dear to me, had established the Islamic Scout Movement and an orphanage in Lebanon. He also headed the board of trustees of the Islamic school system (Al-Maqasid). As I was growing up, my father brought me a sheikh to teach me the Qur'an, so I was reading it very early on and having discussions with the sheikh about what I read. This approach both educated me in religion and also in the skills of the classical Arabic language. It was a very important time in my life to be rooted in all of these important experiences.

At the same time, however, there was something very unusual happening in my home. My father was being very protective of me, almost restrictive. And he always did it in the name of religion. Much later I realized that having lost my mother when I was three years old, my father decided that he was not going to lose me. He became very possessive, but he used the religious argument to justify his actions. So as I grew up, I felt that I was suffocating and that perhaps all his claims about religion were also suffocating me.

When I finished high school, my male cousin Usama interceded with my father to let me go to college. My father, who believed strongly in education, was concerned about my well-being in a coed university. Usama then promised my father that he would look after me and I would be okay at the university. So I was permitted to attend the American University of Beirut. There I noticed that my other cousins, and other students as well, were living a little bit freer life than my own. This is how I first became exposed to secular, western culture.

After finishing my undergraduate degree at American University, I came to the United States to continue my education, and this is where I actually started a full-fledged rebellion. I never totally gave up my religious beliefs—these beliefs were very deeply entrenched—they were just submerged for a while, as I became Marxist, thanks to my professors.

On my way to the United States, just a few months before I came here, something happened. I was the president of the debating society at the American University, and a distinguished American guest passed through Beirut. Our club invited him to speak on campus. The dean of students at our university said, "We don't think he should speak on our campus." And I went and asked him, "Why not?" He said, "He'll give a very bad impression of life in the US; there is no need to show our dirty laundry in Lebanon." We insisted on our right to freedom of speech, and Malcolm X did come to campus, and he did speak.

After Malcolm spoke, we corresponded; and he came again. On his second trip, I saw him to the airport, and he gave me a little gift, a book. He wrote in it an inscription that I did not really fully understand at that time. It said basically, "Go on, you'll be a great Muslim woman leader . . . for Muslim women's rights."[1] And I was thinking "What?" I was just a kid then, and he decided to buy me some ice cream and talk while waiting for the airplane. I remember we had a very nice talk, and he invited me to Harlem when I come to the United States. He knew that I had decided to come to the United States to pursue my graduate education.

It was a couple of months later when I heard on the news that my friend Malcolm had been killed. And it was a really bad loss for me. I do not know how many of you have lost parents early on in life, but that scars you for a very long time, and you do not handle the losses after that very well. I remember going into my dorm room, closing the door, and deciding that I was going to starve myself to death. It did not happen. But when I came to the United States, the first thing I did when I arrived in New York was to tell the cab driver, "I need to go to Harlem." And he said, "Why?" I said, "Because I promised to see Harlem." And the driver said, "Okay, I'll take you." So he drove me, and at one point he stopped the car and he said, "You see over there?" I said, "Yeah." He said, "That's Harlem. You don't want to go there." And he drove on.

That set the tone for how I understood American life and how I understood very early on my alliances with various people in the United States. When I came here the civil rights movement was raging, and it was a very simple thing for me to become a part of it, because I had understood what Malcolm X had told me. I also saw the antiwar movement and I became part of it. I arrived here in 1966, and I was able to be part of all these things.

But as I grew up, I felt that there was something missing. In all of these events, I felt that the woman in me wanted to say something, to take more of a central role. I was used to a central role in the country I grew up in. True, my father was restrictive; but I was recognized as a person in the religious arena as much as any of the men around him. Also, one day my aging grandfather, who had many grandchildren, called me. He sat me next to him and said, "You are my granddaughter and you are very young, and probably I will die before you will be old enough. But I want you to remember two things

I'm going to tell you now, and when you grow up, think about them." And then he confided in me two very important ideas that represented his deep thoughts about religion.

As I grew up, not only did I think about these two ideas, but also about the fact that my grandfather did not summon any of my male cousins and put them next to him and say, "This is what I want you to think about as you grow up." It became clear to me that my grandfather had chosen me for leadership in the religious arena. This might be difficult to understand in light of what we see today. But no patriarch in this world who is a Muslim can stand in front of me and tell me that Islam would prevent me from doing what I am doing. There is absolutely no religious backing for such a position, and I know that because I have studied the religion. This is the power I have.

After I came to the United States, and I got seduced by Marxism, I wrote a great deal of secular feminist literature. The first one I remember was in 1975, when I was getting my Ph.D. I read it at the Society for Women in Philosophy (SWIP).[2] That was the first meeting of SWIP, and SWIP has represented a very important force in my history. So did the National Women's Studies Association. These two organizations gave me the family I did not have in the United States, and I remember when we first went to SWIP that some of the women started talking about religion. "Oh God, how boring. Can't they grow up?" I thought, "You know, I was religious too, but now I found Marxism." And then I noticed what the women around me were doing—they immediately fell into a self-criticism mode and realized that there should be a place at the table for everyone and we should respect everyone regardless of whether they were secular or religious, gay or straight, White or non-White—and that was a wonderful, wonderful milieu for me to grow in, in terms of tolerance and in terms of building a family. The same thing happened at the National Women's Studies Association.

So I went on from there to teach feminism at Texas A&M, which was a challenge. In fact, many of my students were from the corps of cadets. Then at one point I felt that I was really committed to change, that I did not want to talk about women's rights, I wanted to get them. I felt that if I continued to be a philosopher and write, I had no idea how to go about changing the world. So I thought a lot about it—I was just about to come up for tenure—and I could have had a very easy life after that, just get tenured and sit in College Station. But instead I decided, "I am going to make an important move. I am going to become a student again." And I went to law school. That was a very tough decision. I had male professors who were committing many logical fallacies as they lectured in class. My Ph.D. was in logic, and I very much wanted to correct their mistakes, but I soon realized that that was not what you do in law school.

Law school was a turning point. When Letty Cottin Pogrebin talked about superstition, she described what I think many of us who are religious feel. We feel that God talks to you, in different ways, but you just have to be sensitive, and listen, and you shall hear. And when I listen, what I find out is that what I want is not necessarily what is best for me. Look for the signs; see what doors open and what doors close. Well, what happened was that while I was in Texas on my way to law school I had a very personal crisis. I sat and thought about it—by then I had a couple of friends from the community, and they were very religious people from Saudi Arabia. I remember telling the wife about my problems, and she would chat with me. Her husband was very religious. So one day I looked at him and said, "Would you please, when you pray, remember me in your prayers? Would you please pray on my behalf?" And he looked at me and he said, "You know, nothing is stopping you from praying. Do it yourself." I thought, "How uncooperative of him." Then I thought, you know, "Who needs this guy, right? I'll go pray."

And then I went home. I remember it was morning, really early morning before sunrise. I was alone in my bedroom, and I decided to pray. I had done it many times before, but I had not done it since I had become enlightened in Marxism. I remember this strange feeling of bowing and kneeling to the floor at home. As I was doing it, I was telling myself, "You Marxist Ph.D. What are you doing?" And then I thought, " But that's exactly why I need to do it." And suddenly I felt a peace I had not felt before. You know how some women speak about the hole in here, in our guts? That hole just disappeared as I prayed, and I knew that I was doing what I was supposed to do. So I went back to religion.

When I went back to religion, I went back on my own terms. I had a special relationship with God. I did not need anybody to teach me the Qur'an because I have done that, I can read it on my own, I can think on my own. I do not need anybody's interference. And so when I went to law school, I went to law school with that in mind. But, at the same time, I thought, "I have rebelled enough. I have talked about patriarchy enough. You know what? I do not even know patriarchy, the patriarchy I'm talking about." After all, I grew up in Lebanon. We talk about western patriarchy, we talk about capitalism and its tools—I had never really personally experienced it; I had never had to work. So I decided that if I was going to speak about something, I better experience it. And so I went to Wall Street and became a corporate lawyer.

It was really quite an experience, including the time when one partner wondered if I could do the dance of the seven veils. But on the whole, I learned a lot that was very important for later life. And then I understood that my mission was not in being there but in teaching. The door opened for me when the editor of the *Case Western Reserve Journal of International Law* contacted me out of the blue and said, "By the way, could you write us an article on Islam and democracy?" And I thought, "What a topic! And why me?" It really came out of the blue. It was not fashionable then to talk about this topic. I thought, "I'll do it." I talked to the law firm, asked them to give me release time, took it, and started researching. There was very little on the subject. Finally I found some ancient stuff and was able to translate it into modern terminology.[3]

The Muslim men in my community were very supportive. In fact, they started giving me more and more ways to improve my research and become a jurist in the real sense of the word. When my article appeared, they actually reprinted it and distributed it. So I felt a great deal of support from some of the enlightened men. I was not fighting against everybody.

To make a long story short, during that period I went to many international conferences, including Copenhagen and Beijing, and there I discovered that the international face of my wonderful feminist sisters that I had known for so long was different from their domestic face. I realized that what they were trying to do was basically to act patriarchal toward my sisters, the Muslim women abroad. It became clear that my Muslim sisters needed to be helped from the onslaught of my western feminist sisters. So I established the organization called Karamah. Karamah means "dignity"—and this name comes from the Qur'anic verse that says, "We have given dignity to the children of Adam" (17:70). That includes men and women. And so Karamah began as an educational organization.

This is what we do: We develop feminist jurisprudence, which is totally based on tradition. We do not invent things. We do not reject tradition. We just show how patriarchal men have distorted that tradition. I have taken my message to no less than fourteen Muslim countries where I sat with legislators, I sat with mullahs, I sat with women lawyers and grassroots women. I explained my message to them. In every place I was well received. There have been a couple of times where I was not so well received until we talked a little bit further. But what I am trying to say is that in the Muslim world, if you come to the problem from a faith-based approach, Muslims are more likely to listen to you than if you come to them saying "You still believe in religion? Why don't you modernize and become secular?" That goes nowhere. And for the longest time Karamah was not appreciated by secular feminists in the United States.

Today our time has come. Today a lot of people are coming asking for Karamah to help, whether domestically or internationally. There are many Muslim women that have asked us to help them start branches of Karamah in their own countries. We have spoken on various personal status code (family law) issues. I have provided a consultation on family law to the Supreme Council for Women's Affairs in Qatar. I have been asked to consult on various family laws in other countries. We are now getting contacted on issues relating to Afghanistan, Nigeria, South Africa, and so on. So Karamah has been growing since the last year in tremendous ways. And our goal is to grow in a way that makes everybody feel that what we are doing is the right thing for Muslim women at home and abroad.

So I am very happy to say that now that I look back on my history, the pinnacle of this history is happening right now, with a lot of young women coming to us and saying "Train us. We want to be the next generation of Muslim women who are going to follow up on the work that you are doing." They are going to bring together the Muslim women around the world. We might even have our first international Muslim women's conference here in the United States. So this is really a very important time for us. We have to understand that basically the most important thing we do is education—that unless we lay the religious foundation properly, nothing is going to get done. We do not work out of the point of view that we need to get into the midst of conflicts. To the contrary, we believe in conflict resolution.

The real challenge for us, and I will finish by addressing this challenge, is the following: There are perceptions of the United States abroad now that are very important, and it is these perceptions we have to take into account as we work. What is the United States doing abroad? Is it a force for democracy and freedom, or is it a force for domination? It is these two alternatives that are going to determine how we are going to work. If we work abroad and we are viewed as being a capitalist tool, we are not going to get anywhere. And if we work abroad as allies of people of faith who are trying to achieve the human rights of the various people in their community, we go much further. How do we balance this without getting caught into a very, very nasty situation abroad? For this, I can only ask that you remember us in your prayers and thoughts. We are now in Karamah at a very critical juncture. We have decided this morning—some of our board members are actually here at Harvard and we had a board meeting this morning—that we are going to go ahead and take wise risks. We cannot sit on the sidelines simply because the situation is dangerous. We are going to do what we have to do, but we will do it with honesty, and hope that God will protect us.

NOTES

1. The inscription read: "To Azizah, You have and are everything it takes to create a New World—leadership is needed among women as well as men—and you have all of the qualities it takes to make people and things move. Brother Malcolm X." The book was Abd-al-Rahaman 'Azzam, *The Eternal Message of Muhammad*, trans. C. Farah (New York: Devin-Adair Co., 1964).
2. This paper has not been published.
3. Azizah al-Hibri, "Islamic Constitutionalism and the Concept of Democracy," *Case Western Reserve Journal of International Law* 24, no.1 (Winter 1992): 3–10.

FOUR

Virginia Ramey Mollenkott

1974 Founding member, Evangelical and Ecumenical Women's Caucus

1977 Author, *Women, Men, and the Bible*

2001 Author, *Omnigender: A Trans-Religious Approach*

FOR THE FIRST THIRTY-SOME YEARS OF MY LIFE, THE CHRISTIANITY I learned from my Protestant fundamentalist family was enough to strangulate my desire to celebrate my own particularities and thus to embody God in just the way She had created me to do. But during those same years, the keys to my eventual liberation were also being provided. Although many right-wing Christians despise what I have done with the keys they put into my hands, the fact is that the same Bible that deeply oppressed me has also been the most vital element in setting me free. It is not an overstatement to claim that I have been radicalized by the Bible.

I was born in 1932 into a working-class Philadelphia family. We attended church three times on Sunday and every Tuesday evening at a storefront assembly of Plymouth Brethren. These Brethren have been immortalized by Garrison Keillor as the major alternative to Lutheranism in Lake Wobegon, but our assembly's doctrines were a little less benign than anything I've heard Keillor describe. I was taught that I had a deceitful, untrustworthy heart, but that Jesus loved me anyway. Only by asking Jesus to come into my evil heart to wash my sins away could I ever be made worthy of Heaven. My worth would never stem from any merits of my own, but only from Jesus' paying for my sins vicariously, bearing the punishment I deserved by dying on the cross for me.

While I was still quite young, seven or eight at the most, one of my Sunday school teachers gave our class a graphic description of Jesus' crucifixion. Having been assured that even had I been the only person on earth who ever needed salvation, Jesus would have submitted to this torture to satisfy his Father's righteous anger at my sins, I began to cry. Although I was a compliant child who desperately wanted to please my parents, my mother had her own reasons for administering frequent whippings. So I knew what undeserved punishment felt like—and I could not bear the thought that Jesus' Father would require him to be tortured to death because of my evildoings.

Many years later, at the first Re-Imagining Conference in Minneapolis, I would publicly take my stand with the womanists and feminists who reject the theory that Jesus' death was a vicarious payment for the sins of humankind. We did so on the basis that it looks like child abuse perpetrated by God and thus sanctifies violence in general as well as rape and domestic violence. But at age seven or eight, all I knew was that I could not *bear* for someone else to be punished for evils I had allegedly committed, even though I could not conjure up any thought, word, or deed bad enough to merit such punishment. On that memorable morning, once Sunday school had ended, grown-ups gathered around to see why I was sobbing so uncontrollably. They seemed strangely amused that I should have taken the lesson so seriously. I remember feeling puzzled that anybody could know about such horrible injustice *without* taking it seriously.

BELIEF IN DEPRAVITY AT THE CORE

Although I was not clear about what I had done to cause Jesus' crucifixion, I found it easy enough to believe in myself as boundlessly evil. Protestant fundamentalist theology only reinforced the sense of damnation I felt as a victim of mother-infant incest. At a very early age I noticed that other children were not conscious about their bodies the way I was, and I assumed that the difference stemmed from their being clean-minded, whereas I was filthy-minded, aware of sex while the others remained innocent. Mother ceased her inappropriate attentions when I reached age three, because she feared I would remember; and by the time she resumed her attempts in my eleventh year, I was already too experienced to permit anything further. Although she forced me to sleep in the same bed with her, I clung to my side of the bed and said no loudly enough for my brother to hear if she attempted anything. Not one to give up easily, she continued to make passes well into her eighties and my fifties. Fortunately for me, she had a near-death experience in her mid-eighties, and during the last four years of her life I had a beloved mother and a healed relationship.

I have no trouble believing research statistics that claim that child abuse, including incest, is more frequent in religiously right-wing homes than elsewhere. A belief in total depravity tends to stimulate the sensation that having the name, one might as well play the game. And the sense of an easily angered, removed, authoritarian God encourages power—over relationships not only between men and women, but also between parents and children. I am convinced, however, that mother-daughter incest is far more common than most of the literature acknowledges, especially in religiously conservative homes. In such homes, many housewives feel powerless over anything and anyone except their own little children.

My brother and I were the first generation in our family to attend college. Mother always said she would send us both to college if there were enough money, but if not, of course my brother would be chosen. This was in accord with the Plymouth Brethren belief that men are divinely ordained to head the home, church, and society, and therefore need greater education than girls and women. Since I was more intellectual than my brother, I chafed under these teachings and resolved to become a missionary. I knew that on foreign mission fields, women could assume leadership roles left vacant by men who had no desire to live under adverse conditions. I also vowed to myself that nothing—nothing!—would stop me from getting a good education.

When I was eleven I entered into a lesbian love relationship with a twenty-one-year-old woman in our assembly. She was of course committing statutory rape, something I had never heard of at the time. But to me the relationship felt affirming because for the first time in my life an adult person had shown an interest in what I was thinking and feeling. I am not defending statutory rapists or sexual predators; I am simply stating that in my particular case, the relationship turned out to be a validating and helpful one. It empowered me to say no when Mother tried to renew her inappropriate behavior; and I would not have responded to the relationship with the twenty-one-year-old in the first place had I not already been oriented toward same-sex love. Both my personal experience and my research have taught me that no one can recruit anyone into a sexual orientation that is foreign to their own inclination. People can be lured or forced into an alien experience for a while, but eventually they will revert to expressing their own authentic desires.

When Mother found out about my secret relationship, she sent me to a Southern Presbyterian boarding school near Orlando, Florida, "outing" me to everyone before my arrival. At that school, chapel was a daily requirement, during which we were taught the same fundamentalist theology I had always heard. But there was one significant additional teaching: namely, that whenever a woman dared to "do theology," the result was always heresy. The story of Jezebel provided the sole biblical "proof text" for such assertions, but they shamed me deeply. Various administrators also took enormous interest in my lesbianism, frequently reminding me that although my condition was unchangeable and incurable, God had no time for people like me. They told me that according to Romans 1, we homosexuals were "without God in our minds." Privately I cried out to God, asking how "He" could be absent from my mind when I memorized so much scripture—the whole of Ephesians, Philippians, and Colossians, the Epistle of First John, and so forth.

After months of being forcibly isolated from the other students, falsely accused of molesting a student, and profoundly shamed in various other ways, at age thirteen I tried to kill myself, just as many other lesbian, gay, bisexual, and transgender youths have done. My suicide attempt was foiled by a student who thirty years later phoned to tell me she also had been lesbian all her life and had felt sorry during high school that I was taking so much abuse "on her behalf." While I was imprisoned in the school infirmary, the administrators required me to read a book about Satan, which of course only deepened my desperation. What assisted my recovery was the love of my fellow students, expressed in notes that were wrapped around hard candies and tossed over the infirmary transom.

I went to Bob Jones University (BJU) because it was more affordable than Wheaton College (Illinois), the only other college my family knew about that was right wing enough to be considered. I was able to navigate the rough waters of BJU's infamous disciplinary policies because the administrators knew nothing about my love nature and consequently did not harass me about it. But every day in chapel we were forced to recite a creed asserting that we believed in "Christ's vicarious atonement for the sins of mankind by the shedding of His blood on the cross." I tried not to think too much about that, focusing instead on the thrilling insights I was picking up by studying British and American literature.

MARRIAGE: UNPAID SERVITUDE

By my senior year, the social pressure to date a man and move toward marriage became very strong. I confided my same-sex attractions to one of my professors, who assured me that if only I would pretend to be heterosexual long enough, eventually heterosexual feelings would emerge. A high school teacher had said something similar; and although I didn't really believe it, I hoped that it just might be true. Besides, I knew that the only escape from living with my mother was to marry. So I began dating Fred Mollenkott and even taught at BJU for a year after graduation while he was still an undergraduate there.

During summers I attended Temple University, where I studied chiefly under the tutelage of Professor Elisabeth Schneider, the first world-class literary scholar I had ever encountered. The fact that she was also an atheist shook my fundamentalism to its foundations. I began extensive reading in some of the great American Unitarian and Transcendentalist thinkers, mentally contrasting their views to those of the Plymouth Brethren with whom I still met four times a week. I contemplated a complete revolt from Christianity. But something inside kept warning me that no plant grows by cutting itself off from its roots. Rather, growth comes from deriving whatever sustenance one can garner from those roots, emphasizing the most nourishing factors in order to develop into something larger and more free. The Bible (interpreted through the fundamentalist grid) had been my deepest taproot, and throughout my Ph.D. work and forty-four years of teaching college and graduate literature, I refused to walk away from the Bible, refused to "trash" it, learned to read it through the lens of liberation, and found myself transformed by those ancient texts.

Before I describe some of the major processes and defining moments of that gradual transformation, I want to comment on my fundamentalist marriage and extrication from it. When I walked the aisle in 1954, I did not have a clue about the implications of the patriarchal trap I was entering. As I discovered rapidly, but especially during my divorce proceedings in 1973, everything was tilted in favor of the male. Although I paid all my own bills and most of his, I needed his permission to get a loan, and he did not need mine. And although I had used New York University merit scholarship money for the down payment on our house and then paid most of the mortgage as well, at the divorce I had to split the equity equally with Fred because, as I was told, "that was all part of the marital bargain."

Fred believed that I was divinely obligated to pick up his dirty clothes wherever he dropped them and to return them to his bureau ready for wear. And although as a college professor and eventually a mother my working hours far exceeded his, I was obliged to make all meals and clean up afterward. But at the divorce, I merited no alimony for all those years of theologically driven servitude, because after all I had a good career and could support myself. I was fortunate to escape with custody of our son without having to subsidize Fred. Although I often subsidized him voluntarily between our divorce and his death nine years later, to have been forced to do so would have felt like the ultimate in androcentric insults.

JOHN MILTON: LIBERATIONIST MENTOR

Fundamentalist moralisms leave no room for divorce, so it was truly a breath of hope when I discovered that in mid-seventeenth-century England, the great Puritan poet and theologian John Milton had written four tracts in support of divorce for incompatibility—something New Jersey legislators didn't get around to for three additional centuries.

Unabashedly, Milton took the law of love as his measuring stick for interpreting anything else he read and, on the basis of that law, argued *from scripture* that a loving God would never have consigned people to lifelong cohabitation on the basis of a mistaken commitment and/or a sexual act. From those tracts, and from Milton's other works, I learned how to read the Bible through liberationist lenses, and began my own gradual extrication from the fundamentalist mind-set.

In recent years, while learning a great deal from feminist academic research, I have often felt grateful that it wasn't available to me at the time when I was enmired in my androcentric marriage. Had I read the work of highly respected feminist scholars who assert (for instance) that Ephesians 5 really does require of women a secondary role in the home, church, and society, and really does order married women to live in one-way submission to their husbands, I would have been filled with despair. The fact that feminist scholars could offer no *biblical* way for a woman to find freedom—the fact that they *agreed* with the patriarchal interpretations I had learned in my youth—would have drained me of hope. It would not have helped to know that feminist scholars *disapproved* of the heteropatriarchal meanings they found in the Bible. I was not free to turn away from the text; what it "really said" was what mattered to me. So if androcentric fundamentalist and feminist biblical scholars agreed about the meaning of passages like Ephesians 5, I would have reasoned that they must be right and that the only way to freedom would be to jettison Christianity and its Holy Book entirely.

Instead, I learned from my graduate studies at Temple and New York universities, and especially from Milton's hermeneutics, how to recognize in Ephesians 5 certain attempts to subvert an unjust system that could not easily be changed or even challenged too directly. I learned to notice, for instance, the details of a larger context, such as the fact that Ephesians 4:15 instructs all followers of Jesus to grow up in all ways into the one who is the head, into the Christ—and to realize therefore that the following chapter's comparison of husband to head and wife to body could not in such a context be intended to validate a domestic hierarchy. No less than their husbands, Christian wives were expected to grow up "in all things" into the head, leaving no space for primary or secondary identities.

From Milton's method I learned to pay attention to the central impact of literary images, such as marriage's being depicted as the union of head and body in one flesh. Asking myself which I would prefer to sacrifice, my head or my body, enabled me to feel the impact of that imagery—certainly never intended to establish hierarchy, but to get readers to glimpse the organic unity of head and body, either one dead without the other.

I learned also to interpret analogies only within the context where they originally were presented, since every analogy breaks down somewhere. I noted that the wife is told to submit to her husband only within the parameter of Christ and the church, a relationship in which there is no coercion; and that even *that* analogy is drawn only within the commandment that every Christian should submit to every other Christian out of reverence to the Christ nature within everyone (Ephesians 5:21).

I learned also to notice linguistic anomalies, such as the fact that the Greek of Ephesians 5:22 does not contain any verb signifying the wife's submission, but instead piggybacks on the verb in the previous verse, the verb that commands *mutual* submission.

And I learned to avoid reading contemporary definitions back into the biblical text. To the Ephesians author as to other biblical authors, it was the heart and not the head that made the decisions from which issued the quality of a person's life. So apparently the author did not intend to pronounce the male the ultimate decision maker; that interpretation is anachronistic, finding support only in modern understandings of the function of the cerebral cortex.

From Milton's method I also learned to pay attention to the historical circumstances surrounding the text. The Ephesians author understood that because males held the power in that place and time, of necessity the husband would have to be the head or source of Christianizing the marital structure by laying aside his patriarchal privileges in favor of *mutual* subjection.

I am grateful that because of John Milton's poetic example, keen eye, and liberationist tendencies, I learned to lift up certain textual details that would subvert the androcentric expectations of the author's target readership and thus provide for them, and for future readers like myself, a way to shake ourselves free from oppressive social systems and assumptions. I found it ironic that some of the feminist professors at William Paterson College wanted Milton dropped from the literary curriculum, presumably because of his portraits of Eve and Dalila and of Adam's and Samson's misogyny when they were angry at their partners. Apparently my colleagues could not recognize the subversiveness of those portraits.

I plead with those of you who are professional feminist theologians and biblical scholars to bear in mind, when you publish your books and articles, that your work might be read by women who are located today where I was located decades ago. There are many thousands of such women. For their sake, when you deal with scripture, please take the most respectful, egalitarian, and liberating interpretation you can achieve without compromising your integrity. Please remember that as soon as you refer to the Bible dismissively, these women can no longer trust you.

LEARNING TO TRUST
PERSONAL EXPERIENCE AND INSIGHTS

There were many processes I had to work through in order to transform myself from a fundamentalist to a feminist. These processes and defining moments sometimes took place several at a time, nothing like as neatly as they will sound as I describe them. But such is the nature of autobiographical writing.

My first and most basic process was that of learning to trust my own experience and respect my own intellect and motives. Not only did I have to transcend the teaching that my core self was deceitful, desperately wicked, and totally untrustworthy; I had also been taught at Bob Jones University that female thought processes are naturally inferior. Women tend to think relationally, the professor said, whereas men break matters into their component parts and therefore are able to comprehend reality more clearly. At the time I figured there must be something flawed about that evaluation, but I lacked the confidence to defend women's ways of knowing.

I have always been fascinated by theology, and would have entered that field professionally had that ever been named as a possibility in my little corner of the world. Instead I found that my fascination with human behavior and relationships were drawing me toward the study of literature, the only place in the curriculum where we were discussing human motivations and the way diverse people actually live. It was not until the 1970s, when I became aware that feminists were strongly impacting the field of theology, that I began to teach myself that discipline and to make my own contributions to it. At that time I still needed male permission to venture beyond fundamentalist sex/gender roles, and it was supplied to me by Professor Paul King Jewett of Fuller Theological Seminary. He told me that my literary background was perfect preparation for doing theology and invited me to write the introduction to his book *Man as Male and Female*.[1]

I found it easier to learn respect for my intellect than to trust my own experience, convoluted though that may seem. It was especially difficult to believe that we are intended to be, as II Peter 1:4 claims, "participants of the divine nature." When I was reading John Calvin's *Institutes of the Christian Religion*, I was startled to come across a reference to this II Peter statement and immediately checked my Bible to see for myself.[2] Finding Calvin's reference correct had two effects on my consciousness: It increased my distrust of those who had never told me such good news, and it gave me a glimpse of what it would feel like to trust in goodness at the core of myself.

I read a lot of psychology in those days, but experienced cognitive dissonance when authors spoke about fundamental goodness at the core of the human psyche. Scripture passages like II Peter 1:4 were a help; but because we human beings tend to see only what we expect to see, I did not find a wealth of such passages during my fundamentalist years. What really changed me were my dreams. During my thirties and forties I had many Big Dreams that I would then interpret with the help of a psychotherapist and books like Carl Jung's translation of the *I Ching* and Jung's work on archetypes.[3]

Repeatedly I had the experience of assuming that a dream had casti-gated me for my faults, only to discover a beautiful and encouraging inter-pretation that fit the dream symbols much better than my initial frightened interpretation.

For instance, I once dreamed unmistakably that I was a Fool. I took this as a humiliating rebuke, but my therapist suggested that I study literature about the Fool card in the tarot deck. I found that like the Fool in *King Lear,* the Fool archetype personifies the central core of the psyche, the guiding force of the soul, which Jung refers to as the Self.[4] The Fool is unconventional and can be a windbag, and because the Fool lives outside the cozy anonymity most people enjoy, the Fool is often sad and lonely. But that very same outsider sta-tus enables the Fool to discover resources that are deep within.

I found that the number associated with the Fool card in the tarot deck is zero—and true to my early training, I at first assumed that fact to be indica-tive of my utter worthlessness.

But then I learned that when the Fool card is combined with any other card, it augments that card's value. So "nothing" turns out to be "something" after all! And I learned as well that the Fool card is esoterically understood to be the card of love and that alchemically it symbolizes the marriage between divine revelation and human wisdom[5]—exactly the kind of marriage I was trying to teach my students at the time.

Because my dreams were something I did not know how to manipulate with my conscious mind, I was able to trust them as coming from the Holy Spirit. Gradually, gradually, that series of Big Dreams released me from the fearsome theology of self distrust and brought me into the glorious liberty of a daughter of God.

SOME DEFINING MOMENTS

A pivotal moment in my transformation from fundamentalist to Christian feminist occurred during the 1960s when I was reading a book that men-tioned two distinctly different creation stories in the first two chapters of Genesis. By this time I had been teaching college-level literature for over a decade; so I checked my Bible, and indeed found two very different plots, presented at a different pace, with a different emphasis and different tone. I was horrified: How could all those obvious differences have previously escaped my attention? At last I realized the truth: When I read Chaucer, Shakespeare, Hawthorne, or Dickinson, I read on all my cylinders, with all the critical techniques I had learned in college and thereafter. But when I picked up the Word of God, unconsciously I also slipped on my fundamentalist blinders to assure myself that there could be no errors or contradictions in the sacred text. On the spot I vowed that henceforth I would read the Bible with the same attention to detail that I gave to other literary works. And on that very same spot, my radicalization by the Bible began.

Shortly thereafter I had another defining moment. New York University's professor of seventeenth-century poetry, J. Max Patrick, stated in class that the New Testament mandates the death penalty for certain offenses, and I blurted out that it does no such thing. Dr. Patrick did a double-take, unused to any student who knew the first thing about the Hebrew or Christian scriptures, let alone had the nerve to challenge him in public, since he was known for his ability to demolish students with withering contempt. He asked if I was sure.

I explained that he might be referring to St. Paul's opinion that those who did not acknowledge God and were filled with heartless wickedness "know God's decree, that those who practice such things deserve to die—yet they not only do them but even applaud others who practice them" (Romans I:32). I said that this opinion relied on certain laws in the Hebrew scriptures, "but certainly was not a New Testament–legislated death penalty." Professor Patrick looked at me searchingly and thereafter treated me with a respect he rarely accorded to any student, especially female students. From his respect, I in turn learned to appreciate the fact that despite the horrors of the theology I had been taught, my grounding in many surface facts of the Bible was valuable. It would save me lots of time as I learned to put those facts together in different configurations in order to achieve feminist conclusions.

Along the way during the decades to follow, plenty of people have accused me of twisting scripture to suit my own purposes. Being a conscientious scholar, I have asked myself how it was possible that the same words on a page would mean so differently to me than what they mean to androcentric and heteronormative traditionalists. Like Professor Laurel C. Schneider of the Chicago Theological Seminary, I have come to question why the burden of proof about the social construction of all interpretations should fall exclusively on the shoulders of those in the social location of "outsider." And like her, I have concluded that "queer commentary on Scripture is not more laden with the interpreter's desires than any other kind of commentary."[6] The fact is that "queer readings dispose of the presumed infrastructure of heteronormative stability, thereby revealing the desire that established the presumptions of that stability at the core. *Desire funds the theological imagination*, whether outside or inside the bounds of heteronormative presumption."[7] The same could be said of feminist theologies: Desire funds the theological imagination, whether outside or inside the boundaries of androcentric presumption.

To this day I keep many conservative and even fundamentalist commentaries in my biblical library. I utilize their insights with a healthy feminist skepticism, always asking myself who is being empowered by which interpretation. The conservative and liberal and various feminist and queer approaches counterbalance one another, each lifting up textual aspects unimportant to the others. Evaluating these various perspectives, I often think of Alexander Pope's advice: "Trust not thyself, but your defects to know/Make use of every friend—and every foe."

It was Professor Patrick who suggested that I write my doctoral dissertation on Milton and the Old Testament Apocrypha.[8] And that in turn led to several other defining moments.

I did most of my research at the central branch of the New York Public Library, and will never forget the day I first approached the file drawers cataloging the library's holdings in biblical scholarship. It took an entire huge *wall* of drawers! I had been taught that all I really needed to know was the Bible, particularly the Schofield Reference edition of the King James Version. After all, I had been told that the great Reformers—Luther, Calvin, Melancthon—had taken as their motto "Sola Scriptura" (the scriptures alone). But on that memorable day, feeling very excited as I examined the contents of that tremendous card catalog, I realized that the Reformers had referred not only to the sixty-six books universally accepted as canonical, but also to the apocryphal or hidden books surrounding that canon, and all the scholarship that illuminated the canon and apocrypha in all the various translations throughout history, and all the classical and scientific scholarship that threw light on the pages of Holy Writ. Like John Keats when he first discovered Chapman's translation of Homer, "Then felt I like some watcher of the skies/when a new planet swims into [her] ken."[9]

MY EXPANDING UNIVERSE

My mind-opening experience with the biblical studies card catalog was a paradigm for similar experiences I have had in other fields. After fourteen years of post–grade school education in which the only women's literary works ever assigned were a smattering of Emily Dickinson poems and one novel each by Virginia Woolf and Elizabeth Bowen, I began to discover the rich smorgasbord of women writers. And after the same fourteen years of studying only European or American White authors, I began to discover an astonishing wealth of African and Caribbean, Latino, and other "Third World" as well as African American authors, especially Black women such as Gloria Naylor, Toni Cade Bambara, Alice Walker, and Toni Morrison. Furthermore, after fourteen years of being taught (by both commission and especially omission) that every important author, composer, artist, or high achiever was heterosexual, I began to stumble on evidence that a significant percentage of my favorite authors, composers, artists, and historical leaders had in fact been gay, lesbian, bisexual, and/or transgender. This has been one of the more exciting aspects of my life: What began with such a cramped and fear-filled view of humankind has been expanded again and again to embrace more and more diversity.

Each time my horizons have expanded, I have learned to honor some previously unaccepted aspect of myself. At the New York Public Library, my world blew open to enable me to interpret the Bible liberatingly. Discovering the rich contributions of women, I learned to honor my own gifts and those of my foremothers and sisters. Discovering the brilliant contributions of people of color and those from non-western cultures, I learned to honor the colorful shadow aspects of my own nature, acknowledged my White privilege, and took responsibility for uprooting racism in my consciousness and opposing institutional racism in my culture. Discovering the way lesbian, gay, bisexual, and transgender contributions had been erased from traditional history, I came to appreciate my own lesbianism and (eventually) my transgender qualities, and above all to revel in the gorgeous diversity of God's creation.

One other defining moment in my journey from fundamentalist to feminist also occurred at the New York Public Library. Upon producing the requisite letter from a recognized scholar assuring the library that I was a bona fide researcher, I was admitted to the inner sanctum of the Rare Book Room. A first edition of the King James Version was tenderly placed on a soft cloth on my desk. I was told how to handle the pages so as not to cause any damage, then locked into the silent sanctuary to do my work in awed solitude.

I had always been told that the apocryphal books of the Hebrew Bible were not worthy for the establishment of any doctrine—indeed, that they were worthless, full of wild stories and heretical notions such as praying for the dead. No one had ever hinted that these "hidden" books, accepted as canonical by Roman Catholics and as secondary but valuable by many Jews and Protestants, had exerted an extensive and positive influence on the Christian scriptures. So I was astonished to see in this first 1611 edition not only the apocryphal books themselves, but a wealth of marginal notes indicating the influence of the Apocrypha (especially the Wisdom of Solomon) on the authors of the New Testament. The Apocrypha had been so unmentionable among fundamentalists that in high school I had come across and read some of the books with all the glee of swallowing forbidden fruit. But seeing for myself that respected seventeenth-century Protestant scholars had valued the Apocrypha enough to translate it and acknowledge its influence on the Christian scriptures caused me to resolve more than ever to trust my firsthand experience more than traditional but unsubstantiated opinion. In that sense, I left the Rare Book Room far more feminist than when I entered it.

As noted earlier, while I was writing my dissertation on *Milton and the Apocrypha* I picked up from Milton many techniques for reading the Bible in a way that liberates rather than oppresses. I got my first hate mail for writing an article about White racism that was published in *Christianity Today* and my first death threat while serving on the National Council of Churches' Inclusive Language Lectionary Committee.[10] Although I have not read them, I am told there are hundreds of hateful remarks and outright lies about me on the Internet: that I was fired from this school or that committee, that I single-handedly turned the New International Version (NIV) of the Bible into a gay-friendly text, and so forth. I am particularly puzzled by that latter allegation: first, because anybody should be able to see that the NIV is not more gay-friendly than any other version; second, because I was only a stylistic consultant, not a translator; and third, because I'm told that another oft-repeated lie is that I was on the NIV committee for only several months before they discovered my lesbianism and dismissed me. Perhaps I should have known to expect such hatred, since my mentor, John Milton, was vilified for his liberationism during his lifetime, especially by those who said his adult-onset blindness was God's judgment on his evil ways.

It would seem that using the law of love as one's central interpretive measurement is an abomination to many people. Yet it seems to me precisely the practice Jesus recommended when, after identifying as the greatest commandments the two that said to love God and then to love one's neighbor as oneself, he commented, "on these two commandments hang all the law and the prophets" (Matthew 22:40). I take that remark to mean that the Hebrew scriptures—the entire Bible of Jesus' day—were to be interpreted, and then either implemented or taken as warnings, according to those two similar love commandments. And because there is no love where there is no justice, interpreting in that way involves applying the hermeneutic of suspicion and an analysis of power relationships in any given passage of scripture—or, for that matter, any other words or actions whatsoever.

FROM INDIVIDUALISM TO COMMUNITY

This essay would be incomplete without some description of how I moved away from the fierce individualism of fundamentalism (and capitalism) and toward a sense of community. To Protestant Christian fundamentalists, salvation is a private matter between the individual soul and God. It has no public or systemic component; sin is exclusively "personal" rather than also corporate. Even the recent right-wing attempts to "reclaim America for Christ" are fueled by a strongly individualistic drive to make heteropatriarchal values normative so that only people with those values would be accorded first-class citizenship.

In our Plymouth Brethren Assembly, every family tried to look prosperous and trouble-free because that in turn would imply their "rightness" before God. People did not talk about their deepest fears, their shame, or their painful emotions; and seeking psychotherapy was such a failure of faith that if anybody succumbed, nobody mentioned it. So for me it was a revelation to discover genuine community, places where people could be frank about their failings without risking loss of respect and frank about their disagreements without jeopardizing their relationship.

I'd like to be able to say that every feminist organization is a place to experience such community, but for me that has not necessarily been true. I have learned the wonders of mutually supportive community from various conferences at Kirkridge Retreat and Study Center; from interreligious dialogue during the 1980s and early 1990s; from a monthly faculty group concerned with race, sex, and class at William Paterson College (now University); from the editorial staffs of social justice journals like *The Witness* and *The Other Side;* and elsewhere. But for me, the greatest ongoing experience of community has come from the Evangelical and Ecumenical Women's Caucus. Through the sisterhood of these great women and men and various transgenderists, all of whom are warmly welcomed, I have come into myself by joining with others in a way that could not have occurred without such a nurturing context.

The Evangelical Women's Caucus (EWC) was born in 1974 at the second Thanksgiving Workshop of Evangelicals for Social Action (ESA). It was conceived as an implementation of ESA's 1973 Chicago Declaration, part of which stated that "[w]e acknowledge we have encouraged men to prideful domination and women to irresponsible passivity. So we call both men and women to mutual submission and active discipleship."[11] I was asked to present a basic biblical feminist exegesis at the first EWC conference held in Washington, D.C., in 1975, and out of that presentation grew my first fully feminist book, *Women Men and the Bible*, followed by other works such as *The Divine Feminine: Biblical Imagery of God as Female*.[12]

From the beginning, EWC affirmed my gifts. But after Letha Dawson Scanzoni and I coauthored *Is the Homosexual My Neighbor?* and began to lead workshops on the topic, some members of EWC made a point of shunning me, or tried to undermine my authority by asking intrusive questions about my sexuality before I was ready to emerge from the closet.[13] Eleven years into the life of the organization, I was wondering whether I should withdraw my time and energy from a group that would not defend my civil and human rights. Finally, at the Fresno conference in 1986, the Evangelical Women's Caucus passed a resolution in support of those rights. At that time we lost at least half of our membership, who then proceeded to found an organization for heterosexual feminists only. But those who stayed in EWC have become my deeply appreciated "sisters of summer."

Although most of us see one another only in July of every other year, many are able to meet in local chapters; and we keep in touch via phone, Internet, and our excellent newsletter, *EEWC Update*. Some years ago we changed our name to the Evangelical *and Ecumenical* Women's Caucus to reflect the fact that some of our members are Roman Catholic or come from other traditions that would not claim to be evangelical. Yet we retain the term "evangelical" in the hope of reaching women from the religious right, women like Andrea Yates—we hope before androcentric theology drives them to commit mad acts such as the killing of her children that put Yates behind bars for life.[14]

Since my retirement from William Paterson University in December 1996, I have been studying transgender issues and have published a book called *Omnigender: A Trans-Religious Approach.*[15] It is my most radical book, and forms a good illustration of the way I have been radicalized by the Bible. The thesis is that because inequities between women and men are supported by overemphasizing differences between them, and because the presence of intersexuals, transsexuals, bisexuals, and other transgenderists proves that our culture's male-female polarization does not match reality, eventually society must move toward a sex/gender continuum that I have called omnigender. Although I did plenty of medical, psychological, and cross-cultural research for this book, for me the heart of the matter is biblical.

Genesis tells us that both male and female were made in the image of the Holy One, whose sex/gender, however metaphorical, must therefore somehow be inclusive of both male and female. And many Hebrew scholars posit an original Earth Creature who never became a human male until the human female was drawn from its side—in other words, an androgynous or intersexual original Adam, made in the image of an androgynous or intersexual Godhead. That hypothesis fits well with the facts of the Genesis text and helps to resolve several apparent conflicts between chapters 1 and 2.

As for the second Adam, Jesus the Christ: If the gospel statements that he was born of a virgin are taken literally, then like every other parthenogenetic birth, Jesus was genetically female, although as in many such births there was a sex reversal that caused Jesus to look and act like a statistically normal male. No wonder the Christian scriptures use a great deal of transgender imagery to describe Christ's body the church: all Christians, men as well as women, being termed Christ's bride; all Christians being instructed to put on Jesus like a garment, which for women amounts to a metaphor of cross-dressing; and so forth.

At the most recent national EEWC conference (July 2002), I mentioned from the platform that I consider myself a transgender lesbian. Afterward, people asked me why I called myself transgender: lesbian they understood, but in what sense transgender? I explained that I regard myself as a masculine woman, and I think most liberated people, heterosexual or otherwise, are transgender because they do not match society's traditional expectations for men and women. The response I got was genuinely feminist and genuinely human and loving. They nodded thoughtfully, and then during the author book-signing session lined up to buy copies of *Omnigender*. Apart from my experience of God Herself and my partnership with Suzannah Tilton, it was perhaps the most joyous experience of unconditional love that I have every known. Blessed be!

NOTES

1. Paul King Jewett, *Man as Male and Female: A Study in Sexual Relationships from a Theological Point of View* (Grand Rapids, Mich.: Eerdmans Publishing Co., 1975).

2. John Calvin, *Institutes of the Christian Religion*, 1536 ed. (Grand Rapids, Mich.: Eerdmans Publishing Co., 1975).

3. Richard Wilhem, Cary Baynes, and Carl Jung, trans., *I Ching* (London Routledge & Kegan Paul Ltd., 1951), 2 vols.

4. William Shakespeare, *King Lear*, 8th ed. (London: Methuen & Co., 1955).

5. *Meditations on the Tarot: A Journey Into Christian Hermeticism* (Ammity, N.Y.: Amity House, 1985), p. 621. This learned book was written anonymously in French and translated anonymously.

6. Laurel C. Schneider, "Yahwist Desires: Imagining Divinity Queerly," *Queer Commentary and the Hebrew Bible*, ed. Ken Stone (Cleveland, Oh.: The Pilgrim Press, 2001), p. 210.

7. Ibid., p. 214, emphasis mine.

8. Virginia Ramey Mollenkot, "Milton and the Apocrypha," Ph.D. diss., New York University, 1964.

9. John Keats, "On First Looking into Chapman's Homer," *Poems* (London: Printed for C. & J. Ollier, 1817).

10. Virginia Ramey Mollenkott, "Up from Ignorance: Awareness-Training and Racism," *Christianity Today* 15 (March 26, 1971): 6–8.

11. Sandra Sue Horner, "Becoming All We're Meant to Be; A Social History of Contemporary Evangelical Feminist Movement, A Case Study of the Evangelical and Ecumenical Women's Caucus," Ph.D. diss., the Joint Program in Religious and Theological Studies at Northwestern University/Garret Theological Seminary, December 2000, p. 74.

12. Virginia Ramey Mollenkott, *Women Men and the Bible*, rev. ed. (New York: Crossroads, 1988); Virginia Ramey Mollenkott, *The Divine Feminine: Biblical Imagery of God as Female* (New York: Crossroads, 1983).

13. Letha Scanzoni and Virginia Ramey Mollenkott, *Is the Homosexual My Neighbor?: Another Christian View* (San Francisco: Harper & Row, 1978).

14. Andrea Yates was found guilty by a Texas court and sentenced to life in prison for drowning three of her children in a bath tub on March 13, 2002. Before marriage Yates had been a successful nurse, but quit her job and bore five children in quick succession in accordance with religious teachings against birth control. Out of Christian submission to her husband she lived in isolation, home-schooling the children with little contact with the outside world. Anne Eggebroten, "A Biblical Feminist Looks at the Andrea Yates Tragedy," *EEWC Update: Newsletter of the Evangelical and Ecumenical Women's Caucus* 25, no. 4 (Winter 2001–2002), www.eewc.com/update/.

15. Virginia Ramey Mollenkott, *Omnigender: A Trans-Religious Approach* (Cleveland, Oh.: Pilgrim Press, 2001).

FIVE

Rosemary Radford Ruether

1965 Joined faculty, Howard University School of Religion
1972 Taught first course on feminist theology at Harvard
    Divinity School
1975 Author, *New Woman, New Earth*

THERE ARE MANY STORIES THAT I COULD TELL ABOUT THE BEGINNINGS
of the feminist movement and feminist theology in my experience, but I wish to
focus on my experience with the African American community in particular. For

me these early experiences in the civil rights movement and then in living in a predominately Black neighborhood in Washington, D.C., and teaching at Howard University were very formative in grounding my understanding of feminist theology as situated in an interconnected class, race, and gender analysis. I want to focus on this theme because I think it has been largely misinterpreted or forgotten by feminists in the academy and theological schools who began their work in the 1980s or 1990s, or the beginning of the twenty-first century.

The story line that I find among my students in theological schools today, a story line that has been reinforced by several widely read books and articles, is that "in the beginning"—that is, sometime in the late 1960s or early 1970s—"whitefeminists" (written as one word) were oblivious to race and class difference between women. They spoke about "women's experience" as if it were a generic experience common to all women, and made White women the normative female identity. They then were critiqued by a growing cohort of Black and Hispanic women who began their own contextualized expressions of women-centered theologies (womanist, mujerista). Now the current "wave" of feminism knows better and is striving to incorporate this understanding of "difference" between women.

I have no doubt that this is very much the way this situation was experienced by Black and Hispanic (and Asian) women in theological schools in the 1980s, as feminist theology has gained something of a foothold in theological schools and women's studies had become an established discipline in universities. What I want to point out here is that this scenario violates and indeed erases my own experience and that of a cohort of other feminist theologians (such as Letty Russell and Beverley Harrison) who began our work in the late 1960s and early 1970s.

It is important to point out that there was a diversity of feminisms at the time, not some simple unity. Specifically there were two quite different contexts in which the feminist movement arose in the mid- to late 1960s. One was the movement among women lawyers, government workers, and writers from which the National Organization for Women (NOW) arose. This movement was open to issues of class, but was not particularly sensitive to race, and at least some leaders—Betty Friedan in particular—were threatened by the lesbian movement, which Friedan spoke of conspiratorially as the "lavender menace." A second movement arose out of the civil rights, antiwar, New Left, and the Black Power movements. It was this context in which my own feminist perspective emerged.

The scenario of a White feminist oblivious to class, race, and global contexts undoubtedly reflected realities of many contexts in the 1960s, particularly the beginnings of NOW. However, we need to remember that a Black civil rights lawyer, Pauli Murray, was on the original NOW board and also was the key person who secured the passage of the civil rights law that included the word "sex," the legal basis for much of the NOW early work in gender discrimination.

However, my own experience was very different from the Betty Friedan *Feminine Mystique* world, in which educated White middle-class women sought to break out of their suburban captivity to enter interesting professions.[1] In the 1960s, as a young mother and graduate student, I became immersed in the civil rights movement. In 1965, along with a group of other students and chaplains at the Claremont Colleges of Claremont, California, I decided to spend the summer as a volunteer for the Delta Ministry in Mississippi. This was a scary decision. The previous summer, during the "Mississippi summer," three young civil rights workers had been killed and their bodies hidden by local Whites.

We went to Mississippi with a conscious awareness of risking our lives. I remember thinking as we crossed the state line into Mississippi in our battered car that I might die and deciding that I needed to face this possibility. Let me say that I had no desire to die. I was a young mother of three small children, and I have no yearnings for martyrdom. But there are moments where you have to look the possibility of death in the face and decide that you are going to go on, and that was such a moment for me.

For me the 1965 summer in Mississippi was the critical turning point of my life. For the first time I experienced what white America looked like from the context of Blacks in the South. I came to recognize Whites as threatening people who would kill Blacks at the drop of a hat and would be ready to kill Whites who took their side. Our group of volunteers was based at a former Black college in Beulah, Mississippi, where many programs were based. I decided to volunteer with the Head Start program. I traveled around rural Mississippi with an African American woman volunteer from Brooklyn, visiting Head Start programs. We were very aware of the danger of simply riding together in the same car as a White woman and a Black woman. Mississippi White men had been known to run such cars off the road and beat up the passengers. We kept our eye out for White men in pickup trucks who typically carried a rifle across the back window.

Shortly before our group had arrived, a group of Whites had driven through the campus, shooting at the dormitory windows. After that we mounted a night watch, taking turns staying up through the night to guard against another such invasion. Our defense was to ring a bell so that everyone could dive under their bed if such Whites drove through again. During my travels through Mississippi, my colleague and I decided to go over to Bogalusa, Louisiana, for a couple of days, a town then being besieged by the Ku Klux Klan. Here I had an even more dramatic taste of what it meant for Blacks in America to literally live under siege by Whites.

When I returned from Mississippi, an African American woman friend, Minnette Lall, who had also been in Mississippi, and I became volunteers in Watts, a Black neighborhood in Los Angeles, which had gone up in flames that summer. We worked with militant Black and White clergy who trained us in proper ways of work in the Black community, as well as in nonviolent methods of resistance in marches and sit-ins. The following summer my family and I moved to Washington, D.C., where I took a job teaching at the Divinity School of Howard University, a historically Black university. Our family committed itself to live in a predominantly Black neighborhood in Washington.

We added work against the war in Vietnam to our commitment to work against racism. My kids grew up going to marches in downtown Washington. I think they believed that you go downtown to picket the White House or march with banners down Pennsylvania Avenue. During this period I became steeped in a critique of racism, class hierarchy, and American neocolonialist interventionism.

It was not race, class, and global awareness, but gender analysis that was not welcome in the circles that had mentored me in critical consciousness in the 1960s and early 1970s. My mentors in the civil rights and antiwar movements were White and Black leftist radical males, most of them clergy. Black theology and Third World liberation theology were being founded at that time. I drank in their critique of American classist, racist, and militarist society. Among the first books I wrote was a collection of essays written between 1968 and 1971, *Liberation Theology: Human Hope Confronts Christian History and American Power*.[2] The book contains essays on Black theology, Jewish-Christian relations, and Christian anti-Semitism, on communitarian socialism, on the White left in America, and on Latin American liberation theology, along with two early essays on feminism and on ecological theology. My essay on Black theology is based on the early work of James Cone, while my essay on Latin American liberation theology cites the first book of Gustavo Gutierrez, at that time not yet translated into English.

The working assumption of these essays, as all my subsequent work, is that liberation theology is multidimensional and needs to be looked at across a wide range of diverse contexts. It was in the late 1960s that I first began to add questions of gender to what was then, in the circles in which I moved, an established race, class, and anticolonial discourse. In 1968 I wrote my first major essay on sexism, titled "Male Chauvinist Theology and the Anger of Women," echoing the militant language of Black Power.[3]

However, at the Howard School of Religion, at which I taught from 1965 to 1976, there was little openness to Black theology, much less to feminism. The faculty was mostly older African Americans who had struggled in the 1940s and 1950s to establish a middle-class respectability. They preferred to be called Negroes (capital N) and shuddered at the word "Black," which they saw as close to a racist insult. I was the first faculty member that introduced Cone's writings at the seminary at that time, although one of my colleagues, Dr. Deotis Roberts, would begin to develop a "Black theology" that was consciously more conservative and "reconciling" that Cone.

My early article on Black theology was an effort to respond to this critique from my colleagues and to defend Cone's views, rooted in a positive reading of Black Power. Gender was not mentioned at all in this article. Teaching at a historical Black seminary, gender was a touchy subject from a white woman, but also from Black women. There were few younger Black women at the seminary when I first came. Women students were mostly older Black women in a secondary degree program that was offered to urban pastors without college education. There were no Black female faculty members.

I began to develop my first systematic and historical work in feminist theology during a leave of absence, which I took in 1972–1973 to teach at Harvard Divinity School. I was offered the Stillman chair there at a time when the Stillman chair was being passed out to liberation theologians by Harvey Cox on a year-by-year basis. (At that time the Harvard Divinity School faculty didn't want Catholics as a permanent part of the faculty.) However, when I arrived at Harvard, I found that another professor had argued that I did not have sufficient seniority to hold the Stillman chair. I should be called a visiting lecturer in Roman Catholic Studies, even though

I was being paid by the Stillman chair. I went about that year saying that I was "under the Stillman Chair, rather than in it."

At Harvard I taught two courses to an enthusiastic group of students. One attempted to trace the rise of patriarchy and patriarchal religious world-views in the ancient Near East and Greco-Roman world and the way it shaped early Christianity. The second was on nineteenth-century European misogynist anthropologies and the beginnings of modern feminism. I also taught a course on Christian anti-Judaism, looking particularly at its patristic roots. These lectures became my book, *Faith and Fratricide: The Theological Roots of Anti-Semitism*, published in 1975.[4] The feminists at Harvard Divinity School seemed frankly puzzled that I was also teaching this course. Anti-Judaism in Christianity was not seen as a topic of feminism in those years.

My work on feminist theology in the context of Christian history was developed the next year in a series of lectures at Yale Divinity School. Thereafter I taught this material several times at Wesley Theological Seminary in Washington. I did not try to teach a course on feminist theology at Howard. In a course on contemporary ethical issues I introduced one lecture on gender and asked a Black male friend sensitive to questions of gender in the Black community to lead it. It was evident to me that the topic of sexism in the Black community was a very volatile issue, and as a White woman I dared not address it.

My students at Howard were almost all Black men, not only African Americans, but from the Caribbean and Africa. There were no Black women to discuss gender issues in terms of theology at Howard at that time, but if there had been, they would have had a hard time being heard. I realized this when I asked the Black male cleric to speak on gender. At that point critical perspectives on gender relations could hope to get a hearing among Black males only from another Black male, particularly a cleric. The students listened with skeptical expressions even to him, but as a male clergyman, he was at least accorded respect.

Young Black women were beginning to enter Howard School of Religion in the early 1970s and to express an interest in gender questions. In 1975 a latent tension over the issue exploded. A young Black woman did her master's thesis on a gender critique of theology in the Black church. Our faculty was a small one (eight), and it was customary to have a hearing of M.A. theses with the whole faculty. This young woman was roundly ridiculed by the acting dean of the faculty, with the others passively backing him up. I intervened to defend her, and the hostility was turned on me. The acting dean called me to his office and threatened to fire me. In his view my defense of this woman student had insulted the faculty, namely himself. At that time I had no tenure at the school and was vulnerable to dismissal.

This attack did not worry me too much, because I was privy to two pieces of information that he didn't know. First, I was on the search committee for a new dean, and we had decided to bring Dr. Lawrence Jones from Union Seminary to be the new dean. It was evident that things would change at the seminary when he came. The new generation of Black scholars that identified with a Black theological perspective would doubtless be coming to teach. Second, Garrett-Evangelical Theological Seminary had invited me to go to Evanston, Illinois, and to be the Georgia Harkness Professor of Applied Theology there. Feminist theology would be central to my work.

Garrett had already made a strong commitment to a high number of Black students and faculty and the doing of theological education in the context of what was called at Garrett "the Church and the Black Experience." Jim Cone had done his master's of divinity at Garrett and his Ph.D. in the joint Garrett-Northwestern program in the 1950s and 1960s and was deeply critical of Garrett's lack of attention to race issues in theology. But Garrett heeded his call in the early 1970s and attempted to make the Black perspective in theological education a major commitment. Then-president Merlan Northfelt was sensitive that any feminism introduced at Garrett should be compatible with this commitment to Blacks. He put the Black faculty in a major role in the search and sent two leading Black faculty to interview me in Washington. I was chosen for the position largely because of my experience at Howard and the fact that I had developed my feminist theology in the context of a dialogue with issues of racism.

I also had become convinced that it was time for me to leave Howard, precisely because, as a White woman, I could not initiate the discussion of gender issues there. The new era at Howard School of Theology that I was confident Dr. Jones would develop needed to bring in a new generation of African American women theologians and scholars to develop this discussion in the context of a Black church and seminary. This is very much what has happened at Howard since my time there, with leading womanist theologians, such as Kelley Brown-Douglas, currently teaching there.

By the late 1970s and early 1980s feminism was becoming an established area in an increasing number of theological schools, and women were being hired who had done some work on gender issues. Some of these feminist scholars had emerged, like myself, out of the civil rights struggle, and had race and class as an integral part of our view. This was the case with Beverly Harrison at Union Theological Seminary and Letty Russell at Yale Divinity School. Others had come from a purely academic route and had not had the same experiences of the civil rights movement. This included Mary Daly, who went to Boston College in 1968 after completing a theology and a philosophy doctorate in Europe.

Daly was developing a radical feminist theology that would eventually lead to her rejection of Christianity altogether. But she had not shared the civil rights experience (being out of the country most of the 1960s) and was hostile to discussion of race and class differences among women, which she saw as diverting from a unitary view of all women as equally "oppressed." Her insensitivity to the Black experience in her use of certain symbolism, such as speaking of "castrating" the patriarchal God, led to a critique of her by leading Black feminist poet Audre Lord.[5]

By the mid-1980s, an emerging cadre of Black women theologians, claiming the term "womanism," were adopting a "hermeneutic of suspicion" toward white feminists, assuming that white feminists generally were oblivious to issues of race, unless clearly proved otherwise. Although women like Beverley Harrison and I and many others who had a strong critique of race and class were in theological schools and were working hard to support Black students, male and female, and to hire Black female faculty members, Black women (and Hispanic women) needed to deal with the whole history and system of White racism (as well as Black and Hispanic male sexism). Even those of us with a strong commitment to a race and class perspective were still a part of a White system of privilege. However much we might be committed to supporting Black and Hispanic women, it was they and not we who had to do the analysis of what it meant to be in those contexts of "double or triple oppression," as it was termed in those days.

However, this atmosphere that presumed that White feminists were racists unless clearly proven other wise also led to miscommunications. One painful example of that for me occurred in May 1985. In November 1984 I was asked to give a plenary address at the American Academy Religion on feminist theology, a recognition of its arrival on the academic scene. In my address, published in *Christianity and Crisis*, I tried to make very clear that, as a White woman, I could not speak for women as a whole. I wrote:

I need to acknowledge at the outset that I speak from a white Western Christian context. Theology should overcome patterns of thought within it that vilify or exclude persons by gender, race and religion. But this does not mean that we seek a theology that is universalistic in the sense of encompassing all cultures and religions. Such universalism is in fact cultural imperialism—an attempt by one religious culture to monopolize not theology but salvation, to claim that it alone has authentic access to the divine. Christian patriarchal theology has typically been imperialistic, claiming that white male Christian experience is equivalent to universal humanity.

Feminist theology, by contrast, must be consciously pluralistic. Despite similarities among patriarchal patterns, a Christian feminism will be different from a Jewish feminism, or a Buddhist or a Muslim feminism. Moreover, an Asian Christian feminist or an African Christian feminist or an American black Christian feminist will also have distinct problems and will come up with different syntheses. Pagan feminists, who seek to break with all patriarchal religious contexts and to rediscover an ancient female-centered religion or to create one today, pose yet a different problematic.

Feminist theology, then, needs to be seen as a network of solidarity that exists among feminist communities engaged in the critique of patriarchalism in distinct cultural and religious contexts, rather than one dominant form of feminism that claims to speak for the whole of womankind.[6]

Several feminists, including Carol Christ and Delores Williams, were asked to give comments on this article in a subsequent issue of *Christianity and Crisis*.[7] Unfortunately, the editors had scrambled some of the paragraphs of the article, which misrepresented the sequence of my argument. Specifically they put my claim that all feminists need to be able to claim imagery of the divine as "goddess" out of context, making it appear that I was primarily arguing for speaking of God as "Goddess." They also inserted into my article a large reproduction of a marble head of Athena. This image had nothing to do with anything I said in the article. Delores Williams focused on this image of Athena and my defense of speaking of God as "goddess," and attacked the article as a typical example of White feminists oblivious to class, race, and imperialism. She claimed that I was seeking to establish an idea of God as a "white Goddess," failing to include the perspective of Black feminists.

I replied to the comments of Williams (and others), pointing out the errors of *Christianity and Culture*'s presentation of my article. I said that Williams had misread my article. Her attack on it "was based on a total unwillingness to take seriously what I said explicitly at the outset of the essay: I affirm a plurality of feminist theologies both in various Christian racial and cultural contexts and in various inter-religious contexts and I reject any dominant form of feminist theology that claims to speak for the whole of womankind."[8] Unfortunately, Williams's polemic has been received in literature on the development of feminist theology as a confirmation of the "story line" of White feminists oblivious to class, race, and imperialism, until called to account by womanists and other feminists of color. Several recent books and articles cite Williams's comments as a example of this "story line," lumping me with Mary Daly, and typically failing to read either my original article or my reply to Williams, much less my other books and articles that focus on class, race, intercultural, and interreligious dialogue.[9]

Let me make clear that I do not think that White feminists such as myself are innocent of racism just because we have consciously adopted a certain careful language of pluralism. Race and class biases are deeply embedded in the context in which we all work in the United States (and elsewhere). No matter what my words are—and my words reflect my deep convictions on which I have attempted to live and act for thirty-five years—I still live in a context of race and class privilege that is automatically accorded to me no matter what my personal views may be.

A hermeneutic of suspicion that racism is not being recognized adequately is always appropriate on the part of womanists toward White feminists. White feminists also must constantly be aware of their own race and class privilege and question how they are collaborating with this. Ultimately this is not simply about individual "politically correct" words, although this is a part of cultural change, but of deep systematic economic and cultural changes that create a more egalitarian society. Economically the United States is more deeply split by the gaps of wealth and poverty today than it was in the late 1960s.

The words that I wrote in the article published in *Christianity and Crisis* in 1985 express my views more deeply today that ever. We need more and more plurality in feminist theologies done in every racial, ethnic, religious, and cultural context to explicate the issues of women in as many contexts as possible, as well as a solidarity between this expanding diversity that can help midwife real social and cultural transformation toward justice and mutuality. One of my great delights is the increasing emergence of feminist theologies in many different contexts: womanist, mujerista, Asian American, and lesbian theologies in the United States, diverse feminist theologies in Africa, Asia, Latin America, and the Middle East. Buddhist, Hindu, Jewish, and Muslim women are doing feminist theology in their distinct religious contexts. I have been deeply involved in the last twenty years with both First–Third World dialogue between Christian feminists and interreligious feminist dialogue.[10]

This pluralism is coming to be assumed, although we are still learning how to really collaborate and not to be used to undercut one another. Moreover, feminists in Asia, Africa, and Latin America have experienced something of the same resistance to their thought from male leftists that I and others experienced in the late 1960s and 1970s. Most of the African, Asian, and Latin American feminist theologians began their theological reflection in the context of liberation theologies in their regions. They had deeply incorporated a critique of issues of class, race, and colonialism, committing themselves to a theology in solidarity with the oppressed. But when they sought to bring gender into this discussion, their male leftist colleagues ridiculed them. They insisted that "feminism" is a "White bourgeois, First World issue," and was not appropriate in the "Third World contexts." As a result of this treatment, Third World feminist theologians in groups, such as the Ecumenical Association of Third World Theologians, insisted on having their own "Women's Commission" where they could contextualize feminist theology in their own situations. As these women put it in a founding meeting in Geneva in 1983, "We have to decide for ourselves what Feminist Theology means for us. It is not for First World women to tell us how to do it, not is it for Third World men to tell us feminism is not our issue."[11]

First and Third World women, as well as men, across class, race, and gender divides, have still to learn how to really work together on a liberating agenda in theology and praxis in a way that is fully open and mutual. Questioning of feminists in privileged contexts continues to be appropriate, but it needs to be based on some careful effort to understand one another's histories. Constructing a story line about White feminists (or anyone else) that fails to respect some of our actual experiences is not helpful. Pluralism was not invented for the first time in 1990.

NOTES

1. Betty Friedan, *The Feminine Mystique* (New York: Norton, 1963).
2. Rosemary Radford Ruether, *Liberation Theology: Human Hope Confronts Christian History and American Power* (New York: Paulist Press, 1972).

3. Rosemary Radford Ruether, "Male Chauvinist Theology and the Anger of Women," *Cross Currents* 21 (1968): 173–185.

4. Rosemary Radford Ruether, *Faith and Fratricide: The Theological Roots of Anti-Semitism* (New York: Seabury Press, 1975).

5. See Audre Lorde, "Open Letter to Mary Daly," in *The Bridge Called My Back: Writings by Radical Women of Color*, ed. Cherríe Moraga and Gloria Anzaldúa (New York: Kitchen Table Press, 1983), 94–97.

6. Rosemary Radford Ruether, "Feminist Theology in the Academy," *Christianity and Crisis* 45 (March 4, 1985): 57–62.

7. Carol Christ, "Feminist Thealogy?" *Christianity and Crisis* 45 (April 29, 1985): 161–162. Delores Williams, "The Color of Feminism," *Christianity and Crisis* 45 (April 29, 1985): 164–65.

8. Rosemary Radford Ruether, "For Whom, with Whom, Do We Speak Our New Stories?" *Christianity and Crisis* 45 (May 13, 1985): 183–184.

9. Mary Farrell Bednarowski, *The Religious Imagination of American Women* (Bloomington: Indiana University Press, 1999), 138.

10. See Rosemary Ruether and Rita Gross, *Religious Feminism and the Future of the Planet: A Buddhist-Christian Conversation* (New York: Continuum, 2001). Also Mary John Mananzan et al., *Women Resisting Violence: Spirituality for Life* (Maryknoll, N.Y.: Orbis Press, 1996), 27–35.

11. See Rosemary Ruether, *Women and Redemption: A Theological History* (Minneapolis, Minn.: Fortress Press, 1998), 241–243.

SIX

Ada María Isasi-Díaz

1967 Learned how to read the Bible from the poor in Lima,
   Peru
1975 Realized sexism is oppression at the Women's Ordination Conference
1988 Author, *Hispanic Women: Prophetic Voice in the Church*

I WAS BORN A FEMINIST ON THANKSGIVING WEEKEND 1975 AT THE
first Women's Ordination Conference (WOC). I was at the time living in

Rochester, New York, and had driven with a group of friends to the conference in Detroit. A friend in charge of religious education for the diocese knew about the conference and insisted I should go. After nine months as a salesperson at Sears, I had recently started to work part time in an inner city parish while beginning my studies on a master's in medieval history. I had no money to go to Detroit, stay in a hotel, and pay the conference registration fee. "Several of us are going by car so you can just come with us," answered Denise Mack. "And you can just stay in our room. Don't worry about it." Regarding the conference fee, she said she would talk with Lyn Sommers, another Rochester woman who was responsible for organizing small discussion groups for the conference. Lyn called me. "I need one more facilitator for the small groups," she said. If I could do that task, the conference fee would be waived. "Sign me on," I said, with a sense that there was no way of avoiding this conference.

Friday after Thanksgiving, hours before the sun rose, my brother-in-law drove me to the group's gathering point. We started the long drive to Detroit. Little did I know, as I sat in the backseat on that cold November morning, that this conference would influence radically my worldview and give direction to my life for the rest of my days.

The sense of excitement and possibility that filled the hallways of the hotel where the conference participants gathered was incredible. The process that had been designed for the conference remains one of the best I have worked with. The small groups in which we gathered after the plenary sessions were geared to allow participants to discuss the issues presented and to enable them to begin to move to action. Given what we had heard and what we were discussing, what did each of us want to do? Little by little the small groups dissolved as people moved to various caucuses being formed according to the interests of the conference participants. I facilitated the small group to which I was assigned, and after the second plenary session the group had dissolved. I was jobless, but not for long!

My conference name tag identified me as a facilitator, and as I stood in one of the hallways drinking a cup of coffee, a tall imposing woman asked me in quite an abrupt manner, "Where is your group?" Learning that my group had already dissolved, she thrust papers and markers into my arms and said while rushing on, "Then come and help me." Marjorie Tuite, a nun well known because of her work against racism, was facilitating a caucus formed to consider establishing an organization on the issue of women's ordination in the Catholic Church, and she needed someone to take notes. I followed her without saying a word, fascinated by the energy she exuded. During the next hour I had the most intense lesson of my life in group dynamics.

Never losing sight of the task at hand, Marjorie allowed everyone to speak. Her no-nonsense attitude invited people to think before they spoke, and the meeting moved along at an incredible pace. She was constantly summing up where we were as I did all I could to write down every step we took. When the meeting was over, she briefly checked what I had written, told me to whom to give the notes, and left the room with a woman who had come for her. Later, at the last plenary session, the assembly was asked to consider the resolution from our caucus. I felt a certain awe when I heard read the words I had written.[1]

My birth as a feminist took place at the ending ritual of the conference. When those who believed themselves called to ordination were asked to identify themselves, I knew I had to be honest and stand. However, a battle was raging within me. I felt caught between a sense of vocation—what I wanted to do with my life—and a sudden awareness of the intense struggle that lay ahead. I turned to Mary Walden, an Ursuline sister whom I had met fifteen years earlier, only three days after arriving in the United States as a refugee from Cuba. In tears I said, "Mary, I do not want to stand. I am tired of battles." She smiled at me reassuringly. Almost forced by the belief that I was called to be ordained, I was among the last ones to stand. When I looked around, I found myself surrounded by a "cloud of witnesses." In this battle, at least, I would not be alone. After a few seconds I sat down thinking, "I have been born, baptized, and confirmed in this new life all at once!" As I left the assembly I signed a paper indicating my interest in working on the ordination of women in the Roman Catholic Church.

Back home working in an inner city parish and my studying at the university kept me very busy. A few months went by. One day the phone rang and it was Rosalie Muschal-Reinhardt, a member of the task force that had organized that first Women's Ordination Conference. "You signed the list of those interested in forming an ongoing organization, and I am calling because we are doing just that," she reminded me. The first meeting was going to be at Rosary College (now Dominican College) outside Chicago, and once again I simply did not have money for an airline ticket. "We have vowed," said Rosalie with her characteristic passion, "we will not meet again without women of color participating." I was to save the date, she insisted, and she somehow would find the money to pay for my ticket. She did and I became involved as a volunteer for several years and eventually worked as a paid staff member of WOC. It was in the women's movement in the Catholic Church that I began to learn about gender oppression. The Catholic Church with its oppression of women turned me into a feminist!

In the 1960s I had been a missionary in Lima, Peru, and there the poor had taught me the real meaning of religion. They taught me that if religious beliefs are not the basis for the struggle for liberation, they can indeed become the "opium of the people." They taught me that God stands with the poor and that liberation and salvation are inseparable, that "poverty is a slap on God's face." In 1970, when I left the convent and came back to the United States, I had the sense that I was starting life anew. Those were difficult years for, despite the love and support of my family, I simply did not feel at home and did not know what to do with my life. I knew that leaving the convent did not absolve me from my vocation to ministry—redefined by my experience in Peru as ministry with and for the poor. Every week I would read the *National Catholic Reporter,* a liberal Catholic newspaper, looking for clues as to how I could get involved in the church. As I read news of the church in the United States, nothing seemed important to me, nothing seemed to resonate with me. One day I noticed a small announcement that ran every week. It talked about the Deaconess Movement: Write, it said, and they would send a newsletter. After I saw it three or four times, I am not sure why I did it but I responded. Soon I received a homemade newsletter written by Mary B. Lynch, a Roman Catholic laywoman.[2] A few years later I learned that she was the one who called together in Chicago a group of women who organized that first Women's Ordination Conference. I found the newsletter interesting, but it did not touch what then was at the heart of my personal struggle: looking for ways to get involved in stopping poverty and the exploitation of Latin America by the United States.

During 1976, the first year of my life as a feminist, I worked hard at educating myself. Though I knew next to nothing about feminism and gender analysis, I understood early on that I could apply the same processes and categories of analysis I had used to learn about poverty and its relationship to the gospel message to the oppression of women. There was not much available to read, but I have always learned best from experience. I began to wear my newfound gender-analysis lens all the time. Soon a group of us started to meet locally to see what we could do to move the church in Rochester to deal with the issue of women's ordination. Local and national involvement provided me with a community of women with whom I could learn. Many of them were veterans of the social movements of the 1960s. In Lima I had been thoroughly involved in advocating for the poor with civil authorities and in church circles. As I heard other women draw from their experiences in previous social movements, I could parallel their moves and draw from my own experiences in Lima. During this process of learning I led with my heart: I kept in mind at all times the commitment I had made when I stood at the closing ritual of the Detroit conference for women's full participation in the church. Group reflection and reading began to provide me with the intellectual tools I needed to see the connections between poverty and sexism. My vision became clearer but my world became more complicated as the days went on. Soon I could sing with full conviction, "I wish my eyes had never been opened."

Much of the work we did in those early years of WOC fell into three categories. First of all we were hard at work creating an organization, trying desperately to expand our membership, to create an economic base for our work, and to set up procedures for communication and decision making that followed feminist understandings of group process. Eventually, when I became part of the WOC office team, my job was to expand our membership and work with local WOC groups. Second, we also did all we could to keep the issue alive publicly. The fact is that both the secular and the religious press were kind to us. We worked hard to provide all the background they needed on the issue of women and the church and to accommodate their requests to the best of our ability. Many of the reporters we worked with let us know they were sympathetic to our cause and did all they could to keep our issue in the public eye. For example, when John Paul I died a few weeks after being elected pope, one of the main television networks decided, instead of rehashing the church's procedure for electing a pope, to look at issues facing the church. WOC was contacted and I was selected to be the one interviewed on a popular morning show, *Good Morning America*. I learned much from this experience and was happy to have played a role in having our message reach millions. Soon surveys were saying that over 60 percent of Roman Catholics wanted women to be ordained.

The third area of our work, which undoubtedly caused us the most frustration, was dealing with the Roman Catholic bishops. Some of them were convinced that women should be priests, but they did little to move the issue within church structures. With the help of Bishop Charles Buswell we were able to pursue a two-year dialogue with the bishops' committee that dealt with women's issues. I was one of the WOC dialoguers during that process and learned much about church politics.

One night I was in the elevator with a bishop involved in the process. We considered him a friend and yet I sensed that he was not understanding our arguments. As the door of the elevator closed I said to him, "Why do you not understand what we are saying?" With a painful expression he said to me, "Ada, don't you see that if I understood, I could not remain a bishop in this church?" I wanted so much to ask him why he wanted to be a bishop if that meant compromising the truth. It was a crude awakening for me to realize that truth does not always carry the day, that knowing does not necessarily lead to action. The dialogue with the bishops taught me much about the insidiousness of power and the need for power to be reconceptualized as a capacity to bring about justice instead of a faculty to control and dominate. I believe we need to understand that power belongs to the community, to those invested in the organization or institution in question and not solely to its leaders. Leaders must understand that they are only given the opportunity to exercise power by the community and for the good of the community and that, therefore, they have to be accountable to the community. Unless power is understood this way, it will continue to be used to oppress instead of to liberate. The reconceptualization of power is a task that feminist theory, feminist theology, feminist sociology, and feminist organizations have not focused on. Until we do, we will continue to undermine the work we do on behalf of justice for women.

I have never known how to proceed in life without seeing what I do as either a way of surviving (like washing dishes or working at Sears as a salesperson when I could find no other jobs) or as part of my vocation in life. I was not surprised, therefore, that I began to find work on the issue of women's ordination, which I soon saw as but one way of working against sexism, as part of my vocation. The experience of a women involved in WOC in the early days helped me realize this. She called one day and said that she needed a break; she felt burned out. What she said impacted me greatly: The fact is that it scared me out of my wits! For weeks I chided myself for perhaps not taking the issue seriously enough, for I certainly did not feel anywhere near exhaustion. On the other hand, I did not want to become so drained that I had to step away from my commitment to the women's movement. I had gotten involved thinking that women would get ordained within a decade or so and then I could once again concentrate on working with the poor. But what if involvement in this issue left me psychologically spent?

One day, as I drove home from work in the middle of a snowstorm, three things became clear for me. First of all, I realized that sexism was a category of oppression and that it did not exist apart from poverty but compounded it and vice versa. (Soon, Rosalie Muschal-Reinhardt, Marjorie Tuite, and I designed a visual to explain the interconnections of sexism, racism/ethnic prejudice, and classism.) Second, as I slowly inched ahead on slippery roads, I could hear my mother saying the words with which she always ended her letters to me: as long as God gives us the energy we need for the struggle, we will be all right. Mamá has always insisted we should not ask God to free us from struggling but rather we should be happy to have something to struggle for. What we need to do is ask God to give us *fuerzas para la lucha*, strength for the struggle. (Years later I would work on developing *la lucha* as a category of analysis and as a theo-ethical category.) Third, the snow-covered windshield of my car became like a movie screen where I could see my next-door neighbor in Lima, a woman who lived in extreme poverty yet never lost her sense of dignity and purpose of life. I remember the steadiness of her struggle: Day after day she dealt with the reality of the present and survived that day in order to be able to face the next. (That reflection has led me to develop the category of *lo cotidiano* as the main site for struggle, as the site that reveals oppression at the same time it illumines the preferred future.) What I realized that day I came to understand more and more as I discussed it with my women friends in Rochester. From that day forward I have never been scared of burning out, often singing to myself, "I ain't no ways tired. I've come too far from where I started from. Nobody told me the road would be easy." And, as to burning up, that is what life is all about, isn't it? For me life is about being passionate for justice! That is what fulfills me; that is what gives me energy and creativity.

In 1976, to celebrate the bicentennial of the founding of the United States, the Catholic bishops organized a consultation process to define the main issues that the church needed to address in the years ahead. The process finished with a conference in Detroit. Initially Women's Ordination Conference was not invited, but several of the leaders of the organization pressed for inclusion and eventually we were allowed to participate. Our work at this conference, called "Call to Action," was the first public action of

WOC. We worked hard to be a positive presence at that meeting. For me personally, "Call to Action" was very important for there I met Yolanda Tarango, a Chicana nun from El Paso, Texas.

After the Catholic Bishops' Conference I asked her repeatedly to join WOC. Yolanda was not eager to do so, and little by little I learned the reason. At the end of the WOC conference the year before, two women had read an important statement to the whole assembly. María Iglesias, a nun from New York City who was at the time national coordinator of Las Hermanas (a Hispanas/Latinas Catholic organization), and Shawn Copeland, then president of the National Black Sisters Conference, had spoken to the largely White women's assembly. Shawn had warned conference participants not to rebuild the walls of Jericho to keep Blacks and Latinas out once White women made it into the priesthood. "One of the other parts to the story of Joshua is that after the people took the city of Jericho, Yahweh said to them, 'Never build in this place again, a city like this.' So if you go through the walls and you take the city, then don't build the same city again."[3]

Now, with Yolanda's help, I began to analyze and study the issue of racism/ethnic prejudice in the women's movement. In the summer of 1978 Yolanda invited me to participate in the national meeting that brought together Hispanic priests and members of Las Hermanas. At that meeting I began to understand the complexities of the ethnic prejudice against Hispanics in the United States, its connection with racism, how ethnic prejudice is present in the women's movement, and the role it plays in oppressive structures. That meeting also made me realize that, given that the vast majority of Hispanas/Latinas in the United States are poor women, working for justice for women in the church could be an effective way of working for justice for women in society. I left that meeting with two firm convictions: First, I needed to listen to grassroots Hispanas/Latinas just as I had learned to listen to the poor in Lima. (Years later Yolanda and I developed a method for doing *mujerista* theology that starts with the voices of grassroots Latinas. Several key theological claims have arisen from this conviction: *mujerista* theology is a liberative praxis; grassroots Hispanas/Latinas are organic theologians for they are admirably capable of explaining their religious understandings and the role religion plays in their daily struggles; the lived experience of grassroots Hispanas/Latinas is the source of *mujerista* theology.) Second, I needed to begin to bring to the table of WOC and other organizations in which I was participating the voices I was listening to: I needed to voice the perspectives and issues of Hispanas/Latinas.

Many of the women I worked with in WOC, almost exclusively White women, were committed to the struggle against racism. I believe many of them came to understand the particulars of the struggle of Hispanas/Latinas in this society. However, as I began to speak more and more as a Latina from that special perspective and as I attempted to link sexism to racial/ethnic prejudice, I began to become invisible in the movement. Jamie Phelps, an African American nun active in WOC in those early days, offered me advice time and again. "Girl," she would say, "be careful. They will sideline you as soon as you become too vocal as a Hispanic." How right she was! After five years of being at home in the women's movement struggling for justice in the church, I began to feel alienated. I had left my parish job and was working as a paid staff member at the WOC office. Disagreements regarding priorities, styles of leadership and strategies, and struggles for control of WOC together with my own personal shortcomings created a most difficult situation, and I was asked to resign from my job with the organization in which I had been involved for seven years. Distraught by what had happened, I spent time analyzing the reasons for it and trying to learn from it. It seems to me that, though we had struggled to wield power in nonoppressive ways, when difficulties arose we fell back into the way we had been treated all of our lives in patriarchal structures: We turned disagreement into confrontation and we wielded power to control and dominate instead of to enable and facilitate. However, though wounded and disillusioned, I was not about to turn my back on the struggle for justice for women. That had become part of my vocation in life, of who I am. I simply needed to find new avenues for involvement, new ways of contributing to the liberation of women.

Religion always has been a central part of my life. Religion, in particular Roman Catholicism, is a key element of Latina culture. It is not at all exceptional for me, therefore, to have become aware of gender discrimination through my involvement in the church. Nor is it remarkable that a church issue, the ordination of women to a renewed priestly ministry, provided for me the opportunity to struggle for justice for women. My awareness of how sexism operates in the Catholic Church and how it influences our religious understandings and practices has never created for me a crisis of faith. My religious beliefs, on the contrary, seem to grow stronger. The injustices I have suffered in the church, the many pitfalls it harbors, have led me to a deeper understanding of myself and my vocation in life. Since I was young I have always distanced the divine and my relationship with the divine enough from the church (and now from theology) so that what the church teaches and the way it acts do not scandalize me or disappoint me in any way that negatively affects my faith. At the same time, as a young missionary in Lima, I learned that the church has power and influence in society. Though in the United States the role of the church in society is different and though today that role is not what it was even as recently as the 1980s, I believe that churches still have powerful moral influence in society. I believe churches have an obligation always to take a prophetic stance: They always have to be on the side of the poor, the oppressed, the exploited, the marginalized, and the vulnerable. Furthermore, I believe that justice is a constitutive element of the gospel message. The gospel message is intrinsic to my worldview: It is an ongoing source of understanding; it is, most of the time, the backdrop against which I make judgments; it motivates me and sustains me.

While working at WOC I had begun to take courses in the master of divinity program at a seminary in Rochester, New York. As I tried to sort out what to do next with my life after leaving WOC, I knew that it would have to be related to the struggle for justice for women from the perspective of religion. I decided I would finish my theological degree and then return to what has always given me greatest joy: working with grassroots Hispanas/Latinas. I knew I had to look beyond Rochester. My willingness to look for new ways of being involved in the struggle for women's liberation in church and society and the commitment to diversity of women theologians like Carter Heyward led me to participate in the project that produced the book, *God's Fierce Whimsy*.[4] Then, thanks to the sisterly care of Beverly Harrison and Ardith Hayes, in the spring of 1983 I found temporary employment at Union Theological Seminary in New York, and that fall I started my studies there. Yolanda Tarango and I had been working on gathering the voices of grassroots Hispanas/Latinas for publication, and I intended to use the time I was studying to finish this task. Our book, *Hispanic Women: Prophetic Voice in the Church*, was first published in 1988.[5] *Mujerista* theology was born in the many conversations Yolanda Tarango and I had with groups of Las Hermanas all around the country. It emerged from the many struggles we had as Hispanas/Latinas with church structures to have our voices heard and taken into consideration. It came from the conviction that we had to speak for ourselves or we would continue to be invisible or, at best, Hispano/Latino men would speak for us.

But the elaboration of *mujerista* theology never would have happened without the community of which I was a part at Union Theological Seminary in the 1980s. Angela Bauer, Elizabeth Bounds, Pamela Brubaker, Katie G. Cannon, Chung Hyun Kyung, Marilyn Legge, Margie Mayman—how much I learned from all these women as we took courses together, spent time reading each other's work and commenting on it, and cried and laughed together! Then there are the women who used their contacts and influence to open roads for me personally and to insist on including *mujerista* theology as one of the theological voices of women that needs to be included at all times. Among these women, and there are many, I particularly remember Rosemary Radford Ruether, who referred us to her editor at Harper & Row and helped us to get our first book published. Letty Russell made sure time and again at the American Academy of Religion and elsewhere that *mujerista* theology was included. Marcia Riggs and Karen McCarthy Brown helped me become a professor at Drew University. For years when I could not find any other Latina at the annual conference of the American Academy of Religion, it was with Katie G. Cannon, Joan Martin, and other womanist theologians that I felt at home. Their struggles to have their own sessions at the AAR were the blueprint I followed to propose establishing a Latina/Latino theology session there.

Having decided to go on to study for a Ph.D. and to work as an academician, I still had to deal with the fact that it is the work I do with grassroots Latinas that is most life-giving to me. It is from them that I draw creativity and strength to continue to struggle for justice. Through the years I have learned the difficult task of straddling both worlds, the world of the academy and the grassroots Latina community. These two areas of involvement have been my mainstay as I have worked to develop *mujerista* theology.

Also during these last twenty years I have been blessed with coming to know and become friends with women from many other parts of the world who, under much more demanding circumstances than the ones we Latinas face here in the United States, insist at all times on justice for women. Aruna Ganandson, Mercy Amba Oduyoye, Elizabeth Tapia, Mary John Mananzan, Ofelia Ortega, Elsa Tamez, Ana Maria Tepedino—these and many other women have taught me that we cannot struggle for justice for women thinking only of our own communities. They have taught me that if we do, some women will benefit at the expense of others, a tragic development given the fact that no one is truly liberated unless we all are liberated. The dictum "think globally, act locally" is one we need to continue taking to heart as we move ahead in the twenty-first century.

Together with the struggle for justice, friendships and relationships have been central in my life. As a *mujerista* I have come to understand how these two themes are intrinsically linked. Very important to me is the belief that we cannot sustain the struggle for justice for women without a deep sense of commitment to each other as women. There is no possibility of creating just structures in the academy, in the churches, and in society at large if relationships and solidarity do not inform our lives on a daily basis. At least I can bear witness to how much we can accomplish when we come together as community. I can also bear witness to how destructive we are when we forget about each other or use each other and the movement for our own self-aggrandizement. For me, the struggle for justice for women is part of who I am; it is, therefore, a religious issue. My most profound religious experiences have happened in the midst of *la lucha*; and *la lucha* is what gives meaning and joy to my life. In *la lucha* I find God time and again. Yes, for me, *la vida es la lucha*: We must struggle to create community if we are to contribute to making justice for women a reality in our lives and our world.

NOTES

1. Anne Marie Gardiner, SSND, ed., *Women and Catholic Priesthood: An Expanded Vision: Proceedings of the Detroit Women's Ordination Conference* (New York: Paulist Press, 1976).
2. The newsletter is *The Journey*, published by The Deaconess Movement from 1970 to 1976.
3. Gardiner, *Women and Catholic Priesthood*, p. 189.
4. Katie G. Cannon et al., *God's Fierce Whimsy: Christian Feminism and Theological Education* (New York: Pilgrim Press, 1985).
5. Ada María Isasi-Diaz and Yolanda Tarango, *Hispanic Women: Prophetic Voice in the Church* (San Francisco: Harper & Row, 1988).

SEVEN

Carol P. Christ

1971 Founder, Women's Caucus, American Academy of
   Religion
1979 Coeditor, *Womanspirit Rising*
1998 Author, *Rebirth of the Goddess*

I WENT FROM A LOWER-MIDDLE-CLASS HIGH SCHOOL (from which
only a few students went on to four-year colleges[1]) to Stanford University
from 1963 to 1967 on a combination of scholarships, work-study, summer

jobs, and much sacrifice by my parents.[2] I got to Stanford because my high school counselor,[3] Pauline Richter, insisted to my parents that my grades and scores dictated that I should get out of "Dodge" (in this case, Northview High School in Covina, California[4]) and go to a private university. In those days it was expected that students from Republican homes would become liberal Democrats in college. Many of my classmates and two of my religion teachers, Robert MacAfee Brown and Michael Novak, as well as the dean of the chapel, B. Davie Napier, were involved in the civil rights and antiwar movements. I maintained my parents' conservative values until I graduated, for to do otherwise would have seemed like betraying them. I majored in humanities with a concentration in religion because I was trying to figure out why my baby brother had died when I was thirteen years old.[5]

Graduating during the Summer of Love, I spent much of the time I was supposed to be learning German debating values and politics. By the time I began graduate school in religious studies in the fall of 1967 at Yale, I was deeply committed to civil rights, ending poverty, and stopping the Vietnam War. I believed that my new value commitments were called for by the Christian faith of my childhood and college studies.

Though I had been warned by B. Davie Napier not to go to Yale because "they don't like women there," I couldn't believe that they wouldn't like me.[6] After all, I was as smart as any man. Coming from the West Coast coeducational atmosphere of Stanford, I could not have imagined the East Coast men's club ambience of Yale in my wildest dreams. Everything about Yale, from the dark wood paneling, leather chairs, and portraits of male professors in academic gowns on every available wall space, to the swirls of cigar and pipe smoke in the seminar rooms, conveyed message that women were not welcome there.[7] At our first meeting, I eagerly told my new graduate advisor, Brevard Childs, that I was interested in interpreting the Hebrew Bible using literary methods. "Miss Christ," he replied coldly, "then why didn't you go into comparative literature?"[8] My reception by the other faculty was not much better. Whenever I spoke of the things that mattered to me, I was dismissed. Buber and Tillich were "poets," not "theologians," I was told.[9] The entire faculty supported the war in Vietnam, and none of them seemed to think that civil rights or poverty had anything to do with the study of theology. The faculty spoke about what "a man" would do when he finished his degree. When I pointed out that I was "a woman," they snickered and said that no one expected me to finish anyway, and if I did, of course "a man" would need a job more because he would have a family to support. I was told that when I entered the Divinity School's common room or dining hall, the men in my program frequently made bets about where I would sit, while salaciously eyeing my blond hair, miniskirts, and long legs.

There was only one other woman in my class, Margaret Farley, a Roman Catholic sister[10] who (luckily for her) did not socialize with the other students. Most of the male students were at least five years older than I was, having completed ministerial degrees and in most cases getting married before beginning work on the Ph.D. I had little in common with most of them. My parents disapproved of my new political and social values. I felt very alone. I spent a whole summer crying. The reasons for this were many, but the most significant one was the gap between the way I perceived myself (as an embodied female thinker) and the way I was being perceived (primarily as a female body). Given my experience, it is not surprising that issues concerning the female body have been central in my subsequent work. I stayed in the graduate school because the Danforth and Woodrow Wilson fellowships I had been awarded by virtue of having done little else but study at Stanford gave me confidence in my intelligence.[11] And like others of my generation, I believed that "the times they are a-changin'."

In my second year at Yale, one of my professors suggested that I meet his wife, a former graduate student in the program who was teaching at a local junior college. Violet Lindbeck had never finished her feminist dissertation, because her advisor did not see its value. She handed me some articles that were my first introduction to feminism. Soon I was active in the New Haven Women's Liberation Movement and the Yale Women's Alliance—a graduate student action and consciousness-raising group. We boycotted Mory's, a men's club associated with the university, and put together a feminist guerrilla theater act in which I played the Statue of Liberty. In the spring of 1970, with Violet Lindbeck's help, some of us invited Rosemary Radford Ruether and Claire Randall to speak at the Divinity School. This inspired Judith Plaskow and me to invite the other graduate student women in our department (who until that point had not shown interest in feminism) to tea. This gathering led to a direct action known as "the Liberation of the Shit Room," a sit-in in the Divinity School's only toilet (for men) in the library stacks.[12] Sisterhood was indeed powerful. Knowing that other women felt as I did made me understand that I was not crazy. My growing friendship with Judith Plaskow was life-affirming. We heard each other into speech, read each other's work.

In the spring of 1970, I met Marcia (now Mara) Keller, Virginia Walbot, and Caroline Whitbeck.[13] Keller encouraged us to support a letter she had written inviting the United States Department of Health, Education, and Welfare to investigate Yale for sex discrimination. We founded the Women's Staff, Faculty, and Graduate Alliance, dedicated to improving the status of all women at Yale, including its one tenured and several untenured female faculty members, its beleaguered graduate students, new undergraduates, and a large and underpaid secretarial staff. Caroline Whitbeck and I wrote a Model Affirmative Action Plan that was later published by Bernice Sandler of the Women's Equity Action League.[14] Eventually HEW found Yale guilty of sex discrimination, but the presidents of the ten top universities convinced President Nixon that they should be exempt from censure.[15] I continued to be active in the student protest movement—traveling to Washington, D.C., to attend marches and serving as a marshal in the rally to free Bobby Seale and end racism and the war in Vietnam that followed the closing of the Yale campus in the spring of 1970.[16] My understanding that the personal is the political was shaped by sharing stories in a consciousness-raising group that Carolyn Dobay Forrey and I started by posting a notice on the bulletin board of New Haven Women's Liberation.

In all of these social and political activities other students, not the church, formed my community. Yet I understood my commitment to justice to stem from biblical religion. Religious leaders including the Berrigans and William Sloan Coffin were outspoken in the struggle for peace and justice. I met Coffin in my first year of graduate study through a friend and discovered that he did not consider women at all important. Instead of Yale Chapel, I attended Yale's Roman Catholic folk mass throughout my graduate years. Though I had been baptized Protestant, my father's family were Catholic, and Catholics at Yale shared my class background. The spirit of Vatican II, opening to the world, and love expressed in the sharing of bread, wine, and the kiss of peace, was alive in the folk mass. A priest who entered graduate studies with me delighted in calling me a "practicing Catholic." I grew to feel the power of the Catholic mass in English, particularly in its connections of the cycles of grief and joy to the seasons.

In the summer of 1969 I began a journey of coming to terms with God's relation to the Holocaust provoked by reading Elie Wiesel's *The Gates of the Forest*.[17] As I worked on my dissertation on Elie Wiesel's stories,[18] I came face to face with the fact that the mass that I loved blamed "the Jews" for the death of Christ. Because I had participated viscerally and bodily in the liturgy of the mass, I experienced the unmasking of Christian anti-Semitism in my gut: it made me sick to my stomach. I could no longer joyfully take part in the Easter liturgies, the high point of the religious year. My break with Christianity began here.

In the spring of 1971 I was invited to the first Conference of Women Theologians at Alverno College. Being together with some twenty other women who had studied religion and theology was a turning point for me. For the first time in my experience, the question of women and religion was being taken seriously in community. Another woman and I drafted a short paper on the need for female imagery for God, a subject I would later write much about. Yet at Alverno, the issue of God language was dismissed as trivial.[19] Sometime during the conference, I suggested that we form a feminist group within the American Academy of Religion (AAR). At that time, no more than five or ten women attended the AAR meetings.[20] I was urged to call Harry Buck, then executive director of the AAR, to ask for meeting space. Harry responded positively and provided me with a list of the names of all AAR members who were not obviously male.[21]

I sent out a letter inviting women to come to the AAR meetings. At the hotel where the meetings were held, I was accosted by Harry Smith, the executive director of the Society for Religion in Higher Education, who asked me if we were planning to nominate a woman for president of the AAR. This idea had not occurred to me, but it seemed like a good one. By the time the meetings ended, we had founded the Women's Caucus—Religious Studies, inaugurated the Women and Religion Working Group, and elected Christine Downing as an upcoming president of the AAR.[22] Though I was still a graduate student, I was thrust into a kind of limelight at the age of twenty-five.

When I left Yale in the summer of 1972, I was already feeling alienated from the Roman Catholic mass that had once been nourishing to my spirit. I now felt its sexism as deeply as its anti-Semitism. Every time I heard God referred to as Father, Lord, or King, my stomach went into knots. Liberation theology was in the air, but it did not speak to me. For me the God of Exodus who cast the Egyptians and their horses into the sea in order to rescue the Hebrew slaves was a God of war.[23] The faces of dead and dying Vietnamese children were etched in my mind.

In early 1974 I was up late one night working on my dissertation, writing about Elie Wiesel's anger at God for allowing his chosen people to die in the

Holocaust. My own anger came to the forefront. I began to berate God for letting himself "be named in man's image, as the God of the fathers, as the man of war, as the king of the universe." How could a loving and powerful God let men beat and rape women? I asked. Let them kill each other and women and children in war? Why didn't he send a prophet to save women? When my anger was spent, I lay quietly on my bed. In the silence I heard a voice in my mind saying: "in God is a woman like yourself. She shares your suffering." This experience had the force of revelation for me. I knew I would seek the God who was a woman like myself until I found Her.[24]

Though I was feeling alienated from the Christian God, I was drawn to attend a celebration of the ordination of the first women Episcopal priests at Riverside Church in my neighborhood in New York City in the fall of 1974. When the women walked in singing "A Mighty Fortress Is Our God," affirming a military and male God as their savior, I walked out of the church and never went back. Mary Daly's *Beyond God the Father,* which I studied intently, prodded me to the conclusion that the symbol system of Christianity was the foundation of a patriarchal, hierarchical, and warlike society.[25]

When Naomi Goldenberg, Marcia Keller, and I took a workshop from a then unknown woman named Starhawk in the winter of 1975, I found the Goddess I was seeking. As close to us as our female bodies. The life force flowing in all that is. Energy of birth, death, and renewal. An ethic based on reverence for the deep connections of all people and all beings in the web of life. I was elated to find Starhawk speaking words that expressed my body knowing and the deepest desires of my heart. Not long afterward, I found my search for a female God echoed in Ntozake Shange's incredible play, *for colored girls who have considered suicide when the rainbow is enuf.*[26] I rejoiced when a Black woman as tall as I rose from despair and sang "I Found God in Myself and I Loved Her Fiercely." Because my introduction to the Goddess came in part through Shange, it never crossed my mind (as it is sometimes said) that "the Goddess" is "White." The ritual group that was my spiritual home in the 1980s was co-led by a Latina, and a Black woman who is now a well-known ecofeminist was part of our group. The poster that hung above my desk for years entitled "And God Created Woman in Her Own Image" by Ann Grifalconi pictured God as a Black woman.

I naively imagined that my sisters in academia were longing for images of God-She and Goddess, as I was. It was a big disappointment to find out that they were not. In the New York Feminist Scholars in Religion, a group I founded with Anne Barstow, my sisters told me that Goddess religion could have no ethics or sense of justice, yet my sense of the injustices created by biblical religion was so strong it had made me unable to participate in the faith of my upbringing. My sisters called the God of Exodus and the prophets a Liberator, while I could only see him as a Warrior. I began to feel almost as isolated among my academic sisters as I had once felt at Yale. I had violated a boundary that I did not know existed.[27] I will not elaborate on the pain involved in this story here. However, I note that the conference entitled "Religion and the Feminist Movement" (for which this collection of papers were written) is also organized around the assumption the most significant questions in women and religion are raised by those who remain within traditional religious institutions. Of twenty-seven invited speakers, only two or three (depending on how you count Mary Daly) represented the non-institutional women's spirituality movement, while eighteen are Christian, three Jewish, two Muslim, and one identified herself as a post-Christian humanist. Yet I estimate that at least half of all the women engaged with questions of women and religion in North America have been deeply influenced by the Goddess and women's spirituality movements, among them many women who also identify as Christians or Jews.[28] (Another large group of feminists in religion not represented at this conference are western women practicing nonwestern religions, prominent among them women like Rita Gross, Sandy Boucher, and Miranda Shaw.[29] Many feminists who practice nonwestern religions also identify as Jews or Christians.)

Though I felt marginalized by many of my Christian sisters in academia, I gained the strength to speak my truth from other women were also seeking female images for divinity, including Starhawk, Merlin Stone, Z Budapest, Charlene Spretnak, Hallie Austen Iglehart, Naomi Goldenberg, Ruth and Jean Mountaingrove, Mara Keller, Alexis Masters, Rita Gross, Christine Downing, Susan Setta, Anne Barstow, and Karen Brown.[30] These women are friends as well as colleagues. In 1978 I gave the keynote address before a sell-out crowd of 500 at the conference "The Great Goddess Re-emerging" in Santa Cruz.[31] In the speech I gave there, "Why Women Need the Goddess," I said that the symbol of the Goddess affirms female power, the female body, the female will, and women's bonds and heritage. This essay has been reprinted in scores of collections since then, including in a well-known text on critical thinking, and has introduced tens of thousands of women and men to the Goddess.[32] *Diving Deep and Surfacing*, published in 1980, has sold more than 50,000 copies and has changed women's lives.[33] The anthologies Judith Plaskow and I edited together, *Womanspirit Rising* and *Weaving the Visions*, have together sold over 150,000 copies and have helped to transform the way women and religion is taught in North America.[34] I am proud of the religious diversity reflected in both of the anthologies I co-edited with Judith Plaskow and of the racial and cultural diversity of the second.

As for my own career, my early fame brought me a number of job offers before I had finished my dissertation. I taught for five years at Columbia University in the city of New York, where I developed one of the earliest women and religion courses.[35] But as it became known that I was not Christian, my opportunities shrank dramatically. While employed in Women's Studies at San Jose State University, I also taught several courses at the Pacific School of Religion. When a graduate of the institution asked the female dean why I had not been rehired, she was told that the questions I raised about Christianity threatened the faith of some of the students. I received tenure and a full professorship in Women's Studies at San Jose State.[36] But I was worn out teaching four classes and over 150 students a semester, each of my courses an introduction to Women's Studies, my office hours filled with women telling me personal stories of incest and beating, while others accused me of hating men because I assigned feminist work.[37] In addition, I was writing and speaking an average of three times each month. I had always thought I would be happy "if only I could teach graduate students at a place like Harvard." But when I was as a research associate there in 1986–1987, I was disheartened to learn that women who intended to stay on the faculty were afraid to speak out too strongly. The woman who was assigned to respond to my paper at a women's faculty seminar said it was a great paper combining passion and scholarship, but "we at Harvard" could never be so "bold," a commentary as damning as any that could have been given by a patriarchal male. Earlier, Sallie McFague had advised me that though I deserved a better job than the one I had at San Jose State, I should not expect one, given the conservatism of the academy and the fact that my not being Christian would keep me from being hired in a seminary. After all, Sallie reminded, me, she herself gained tenure at Vanderbilt Divinity School only because she first agreed to serve as dean. Mary Daly had never received a second job offer and thus continued to teach under conditions of duress at Boston College, while Rosemary Radford Ruether's two permanent positions had been in seminaries.[38] After my year at Harvard, I resigned a tenured full professorship and moved to Greece.

Personally, I have never regretted this decision. I live in Molivos, Lesbos, one of the most beautiful places in the world, and am involved in the local environmental movement to save it. I found a nourishing spiritual path and ways to teach creatively leading Goddess tours and seminars in Crete and Lesbos.[39] I continue to write, and my books continue to sell, which means that my work continues to play a role shaping the way we think about women and religion. However, it worries me that the women's spirituality and Goddess movements are marginalized in the academy and in seminaries. Because of this women are not able to study Goddess religions, ancient and modern, in major graduate programs.[40] The insights of women who have left institutionalized religion behind are not heard—and perhaps are feared—by those who hold positions of power in the universities and seminaries. Important groups of women in religion in America are not in dialogue with each other. I believe this is a loss for us all. In *She Who Changes: Re-imagining the Divine in the World*, I suggest yet again that women in religion share much that institutional boundaries mask.[41]

REFLECTIONS ON THE STORIES WE TELL

In the paper she prepared for the conference on Religion and the Feminist Movement, Rosemary Radford Ruether stated that she did not recognize herself in a story that is sometimes told about the women and religion movement. This is the story that the founders of the movement were White feminists whose sole concern was the liberation of middle-class White women like themselves and who had no understanding of race, class, or colonialism. Like Radford Ruether, I do not recognize myself in this story. My awareness of sexism followed my outrage about racism, poverty, and American militarism. I wrote the first literary critical analysis of *for colored girls who have considered suicide* in my first book, *Diving Deep and Surfacing*. At San Jose State in the late 1970s and 1980s, my students included Asian, Asian American, Latina, and Black women. They nudged me to make my courses more and more inclusive of their experiences, and I did so. *Black-eyed Susans, Bless Me Ultima, for colored girls who have considered suicide when the rainbow is enuf,* and *The Color Purple* were included on the reading lists for my Introduction to Women's Studies class, along with many photocopied essays by non-White women, including one called "Korean Picture Bride."[42] I taught Audre Lorde's groundbreaking essay "Uses of the Erotic" when it was still a pamphlet.[43] I insisted that a

Latina and a Black woman be hired to teach in our small Women's Studies program. This does not mean that as a White feminist I knew it all; rather it suggests that I never imagined that I did.

There is another story that is often told in the women and religion movement in which I do not recognize myself. This is the story that Christian feminism is about ethics and social justice while Goddess feminism is about the narcissistic navel-gazing of middle-class White women. This story has been uncritically repeated in a number of recent introductions to feminist theology in both Britain and North America, for example, in *Introducing Feminist Images of God* by Mary Grey and in *Introducing Feminist Theology* by Anne M. Clifford. Both authors cite Rosemary Radford Ruether as a source for this understanding of the Goddess movement.[44] Though widely told, this story ignores and distorts important and well-known facts about the origins of the Goddess movement and the values and actions of its participants.

Z Budapest, whom many consider to have been the first to link contemporary Goddess religion with radical feminism, named her coven after Susan B. Anthony because she believed that Goddess religion had an important role to play in completing the feminist revolution. Because of her feminist activities, including advocating women's right to control our bodies, Z was arrested in the state of California for reading tarot cards. Rather than paying a fine, she argued in court that her arrest was a violation of her right as a woman to practice the religion of her own choosing. Starhawk presented a paper entitled "Ethics and Justice in Goddess Religion" at the AAR conference in 1979 that became the basis for a chapter in her *Dreaming the Dark*, which sold over 100,000 copies. In that book she documented her participation and leadership in the antinuclear movement, in which many other Goddess feminists, myself included, were also active. In recent years Starhawk and other members of the reclaiming movement she founded have been leading voices in the worldwide direct action movement against globalization, and she and others in the Goddess movement have been jailed many times. Charlene Spretnak, author of *Lost Goddesses of Early Greece* and editor of *The Politics of Women's Spirituality,* has been a leader in the Green Party in California and coauthored *Green Politics* with Frijof Capra. Hallie Austen (Iglehart), author of *Womanspirit* and *Heart of the Goddess,* is a founding member of Seaflow, a group dedicated to saving whales and other sea creatures from the deadly effects of sonar waves sent out by military submarines. Vicki Noble, co-creator of the Motherpeace Tarot and author of *Motherpeace,* has been active in the women's health movement. I am a founding member of Friends of Green Lesbos. In *Rebirth of the Goddess*, I devoted a chapter to "Ethos and Ethics" and offered "Nine Touchstones" of Goddess ethics as an alternative to the "Ten Commandments" of the Bible: "Nurture life. Walk in love and beauty. Trust the knowledge that comes through the body. Speak the truth about conflict, pain, and suffering. Take only what you need. Think about the consequences of your actions for seven generations. Approach the taking of life with great restraint. Practice great generosity. Repair the web." In *Introducing Thealogy*, Melissa Raphael dedicated a chapter to "Thealogy and Ethics." Each of us and tens of thousands of other women have been drawn to the Goddess for reasons that are ethical in the broadest sense.[45]

Since all of this is well documented, one has to wonder why the story that Christian feminists are concerned with ethics and justice, but Goddess feminists are not, has been repeated like a litany since the late 1970s. Whose interests does it serve? Surely not the interests of truth, for it is factually untrue. Nor the interests of the widest possible dialogue about feminism and religion, for its function is to exclude certain voices. When the Goddess movement is dismissed not simply as non-Christian but as nonethical, who stands to gain? What is lost when feminist and womanist theologies are defined in exclusively Christian terms? These questions are rarely considered.

One of the results of labeling the Goddess movement as nonethical is that the radical questions it raises about the ethos of biblical religion as shaped by its symbols and images can be more easily dismissed by Christian feminists and womanists. I began my academic career with the naive assumption that all of us together—especially all of us feminists—were dedicated to the pursuit of truth. Yet I soon learned that, in the seminary context at least, raising certain kinds of fundamental questions was not acceptable. Even when most of my syllabus was devoted to the writings of Christian feminists, the mere suggestion that Mary Daly might be right in her critique of Christianity as a symbol system was upsetting to my students at the Pacific School of Religion. Fair enough. It was meant to be. Isn't that what the pursuit of truth is all about? Challenging fundamental assumptions? I raised the question. I did not dictate what the answer had to be. What was surprising was that it was reported to me that a female dean who herself professed to be a feminist found the "upset" of raising questions about Christianity sufficient reason not to rehire me. In the late 1970s a line was drawn in the sand. Feminists in religion received the clear message that it would be professional suicide (at least for those who hoped to teach in seminaries) to ask certain questions. Could this be one of the reasons that the story that Christian feminism is ethical while Goddess feminism is not has such staying power? If the Goddess movement can be dismissed, then the questions it raises do not have to be addressed.

Underlying the criticism of the Goddess movement as not concerned with ethics are two unexamined assumptions. One is that the Goddess movement is concerned with images of God as She only as they relate to questions of women's self-esteem. I have already suggested that this is to narrow and distort the ethical visions of the Goddess movement. The other unexamined assumption is that self-esteem is not itself a political issue. Sometimes this is put in a more subtle way. Concern with images and symbols is important, but it is a luxury that those who are poor or suffering violence cannot afford. Yet this ignores the complex interaction of symbols and social reality in the lives of all women, including those who are poor and suffering violence. How many women are suffering violence in the home the world around because they and their abusers have been taught that God is male and the male is God? How are images of God as a male divine warrior used to legitimate the violence of war? Of God as Lord used to legitimate hierarchies within church and society that leave women out in the cold? If these are questions that cannot be asked because they lead sooner or later to the Goddess, whose interests are being served? Womanist theologian Cheryl Gilkes has written that "many current social problems are often tied to low self-esteem or self-hatred. Self-hatred or damage and brokenness to our inner visions make it impossible for us to make and share effective liberating visions for our community and our world."[46] Building on this insight, Arisika Razak argues that in order to overcome negative images of Black women's bodies purveyed by racist and sexist cultures, Black women need "a God who is Black and female, embodied and divine."[47] Razak and Gilkes agree that in order to become effective social visionaries, women, including women of color, must learn to love ourselves and our bodies. Self-esteem is not a luxury, but one of the ingredients leading to social change.

I ask again: Whose interests are being served by the story that the Goddess movement is not concerned with ethics and social justice? I hope I have made it clear that the answer is that it is not women's. Then whose interests are being served? Those of institutional churches concerned with enforcing standards of orthodoxy? Those of institutional churches concerned that women not go too far? Surely these are interests that feminist scholars in religion should wish to resist. I do not imagine that Goddess feminists and Christian feminists or womanists will always share the same theological, thealogical, and ethical priorities and strategies. Yet I remain convinced that greater openness to dialogue would benefit us all. And I hope that those who write histories of feminism and religion in America will not collude in perpetuating the false story that those of us drawn to the Goddess religion have no concern for ethics or social justice. Nothing could be farther from the truth.

NOTES

1. Far more of my classmates married and had children in their teens than went on to college. My brother was married with two children by the time he was nineteen.
2. I sewed almost all of my own clothing, paying for the fabric with my baby-sitting money. I served meals to the other students in the dining halls in my junior and senior years. I worked as a telephone solicitor in the summers because that was the only job that was available to me. My parents did not go to the doctor and put off needed dental work in order to pay for my tuition. Needless to say I had no spending money while in college. However, because of the exchange rate, I was able to go to Stanford in Italy and to travel on a Eurail pass staying in youth hostels for almost nothing for three months afterward.
3. In the late 1990s I was able to thank her for her intervention and tell her of the success of her counsellee. She was thrilled.
4. Students at Northview High School came from "the wrong side of the tracks" in Covina and also included the Mexican American students from the neighboring town of Irwindale.
5. My brother Alan Peter Christ died of Hyaline Membrane Syndrome at the age of five days at about the same time that the Kennedy baby died of the same illness.
6. Napier was in a position to know, because he had come to Stanford from the Yale Divinity School. How I wish I had understood what he was saying.
7. In 1967 there were no women undergraduates at Yale, enough female graduate students to fill the residence Helen Hadley Hall, only a handful of women in the Divinity School. A letter a friend and I wrote to the *Yale Daily News* comparing the luxurious conditions of the male graduate rooms in the Hall of Graduate Studies to the spartan utilitarianism of Helen Hadley Hall led to the integration of both graduate student residences in the next year. Women entered Yale College in 1969, with the assurance to alumni that Yale would continue to graduate "1,000 male leaders" each year.
8. I did not transfer to comparative literature, but I did transfer out of Hebrew Bible and into theology early on in my first semester.
9. One of the things that kept me sane in this atmosphere was finding Christine Downing's dissertation, "The Theological Imagination: A Study of Martin Buber" (Ph.D. diss., Drew University, 1966) and reading it on microfilm. Downing confirmed my intuitions that Buber was writing theology in a poetic way. Meeting Downing at the Society for Religion in Higher Education reception at the 1970 meetings of the AAR in New York City was thrilling.

10. Margaret Farley was subsequently hired to teach Christian ethics at Yale Divinity School.

11. I cannot underestimate the importance of these scholarships on my self-esteem and also in freeing me from dependence on scholarships from Yale, which after my first year there, surely would not have been forthcoming. The Danforth Fellowship also provided connections to like-minded individuals through their conferences for graduate students and through the Society for Religion (later Values) in Higher Education. Also important was the continuing support of former Stanford professor Michael Novak, who asked me to be a research assistant on his book *Ascent of the Mountain, Flight of the Dove* (New York: Harper & Row, 1971).

12. I published an account of this action in Gloria Kaufman and Mary K. Blakley, eds., *Pulling Our Own Strings: Feminist Humor & Satire* (Bloomington: Indiana University Press, 1980).

13. Mara Keller is director of the Women's Spirituality Program at California Institute of Integral Studies; Virginia Walbot is a world-renowned genetics scientist tenured at Stanford; Caroline Whitbeck is professor of philosophy and ethics at Case Western Reserve University.

14. I no longer have a copy of this document.

15. The exclusion of the top ten universities from censure under the executive order prohibiting discrimination by those accepting federal funds was reported in the press.

16. The letter I wrote to my parents attempting to explain that my participation in the events at Yale that spring stemmed from my understanding of the Christian values I had learned at home elicited a response from my mother that began, "The day I opened your letter was the darkest day of my life."

17. Elie Wiesel, *The Gates of the Forest*, trans. Frances Frenaye (New York: Schocken Books, 1982).

18. Carol P. Christ, "Elie Wiesel's Stories: Still the Dialogue," Ph.D. diss. Yale University, 1974. Available from University Microfilms.

19. I no longer have a copy of that paper. Conference organizers published my paper on Karl Barth's view of women, rather than the one on female God language. I would be happy to receive a copy of either paper from anyone who has access to them.

20. Some of these were wives. Lore repeated to me had it that many of the established scholars in the field considered visits to prostitutes a part of the annual meetings until the formation of the Women's Caucus in 1971.

21. Harry Buck who taught at Wilson College and founded and edited *Anima* was a great supporter of women and our feminist work. He published papers by me, Naomi Goldenberg, Christine Downing, Karen Brown, and possibly others, that were preliminary to our first books.

22. Not surprisingly, AAR election procedures were immediately changed to preclude nominations from the floor. When the Women's Caucus proposed at an open meeting that the 1982 annual meetings focus attention on the nuclear threat (and won), the AAR bylaws were again amended to prevent such a thing from happening.

23. See "Yahweh as Holy Warrior," in *Laughter of Aphrodite: Reflections on a Journey to the Goddess* (San Francisco: HarperSanFrancisco, 1987), 73–82.

24. I first wrote about this experience in "Women's Liberation and the Liberation of God," reprinted in Carol P. Christ, *Laughter of Aphrodite*, 20–26. Also see my *Rebirth of the Goddess: Finding Meaning in Feminist Spirituality* (New York: Routledge, 1998), 2.

25. Mary Daly, *Beyond God the Father* (Boston: Beacon Press, 1973).

26. I must have seen this play for the first time early in the fall of 1976 in New York City; it was published in New York by Macmillan in 1976.

27. Discussions were heated, perhaps because there was a recognition that these questions mattered deeply. Naomi Goldenberg, Anne Barstow, and I were the only proponents of the Goddess, as I recall, while Beverly Harrison was a stalwart proponent of the thesis that Goddess religion could not possibly have a social ethic.

28. The number of women who have been influenced by the Goddess and women's spirituality movements is difficult to estimate, since neither is institutionalized and many women who "worship the Goddess in their hearts" still practice as Christians and Jews. However, given that several of Starhawk's books alone have sold over 100,000 copies each, a conservative estimate would put the numbers in the hundreds of thousands.

29. Rita Gross, *Buddhism after Patriarchy: A Feminist History, Analysis, and Reconstruction of Buddhism* (Albany: State University of New York Press, 1993); Sandy Boucher, *Discovering Kwan Yin: Buddhist Goddess of Compassion* (Boston: Beacon Press, 1999); Miranda Shaw, *Passionate Enlightenment: Women in Tantric Buddhism* (Princeton, N.J.: Princeton University Press, 1994).

30. Works by these women include: Starhawk, *The Spiral Dance: A Rebirth of the Ancient Religion of the Great Goddess* (San Francisco, Calif.: Harper & Row, 1979); Merlin Stone, *When God Was a Woman* (New York: Dial Press, 1976); Z Budapest, *The Holy Book of Women's Mysteries* (Oakland, Calif.: Wingbow, 1989), earlier published in different form as *The Feminist Book of Light and Shadows;* Charlene Spretnak, *Lost Goddesses of Early Greece* (Boston: Beacon Press, 1984 [1978]) and Spretnak, ed., *The Politics of Women's Spirituality* (New York: Doubleday, 1982); Hallie's early work was published under the name Hallie Mountainwing, *Womanspirit* (San Francisco: HarperSanFrancisco: 1983) under the name Hallie Austen Iglehart, and *Heart of the Goddess* (Berkeley, Calif.: Wingbow Press, 1990) under the name Hallie Iglehart Austen; Naomi Goldenberg, *The Changing of the Gods: Feminism and the End of Traditional Religions* (Boston: Beacon Press, 1979); Jean and Ruth Mountaingrove edited the pathbreaking *WomanSpirit* magazine from 1974 to 1984, back issues available from 2000 King Mountain Trail, Sunny Valley, Oregon 97467; Mara Lynn Keller, "The Greater Mysteries of Demeter and Persephone: The Nine Day Initiation Ritual at Athens and Eleusis," manuscript, and "The Eleusinian Mysteries of Demeter and Persephone: Fertility, Sexuality, and Rebirth," *Journal of Feminist Studies in Religion* 4, no. 1 (Spring 1988): 27–54; Alexis and I created rituals to Aphrodite in Lesbos in the 1980s, which I wrote about in *Laughter of Aphrodite*, 183–192, while Alexis wrote a work of visionary fiction inspired by these experiences, *The Guiliana Legacy* (Deerfield Beech, Fla.: Health Communications, 2000); Rita Gross, "Hindu Female Deities as a Resource for the Contemporary Rediscovery of the Goddesss, *Journal of the American Academy of Religion* 46, no. 3 (1978): 269–291; Christine Downing, *The Goddess: Mythological Images of the*

Feminine (New York: Crossroad, 1981); Susan Setta's work on American female religious leaders, many of whom referred to God as Mother, was interrupted by family problems, but at least one of her essays was published in *Anima*; Anne Barstow, "The Uses of Archaeology for Women's History: James Mellaart's Work on the Neolithic Goddess at Catal Huyuk," *Feminist Studies* 4, no. 3 (October, 1978): 7–18; Karen Brown, *Mama Lola: A Vodou Priestess in Brooklyn* (Berkeley, CA: University of California Press, 1991).

31. This conference was envisioned by Charlene Spretnak, Halllie Austen Iglehart, and Carolyn Schaffer; I joined the planning committee.

32. This essay was first published in *Heresies (The Great Goddess Issue)* (1978): 8–11; it was reprinted in Carol P. Christ and Judith Plaskow, eds., *Womanspirit Rising: A Feminist Reader on Religion* (San Francisco: Harper & Row, 1979, 1989), 273–287; in Spretnak, ed., *The Politics of Women's Spirituality*, 71–86; and scores of other times, including in the critical thinking textbook *Current Issues and Enduring Questions*, ed. Barnet and Bedau (Boston: St. Martin's Press, 1993), 700–713, where it is presented as a model for constructing an argument.

33. Carol P. Christ, *Diving Deep and Surfacing* (Boston: Beacon Press, 1980).

34. Judith Plaskow and Carol P. Christ, eds., *Weaving the Visions: New Patterns in Feminist Spirituality* (San Francisco: Harper & Row, 1989).

35. I taught at Columbia from 1972 to 1977; I offered women and religion courses for the first time in 1973. While packing my books to leave Columbia in 1977, Judith Plaskow and I outlined the book that became *Womanspirit Rising*, from the resources we had gathered for our classes.

36. I went to San Jose State in the fall of 1977 and resigned while on leave in the fall of 1987.

37. There were no prerequisites for any of my classes, so no matter what I was teaching, some students angrily resisted learning about women's inequality and oppression; this anger inevitably was visited on me. By the end of the semester the students had settled down and most of them were angry at the system, not at me. This process took a toll on my health, nonetheless. Something about the openness of my heart invited many of my students to tell me stories of incest, rape, and beating for the first time in almost all of my office hours. Though I felt honored that so many women trusted me and I urged them to get help, simply being there with their stories also took an enormous toll on my health. Before I left for Greece in 1986 with dreams of quitting my job, I was operated on for a first-stage malignant melanoma. I was lucky to have caught it early.

38. This conversation occurred when I delivered the Antoinette Brown Blackwell Lecture at Vanderbilt Divinity School in March, 1985.

39. Ariadne Institute (), which I direct, offers a Goddess pilgrimage to Crete and a sacred journey in Lesbos.

40. M.A. and Ph.D. programs in women's spirituality at California Institute of Integral Studies () and New College in California () were founded to fill this gap. At this writing these programs have graduated a number of exceptional students, while remaining understaffed and under funded.

41. Carol P. Christ, *She Who Changes: Re-imagining the Divine in the World* (New York: Palgrave Macmillan/St. Martin's Press, 2003).

42. Mary Helen Washington, *Black-eyed Susans: Classic Stories About Black Women* (New York: Anchor Books, 1979); Rudolfo A. Anaya, *Bless Me, Ultima* (Berke-

ley, Calif.: Tonatiuth International, 1971); Ntozake Shange, *for colored girls who have considered suicide when the rainbow is enuf* (San Lorenzo, Calif.: Shameless Hussy Press, 1975); Alice Walker, *The Color Purple* (New York: Pocket Books, 1983).

43. Reprinted in *Weaving the Visions*, 208–213.

44. See Mary Grey, *Introducing Feminist Images of God* (Sheffield, England: Sheffield Academic Press, 2001), 28–35; Anne M. Clifford, *Introducing Feminist Theology* (Maryknoll, N.Y.: Orbis Books, 2002), 92–97; and Rosemary Radford Ruether, *Gaia and God* (San Francisco: Harper & Row, 1992).

45. Some of the references for this paragraph can be found in note 29; also see Starhawk, *Dreaming the Dark: Magic, Sex, and Politics* (San Francisco: Harper & Row, 1982, 1997) and Starhawk, *Webs of Power: Notes from the Global Uprising* (Gabriola Island, B.C.: New Society Publishers, 2002); Motherpeace Tarot Cards by Karen Vogel, illustrated by Vicki Noble (Stamford, Conn.: US Games Systems, 1997); Vicki Noble, *Motherpeace* (New York: Harper & Row, 1983); Christ, *Rebirth of the Goddess*, 160–177; Melissa Raphael, *Introducing Thealogy: Discourse on the Goddess* (Sheffield, England: Sheffield Academic Press, 1999), 97–115. Information about reclaiming can be found at www. reclaiming.org; information about Seaflow at www.seaflow.org; information about Friends of Green Lesbos at www.greenlesbos.com.

46. *If It Wasn't for the Women* (New York: Orbis Books, 2001), 181, quoted in Razak, see next note.

47. Arisika Razak, "'I Found God in Myself': Sacred Images of African and African-American Women," paper presented at the 2002 meetings of the American Academy of Religion, p. 6.

EIGHT

Delores S. Williams

1980 Director, Anna Howard Shaw Center, Boston University School of Theology

1993 Author, *Sisters in the Wilderness: The Challenge of Womanist God-talk*

1993 Speaker, Re-Imagining Conference

In the following pages I will tell a story. Like most stories, it is personal. It is social. It is probing. It is a different feminist voice rising. I assume in the beginning the political is personal. I have given this story a name:

SEARCHING AN IDENTITY:
OR THE CONDITIONING MOLDING ME INTO MYSELF[1]

I am a Black woman—much too short a statement for such a complex reality.

The conflicts between ought and am, giving and needing, quitting and beginning again. This face in the mirror: my face lined at the corner of the smile, trying to deal with the Black, the woman: their presence, their history, their meaning in me. This search for God, though I doubt as intensely as I believe, circles and dips like a tornado into undiscovered areas of who I am, routing out familiar securities, bringing to the surface an awful uneasiness—then spending itself in the dizzy world of New York life. I begin again.

I am a Black woman—a woman of God, as was my mother and her mother and her mother's mother: the slave. This belief fortified both the blackness and the woman, they taught me. Hard times, God, mean White folks, and hard Black men were as inseparable from life as pain and death. "Nobody knows the trouble you gon' see but Jesus." "God will take care of you." "Precious Lord take your hand and lead you on." "God moves in mysterious ways his wonders to perform." These songs sang by the women of my family proved to them God moved life to a deeper meaning and a greater satisfaction beyond history. They believed: my mother, her mother, and her mother's mother: the slave.

The events of my history and the "facts" of their faith warred at the center of my being as I moved inside and outside the civil rights movements of my time looking for a new way of saying I am a Black woman. Up the dirt roads of rural Alabama. Through hot, southern boulevards marching: marching with the youth of my time, turning over southern mind-sets, getting wounded along the way, singing "We Shall Overcome Some Day." They spat on us. I spat back, showing them the new meaning of Black. Yet there was more of me needing telling: the woman part. Crouching like a guilty child in a kitchen corner she, I, woman glibly repeated Eldridge Cleaver's proclamation: "We shall have our manhood or the earth will be razed in our attempts." She, I, woman had no idea that within the context of this declaration, "Black woman" had no meaning except babies, pain, and "standing behind your man."

Nineteen seventy-three began a weary time. The movement was silenced by the process that rhetoric forgot to mention—the ruthless accumulation of power and its concomitant: the inequitable distribution of goods. The movement left me, Black woman, with a definition forged in the heat of its power politics. "The only position for a woman in the movement is prone," Stokley Carmichael is reported to have said.[2] Many male liberators agreed. My body was much too spent for a pleasant love affair. The events of my history lost solid ground.

I returned to the "facts" of my ancestors' faith strained through a different medium: the distance between me and the movement; my mother's God on wobbly legs; and my stubborn insistence that I am *all* that I am: *Black and Woman*. And I will be! But to make new affirmations about my woman identity, I needed new ideas. I needed a broader worldview, a woman-sustaining and woman-affirming Divinity who didn't require me to sing the sad songs or to believe that Black women's lives achieved greater meaning only beyond history.

Depressed and disillusioned, I stumbled into Union Theological Seminary in New York City looking for a broader context to situate the faith of my female forebears. Long ago I had dismissed the church as an inane institution unable to face the hard tasks of justice-making for women. But there at Union twenty-odd years ago I met Beverly Harrison and her feminist teaching. With love, concern, and friendship she taught me that I must look again at the conditioning that had molded me into myself. This time I should look at myself and my conditioning by giving attention to the social, economic, and political networks of patriarchal power controlled by men and oppressing women. Many of my ideologies were debunked. I realized I had been looking at the world and at my life through male-colored lens. Alice Walker was right. To see the world, a woman had to get men off her eyeballs.[3] My worldview began to broaden as I realized that I was part of a global community of women who lived under the sway of male domination. There was, then, the possibility of communication and support from other women who were trying to understand what had been done to their womanhood by the cultures they came from. I began strengthening my female voice inspired by Audre Lorde's poem telling women we were never meant to survive and our silence would not protect us. Bev's feminist teaching helped me rise up from years and years of sacrifice that had squelched my search to claim myself as artist, as woman, as free.

To look again at the conditioning that molded me into myself was no easy task. There were tensions. There were deaths. My father's death. My husband's sudden death. Overnight I became a single parent with four children. But there were also resurrections. I can truly say this searching my life, this journey from outside myself into myself would not have happened had I not met, been taught by, and had friendship with Beverly Harrison. As I struggled with the conditioning that molded me into my *then-self*, I learned from her (slowly) to claim, to celebrate, to cultivate my woman-self rising. I learned how to begin unsettling the layers of patriarchal conditioning that had so artfully and so subtly hidden me from myself. I learned it is not easy to be born again. But no woman knows herself who has not entered the birth

canal of her own life—who has not faced the fault lines in the first conditioning that molded her into herself. She who breaks the mold breaks the silences
and learns the strength of her own voice.

A FEMINIST IS BORN

I had indeed become a feminist! Now I could proclaim again my original
statement of identity: I am a Black woman! But this time there were qualifiers
to be added from my experience of awakening to myself. I was now a woman
with the right to control my person, my destiny, my body, the definitions of
myself and the world as I saw it. I *was free in a way I had never been free before!*

Yet there was still more of me that needed telling. What was I to do with
the religion of my mother, her mother, and her mother's mother: the slave?
Though it did not accommodate my struggle to understand myself as an
adult Black woman in control of my life, it had played a determinative role in
my conditioning. But now I was bringing new questions to this religious heritage as a result of my feminist transformations and as the result of my so-
journ into Union Theological Seminary.

When the Christian religion and my feminism met, the problem of God
emerged. I searched for new ideas to express my questions about God. I
needed a new way "to language" God, given my experience of awakening to
fuller dimensions of myself and of the world. All of my life I had been encouraged to worship a male God whom I now recognized as a patriarchal
construction. Yet this God was the center of the prayer tradition of Christian
Black women, and I greatly respected this tradition. My mother taught her
children to love Jesus whom she said helped Black people survive and thrive.
But what was I to do with the maleness of this Christian God?

It was as if Rosemary Ruether had anticipated my trouble with the understanding of God from my heritage. Can a male savior save women? she
asked. The conclusion, for me, was that Jesus' maleness was not the point.
The point was that he opposed and challenged the principalities of power
that oppressed women and all people. I soaked in Ruether's christology like a
sponge for the first time meeting water. I began to regard Jesus' maleness as
an accident and his real meaning tied into his inclusive ministerial vision and
action calling women and men to be free and to love.

Then feminist theologian Carter Heyward voiced a christology that
brought Jesus/God out of the clouds, out of the sad songs of "Precious Lord

Take My Hand and Lead Me On." Jesus my brother came forth. This was a Jesus of joy ordaining mutuality in our relationships. Heyward fed my hunger for an understanding of God that could suggest family relation (brother) and could simultaneously suggest equality in the relationship through mutuality. Later the work of Professor Cheryl Townsend Gilkes introduced me to an African American confession of faith claiming a God-family relationship. Slaves sang: God is my father, my mother, my sister, and my brother. Apparently this notion of a relational God had, for a long time, appeared in the African American religious tradition but had not been emphasized in my community of origin. So at this point two sources—one feminist, one African American—began to inform my search for a relational God. After all, I was the mother of four children, one of whom was male. I needed an understanding of God that fostered both inclusiveness and equality. I was determined to raise my children with the new sense of freedom that feminism had afforded me.

Yet the conditioning that molded me into my earlier self rose up again and pressed against my psyche for more consideration. Though Harrison, Ruether, Heyward, Gilkes, and parts of my African American religious heritage had brought some peace and liberative content to my struggle with the God symbol, there were still parts of my faith as a BLACK woman that needed more voice. I was determined that the blackness and the womanness and freedom would not be separated. Black liberation theology met some part of the need with its explication of what it defined as the blackness and justice of God. Its theological attack on White racism was valorous. And its liberation norm was impressive. But this theology, as I first met it at Union Theological Seminary, seemed to me to be hopelessly sexist and exclusively male. Black theologians had not used Black women's intellectual insights in a significant way to fashion their theological positions. In a sense theologian Jacqueline Grant spoke for many Black women when she questioned the validity of a Black liberation theology that did not include Black women's experience in its formulation and articulation. This critique helped energize my search for a God my together BLACK woman-self could know and accept—a God who affirmed the inextricable unity of blackness and womanness and freedom.

Then one day a Black sister-scholar friend, with definite feminist leanings, said to me that "feminist issues are noble, but many of these issues do not fit the facts of Black women's lives." My sister-friend's observations conjured up a memory from my childhood. My southern grandmother, the daughter of slaves, often said—as she recounted stories about lynchings of Black people and burning crosses lit by the Ku Klux Klan—"White folks and us both Christians, but we ain't got the same religion." She never explained what this meant. But now, deep down, I felt her statement did, in some way, resonate with what my sister-friend scholar had said about feminist issues. I asked myself if it was the spirit of the Christian faith rather than its practice that unified Christians in one body? Was it a general religiosity rather than precise Christian theological and ethical positions that molded Black Americans into a peoplehood? Likewise: was it the spirit of feminism rather than its various issues that united its advocates in one force? I had no answers.

However, my questions about the applicability of *all* of what feminists had developed as women's issues were further intensified by a question raised by a Black woman in a church where I talked to women about feminism and the Christian religion. When I finished my presentation, an older Black woman came forward and said this: "Honey [addressing me], I want to say something about this feminism if you can bear with me. [I nodded my head indicating I could.] This all reminds me of the day I went into a fancy dress shop down town and saw a real pretty dress. The colors in that dress blended right. The design was modern and fashionable. The buttons in front looked real pretty with the material. Everything about that dress looked just right. There was only one problem when it came right down to me. The dress was size five, and I wear size twenty. The saleslady told me that shop didn't carry no dresses over size thirteen. I can sew real good, but I knew there was no way for me to alter that dress and still have the same thing. There just wasn't enough material in that dress to make it fit me. Now that's my point, honey. This feminism looks real pretty, but there just ain't enough in it to fit me. And what I'm wondering is if you Black feminists try to make feminism fit me, will you still have the same thing?"

Though I had also used the writings of bell hooks, Angela Davis, and Paula Giddings to prepare my presentation, I could not provide these women with a satisfactory response. They had taken very seriously the racism in the first and second wave of feminism described by hooks, Davis, and Giddings. But their dissatisfaction was larger than race. From what they read in the materials distributed from a variety of White feminist works, they did not see enough of a correlation between their "woman experience" and the "woman experience" defined in some of the material by Anglo-feminists. So I left the church feeling that the women and I had only communicated halfway. I realized that there was more of our Black woman-stuff that needed telling.

A few years later, what seemed to me to be a "divine" manifestation happened. Alice Walker's *Womanist Prose* appeared! Walker described Black feminism with a word she coined. The word "womanist" shook the foundations
of my feminism, and a new variety of feminism was born. For me and for
many other Black women in theological education and ministry, feminism
became pluralized. And in that pluralization, Walker expanded the store of
feminist thought and wisdom about what constituted womanist experience.
Through an array of symbolic cultural codes, Walker presented a description
of a womanist that brought submerged African American cultural traditions
about women to the surface and joined blackness, womanness, spirituality,
survival, and freedom in one sweeping definitive gesture. Thus through an
allusion to Harriet Tubman, Black women's leadership roles in African American liberation history surfaced along with the affirmation of their intelligence and motherhood. With her symbolic references, Walker preserved
Black women's identity as part of an oppressed female-male community while
she simultaneously declared that a womanist could be a separatist "when
women's health" was at stake.

In this definition, issues causing conflict between Black women were in-
sinuated. Skin color prejudice; sexual preference disputes; mother/daughter
tensions; impediments to women's inquisitive nature; and "White criteria"
for measuring Black female beauty coincided with what many Black American women experienced in both the Black community and in the larger context of American life. Walker maintained Black women's kinship to feminism
while she simultaneously registered a difference. For she says, "Womanist is
to feminist as purple to lavender."[4] Finally, Walker did not forget to integrate
Black women's spirituality into womanist identity when she declared that
they loved the spirit. Nor did she fail to indicate Black women's need to love
themselves. Regardless.

A WOMANIST EMERGES

Many Black women and I became womanists! But in becoming a womanist, I
suspected that some of what I had absorbed as a feminist had to be excised.
When I took Walker's definition of a womanist seriously, I realized my Black
roots, some feminist insights, and my new womanist identity had to be made
compatible. I was trying to produce an authentic womanist theological voice
Black Christian women and the Black community could recognize (even

though they might challenge its range). I had assented to some feminist ideas about consciousness raising, woman experience, wholeness, and "having it all" that had to be released if the facts of Black women's lives were to influence my work in significant ways.

CONSCIOUSNESS RAISING
AND WOMAN EXPERIENCE

Anglo feminists had introduced the idea of consciousness-raising groups where women came together to share experiences and to identify and analyze women's experiences of oppression. These groups, as I experienced them, were exclusively female. Though consciousness raising as an idea was useful for both Anglo and African American women, alterations now seemed necessary from a womanist perspective. The alterations concerned two related issues: one involving the inclusion of males in the consciousness-raising groups and the other involving Anglo-feminist understanding of what constituted woman experience. The first issue—our including men—came to my attention at a conference held at Princeton Theological Seminary.

At the gathering, attention was given to the way women scholars interpreted certain biblical texts. We focused on the Hagar-Sarah references in the Old and New Testaments. In the course of events, tension broke out among White women and Black women. Black women identified with the experience of Hagar, the slave. Most of the White women identified with Sarah, the owner of Hagar. The suggestion was made for women to form a group on the spot to deal with the tensions. The White women said that the men attending the session had to leave the room. The Black women said the men must stay and participate in the group's proceedings because men were a major part of the problem. The upshot of it all was that a conscious-raising group was forming around the conflict caused by this Hagar-Sarah identification, and one group of women thought the exclusion of men was necessary in order for women to feel free to share their ideas and experiences. The other group had no problem expressing their ideas and experiences before men because they thought men's consciousness needed to be raised since men were the major designers of women's oppression in church and society.

This exclusion of men from consciousness-raising groups could, for Black women, be related to another issue. How was feminism identifying woman experience? Black women had the double task of giving attention simultaneously to sexist oppression affecting Black women and racial oppression affecting the entire African American community. In her article "Womanist Consciousness: Maggie Lena Walker and the Independent Order of Saint Luke," Elsa Barkley Brown critiqued Anglo feminists for ignoring a major aspect of Black women's experience in feminist definitions of woman experience. Brown wrote that "woman experience" for many Black women activists included both women's struggle and race struggle. Brown chided White feminists for allowing "belatedly, black women to make history as women or as Negroes but not as 'Negro women.' What they [White feminists] fail to consider," says Brown, "is that women's issues may be race issues and race issues may be women's issues."[5]

To my womanist consciousness, this suggested that Black men should not be excluded from conscious-raising groups. Men's consciousness should be raised in order to show them how Black males, in resistance movements and in everyday life situations, continue to oppress Black women—though the men are themselves oppressed by White racism. I did not think this meant that men's issues should become the focus of the consciousness-raising group. Women's oppression should be the central focus. But men need to be "schooled" about how they participate in it and how they could develop strategies to prevent it. They need to see that the oppressed also oppress. Men should hear this story of oppression from women who experience it and not from male mediators. Therefore Black women should facilitate these groups. The broader implication, in a womanist context, is that while the idea of consciousness-raising groups is valuable, they provide limited help for dealing with the awareness of Black women's total experience of oppression if Black men are not part of these groups (not as leaders but as listeners and learners).

As I struggled with feminist presuppositions and womanist definitions, I began to see that many Black women, throughout their history in America, had preserved the relational and nurturing character of their experience in the Black community even as they struggled for women's liberation. Apparently they considered this relational and nurturing element necessary for an understanding of their woman experience, since dedication to family and community was tied into the way many of them defined themselves. Sociologist Cheryl Townsend Gilkes describes an "ethic of familyhood" operative in the African American world. She says, "Aspects of the black religious and political experience in the United States reflect elements of this ethic of 'familyhood.'" Women especially carry this ethic forward. "In both sacred and secular community settings,"

Gilkes claims, "there are powerful and respected older women addressed by the title 'Mother.' . . . Regardless of their institutional offices, these women wield considerable authority in both sacred and secular settings."[6] It is no wonder, then, that Alice Walker begins the definition of a womanist with motherhood, with a mother advising her female child.

As a womanist taking seriously the incidents at the Princeton conference and Elsa Barkley Brown's critique of feminist renderings of Black women's experience, I discerned what had to be extracted from my feminist ideas about consciousness raising. I also asked myself what had to be added so that feminist insights and womanist insights could work together to produce a strong womanist theological voice. Obviously the idea and practice of consciousness-raising groups should be maintained, but the emphasis on "female only" had to be omitted.

However, caution needs to be exercised by Black women. Inasmuch as many of them consider their experience also to be relational and nurturing, womanist consciousness-raising groups need to consider the tensions that can emerge in the Black community when women's relational and nurturing goals and women's liberation goals conflict. How can the community respond to this conflict so that women's liberation activity is not sacrificed? How can the Black woman handle this conflict so that she does not feel guilty for participating in women's liberation struggle?

There is another task to be added to this notion of womanist consciousness-raising groups. Though Alice Walker encourages Black women to be separatist when women's health is at risk, she also defines a womanist as "committed to the survival of a whole people"[7]—women, men, and children. The implication here is that Black people's survival must become an ongoing, collective community concern. Consideration of this issue would certainly mandate female and male presence in consciousness-raising efforts. Both Black women and men need awareness in the area of survival. Social class distinctions and economic inequities in the Black community are deeply embedded in questions about how Black people have survived together socially, economically, and politically and how they have survived economically and politically in the White world. In the context of the sexual and racial oppression of black women, the survival of all Black people would be considered.

A viable consciousness-raising setting, then, could be the Black family since the survival and freedom of every member (including children) are threatened by the injustices woven into the economic, judicial, educational, and health care systems in the United States. Yet the common need for survival consciousness and survival education should not supercede Black women's freedom issues. I realized I could not be naïve. Black women had to be vigilant. The reality is that even within family consciousness-raising groups, women need strategies to prevent Black men from taking over, bonded as many of these men are with men of other ethnic and national backgrounds affirming the necessity of women's subordination.

I reasoned that these strategies could be developed in Black women's periodic separatist sessions (apart from the consciousness-raising groups). The constant challenge to Black women's feminist liberation efforts by Black men and by the White world poses a threat to Black women's physical, mental, emotional, and spiritual health. As a way to counteract this threat, the separatist sessions could emphasize something Toni Morrison once said. She declared that Black women—having neither men nor law nor anything else to protect them—might have invented themselves. It seemed to me that Morrison's reference to Black women's self-invention had universal significance as far as women were concerned. Any woman who openly challenges the domination of male culture and male definitions of reality—any woman who radically redefines women's experience so that women's autonomy, agency, freedom, and survival strategies center this experience—any woman who dares to wrestle herself out of traditional women's roles—that woman is automatically thrown into a process of self-invention. Women engaging this process experience an "archeology" in the mind, body, spirit, and consciousness that has far-reaching social, political, and spiritual consequences. If great numbers of women undergo this self-invention process simultaneously, tensions emerge in the society in which they live, and social change occurs. The emergence of the feminist movement in our time is a clear example of the effect women's self-invention processes can have on society. The "archeology" of self-invention yields new vocabulary and new categories that redefine social, political, religious, and intimate relationships. When women undergo this self-invention process (and the "archeology" involved), they step out of the shadows of androcentric culture into new life possibilities. I began to realize that in separatist sessions women could help each other start the self-invention process. As different ideas begin to connect, strategies for dealing with men in consciousness-raising groups also take shape.

Walker's definition of a womanist and my elaboration on Toni Morrison's reference to Black women's self-invention intersect in two places. One is at the point of Walker's coded reference to Harriet Tubman. The other is where Walker insinuates that self-acceptance is a vital womanist characteristic. Tubman's life and transformations fit every description of self-invention. As a slave she defied the domination of White male culture and definitions of her female slave role by becoming a liberator of other slaves. She liberated more than 300 slaves. Until slavery was over, she lived with a price on her head offered by slave owners. In the Union Army during the Civil War, she crossed the line of traditional role designations for females and males. She led Union troops into battle. Sometimes she served as an army nurse. Often she scouted for the Union in Confederate territory. Her actions refocused Black woman experience so that it could reflect autonomy, freedom, and historical agency. Tubman wrestled herself out of the traditional roles designated for female slaves.

I reasoned that for womanists today, the intersection of Tubman's model of Black women's self-invention and womanist definitions pointed to the demand for Black women's self-acceptance. Black female bodies become important. Black women accept, affirm, and celebrate the size, shape, and color of their bodies. According to Alice Walker, a womanist loves roundness. Many Black female bodies tend to be round, which is a definite departure from the skinny, straight-line manifestation of a female body type American women are encouraged to imitate. Related to the affirmation of the roundness of Black female bodies, the ancestors have taught Black women that variety in skin color is beautiful and valuable. Thus in womanist definition, skin color takes on universal significance, as the child asks, "Mother, why are we brown, pink, and yellow and our cousins are white, beige, and black?" The mother answers that "the colored race is just like a flower garden, with every color flower represented."[8] Therefore womanists must challenge the tradition in the White and Black communities of assigning greater value and beauty to light/white skin over darker-colored skin.

WHOLENESS AND A WOMANIST CONTEXT

Another feminist idea came under review from my womanist perspective. Wholeness was often used in feminist parlance to communicate ideas about connection and/or completeness. In an effort to get beyond the hierarchical, dualistic structure of western consciousness (i.e., rich/poor, male/female, body/spirit, etc.), some Christian feminists offered wholeness as hope for the development of a new consciousness that would conceive of all life (human and human, human and nonhuman) as interconnected and mutually support‑ ive. Interesting theological claims have been made about the significance of wholeness. In the context of her feminist reconstruction of Christian origins, Elisabeth Schüssler Fiorenza described Jesus' mission not in terms of making a righteous, elect group but in terms of making "the wholeness of all."[9] Sallie McFague, connecting humans to an evolutionary ecosystem, writes that "[t]he ecosystem of which we are part is a whole: the rocks and waters, at‑ mosphere and soil, plants, animals, and human beings interact in dynamic, mutually supportive ways that make all talk of atomistic individualism inde‑ fensible. Relationship and interdependence, change and transformation . . . are the categories within which a theology for our day must function." She continues: "To feel in the depths of our being that we are part and parcel of the evolutionary ecosystem of our cosmos is a prerequisite for contemporary Christian theology."[10] Several feminists in the Goddess and Wicca traditions advocate for the development of a holistic consciousness that connects peo‑ ple to the universe on equal footing and gets beyond the dualism characteris‑ tic of western consciousness (a consciousness that has led to the oppression of women, to racism against people of color, to the separation and conflict be‑ tween body and spirit, etc.).

Some womanists also use the word "wholeness," but they have not pro‑ vided definitions of it. I imagine aspects of the African American heritage have prepared Black women to resonate with the feminist claim about the need for the connectedness of all life and things. American Blacks have always main‑ tained a sense of the inextricable and mutually supportive connection among humans, nature, and nonhuman life. When they escaped from slavery many slaves, on the run, dwelled for a time in the wilderness and lived off whatever food the wilderness provided. Some of their slave songs contain testimonies to the goodness and sustaining power of nature and their dependence on it—for example: the song "Nobody Knows the Trouble I've Seen." Yet, for the sake of their survival, slaves and their progeny could not forget the brokenness in their daily existence caused by the disruption of the Black community through the selling of slaves and through maiming and killing members of the Black com‑ munity. Thus regardless of the sense of unity that has shaped Black conscious‑ ness from slavery to the present day, a memory of brokenness prevails, integrated into this sense of connectedness. Though I affirmed feminist cri‑ tique of the dualistic structure of western consciousness and championed their call for a consciousness connecting all life, I realized something more needed to be added in order for wholeness to have enough meaning in it to affect Black women's consciousness. This something more was memory of brokenness. To understand Black women's history in the United States, one had to pay attention to their daily activity of creating and preserving connection (e.g., community) integrated as this connection is by reoccurring moments of brokenness. This memory of brokenness, integrating the unity of African American women's consciousness, is, of course, related to past and present experiences of social, political, and economic oppression. In a womanist reconstruction of consciousness, then, wholeness must be understood to be integrated by the constant reminder of brokenness. Without this memory, Black women may erroneously assume a level of racial and gender comfort for themselves that the United States does not allow Black people. Without this memory, wholeness is an unrealistic, naive hope for the future that Black women cannot afford.

I have begun to shun feminist references to wholeness that are related to "having it all," a phrase that has become pervasive in the language of some feminists. I wonder if they are implying that by "having it all," women have achieved some form of completeness? "Having it all" means that somebody else will have far less. I think that the desire to "have it all" is an imperialistic aspiration. In a domestic context, this phrase refers to women being able to exercise their occupational choices while their homes run smoothly, usually with the help of female domestic workers paid minimum wage or less.

However, I sometimes ask myself if this notion of "having it all" was planted in the feminist movement by those who have tried to backlash feminism into oblivion. I am reminded of an imperative sentence that crept into the African American civil rights movement and the Black cultural revolution at their zenith in the 1970s. That sentence was "Do your own thing." I can't imagine a revolution where the initiators and participants are "doing their own thing." Neither can I imagine a women's freedom movement in which "having it all" becomes the goal of women's struggle for liberation. This sentence and phrase reflect greed and divisiveness. They can contribute to the demise of both African American and women's freedom struggles.

A DIFFERENT THEOLOGICAL VOICE RISING

The problem of God emerged when my feminism and the Christian religion met. When my womanism and the Christian religion met, a heuristic strategy and a biblical issue came into focus. I discovered I was using a particular heuristic technique as I identified what had to be excised from some of my feminist presuppositions and what had to be retained and what had to be added. To relate feminist and womanist ideas, I realized I was using a heuristic strategy I now name "filtering out and factoring in." I was aware of the use of these terms (i.e., filtering and factoring) in certain scientific disciplines and even in economics and mathematics (e.g., factoring). However, my usage conformed to some definitions I discovered in *Webster's New International Dictionary*. Thus filtering, as a verb form, involved removing something from a substance by means of a filter. In my journey, the filter was the developing stages of my feminist/womanist consciousness that removed and/or transformed certain ideas and values. Factoring was a process of replacement by which (to invoke Webster) "something . . . actively contributed to the production of a result." In mathematical usage, a factor is "any of the numbers or symbols . . . that when multiplied together form a product." In her use of symbolic references, Alice Walker's definition of a womanist resonates with this mathematical idea of factoring. Walker factored in Black women's leadership history and ways of being in the world everyday. I have begun to realize that this technique of filtering out and factoring in is not new in the development of African American culture. But it has not been named as such. During the Harlem Renaissance in the 1920s, the "New Negro" was the term Black scholars and artists used to filter out the socially accepted stereotypical image of Black people as ignorant slaves and to factor in an image of the Negro as educated, urbane, intellectually capable, and artistically able.

In addition to the significance of this heuristic for providing different interpretations of Black people's images beyond the Black community, it also had intracommunity usefulness. Black people living in an oppressive social order often unconsciously internalize negative, stereotypical ideas about themselves and about their community's identity, intellect, and morality. A strategy of filtering out and factoring in could help Black Americans extract internalized, negative impressions of themselves and replace these with realistic views of their life and thought.

As I reflected on this heuristic strategy and on the transformations of my consciousness due to feminist and womanist definitions and prescriptions, I revisited the faith of my mother, her mother, and her mother's mother: the slave. I suddenly realized that in the formation of their faith, my female forebears had unconsciously engaged this strategy I am naming filtering out and factoring in. Originally I did not recognize that what I was identifying as sad songs may not be sad at all. Rather, these songs may be some Black women's ways of factoring in healing as a response to an implied brokenness they assumed to be present in the Black female human condition. Without literally naming what had to be filtered out, they factored in God and the religion of song as the healing for Black women's brokenness.

Yet I had to admit their faith seemed grounded in a pie-in-the-sky understanding of Black women's future—a grounding my feminist/womanist consciousness could not accept because pie-in-the-sky could encourage a passive response to the injustices suffered by women and Black Americans. I figured that something else had to be factored in here. But what? Then I remembered something Bernard of Chartres wrote in the twelfth century about the gifts of ancestors to their posterity. He said that what we, the posterity, see as our achievement is not because of "the sharpness of our own sight, nor to the greatness of our own nature but because we are raised aloft on that great mass" of contributions made by our ancestors. When I began to consider my female ancestors' advice and "sad songs" to be gifts to their progeny instead of eschatological missteps, I realized silence shrouded their gifts. And the silences needed to be interpreted if I was ever to produce a strong womanist theology also mindful of the faith my female ancestors passed on.

So I began to dig deeper and deeper into the depths of Black American culture. There I discovered what I took to be the foundation supporting the faith of these Black female ancestors. This foundation was shaped by the way African Americans used the Bible to graft their life situation onto the stories of biblical characters involved in circumstances similar to their situation. God's intervention into the stories of these biblical characters signaled to African Americans that God would express the same concern and action in their lives. Thus Moses, Paul, Silas, the three Hebrew boys (Shadrack, Mescheck, and Abegnego) are a few of the biblical characters appearing in some of the deposits of African American culture. They all represent moments of liberation when God intervened on their behalf. Black biblical appropriations like these support the Black liberation theological claim that God is involved in the liberation struggle of Black people.

However, I was surprised to discover the extensive African American appropriation of the biblical slave woman Hagar. Both women and men had appropriated this figure whose story seemed to mirror the stages and content of

African American women's history, past and present. From slavery to liberation, Hagar—like African American women—experienced brutality at the
hands of her female slave owner, rape by her owner's husband, the birth of a
child as the result of this rape, and running away from slavery. After liberation she experienced homelessness, poverty, single-parent problems in the
wilderness, and a special encounter with God in the midst of her trouble. I
concluded that Hagar served as the Black community's analog for Black
women's historical experience. A strand of activism is manifested in Hagar's
running away from slavery and in her belligerent attitude toward her owner,
Sarah, when she discovers she is pregnant. Hagar's faith in God looms large
(as does the faith of many African American women). I imagined that my
mother, her mother, and her mother's mother (the slave), were modern-day
Hagars whose life struggle taught them that God "moves in mysterious ways
his wonders to perform."

So now I could interpret the silences shrouding my female ancestors'
faith and gift of advice to me. They were silent about this biblical model of
female activism and the belligerence (Hagar) that coursed through African
American history—an activism and belligerence that worked right along with
"God's mysterious ways his wonders to perform." They were silent about
their own resistance activity. Professor Evelyn Brooks Higginbotham's obser-
vation about Black women, the Bible, and the women's social action is in-
structive. She said "Black women . . . drew upon the Bible, the most
respected source within their community, to fight for women's rights in the
church and society at large. . . . More often, however, their efforts represented not dramatic protest but everyday forms of resistance to oppression
and demoralization."[11]

I returned to a question posed earlier. What had to be added to my female ancestors' advice and faith statements in order to source a distinctive
womanist theological voice? Inasmuch as many Black Christians (female and
male) used the Bible profusely to validate their beliefs, their theological positions, and their ethical behavior, I added Hagar to what had originally looked
like eschatological missteps on the part of my mother, her mother, and her
mother's mother: the slave. I decided that I would use the correspondence
between Hagar's story and aspects of Black women's history as a "launching
position" to begin constructing womanist theology. Other relevant theological voices would also be drawn on in order for my womanist theological voice
to resound in more than one context. Years later, this womanist project came

to life in a book I wrote entitled *Sisters in the Wilderness: The Challenge of Womanist God-talk.*[12]

CONCLUSION

My journey through the faith of my female ancestors, through civil rights struggles, through feminism to womanism is far from over. I began this journey looking for a new way of saying "I am a Black woman." Like some feminist theologians, I have had to introduce new vocabulary, language, methods, and concepts so that my Black community experience, feminist experience, and womanist definitions could intersect. I realize there will never be only one way to tell the story of the development of womanist identity. I know that my womanness, blackness, my male relatedness, my religion, my brokenness, and my wholeness will always live in tension with social, political, economic, and religious meanings shifting from time to time. But I assume that womanist theology has a "blood relationship" to all feminist theologies (Asian, Anglo, Jewish, mujerista). And together these theologies can help guide this shift. However, I know womanist theology also speaks in a different and distinctive voice. In my case, this distinctiveness became clearer when African American women's faith and African American appropriation of Hagar's story, together, became the object of theological reflection. Through the lens of this reflection I saw more meaning in the faith of my mother, her mother, and her mother's mother: the slave. And this meaning has yielded a deeper theological voice I hope to bring into dialog with feminist/womanist/mujerista/Asian women.

NOTES

1. A version of the last few words of this title—"Conditioning molding me into Myself"—were expressed in the dissertation of Dr. Robin Gorsline, "Bearing Witness to the Dark: Resources for Anti-White-Supremacist, Pro-Same-Sex(es), Pro-Feminist Theologizing in Queer Modes" Ph.D. diss., Union Theological Seminary, 1999.
2. See Belinda Robnett's discussion of this statement in her book *How Long? How Long?: African-American Women in the Struggle for Civil Rights* (New York: Oxford University Press, 1997), 120–121.
3. Alice Walker, *The Color Purple* (New York: Harcourt Brace Jovanovich, 1982).
4. Alice Walker, *In Search of Our Mothers' Gardens: Womanist Prose* (San Diego: Harcourt Brace Jovanovich, 1983), I.

5. See Brown's article in *Black Women in America: Social Science Perspectives*, ed. Micheline R. Malson, Elizabeth Mudimbe-Boyi, Jean F. O'Barr, and Mary Wyer (Chicago: University of Chicago Press, 1988), 174.

6. Cheryl Townsend Gilkes, "The Roles of Church and Community Mothers: Ambivalent American Sexism or Fragmented African Familyhood," in Gilkes, *If It Wasn't for the Women* (Maryknoll, N.Y.: Orbis Books, 2001), 61.

7. Walker, *In Search of Our Mother's Gardens*.

8. Walker, *In Search of Our Mother's Gardens*.

9. Elisabeth Schüssler Fiorenza, *In Memory of Her: A Feminist Theological Reconstruction of Christian Origins* (New York: Crossroad, 1983), 121. This quotation also appears in Sallie McFague's book *Models of God* (Philadelphia: Fortress Press, 1987).

10. McFague, *Models of God: Theology for an Ecological, Nuclear Age* (Philadelphia: Fortress Press, 1987), 6, 7.

11. Evelyn Brooks Higginbotham, *Righteous Discontent: The Women's Movement in the Black Baptist Church, 1880–1920* (Cambridge, Mass.: Harvard University Press, 1993), 2.

12. Delores S. Williams, *Sisters in the Wilderness: The Challenge of Womanist Godtalk* (Maryknoll, N.Y.: Orbis Books, 1993).

NINE

Elisabeth Schüssler Fiorenza

1964 Author, *Ministries of Women in the Church* (in German)
1983 Author, *In Memory of Her* (translated into twelve
languages)
1987 First woman president, Society of Biblical Literature

I AM OFTEN ASKED AFTER LECTURES, "WITH WHOM DID YOU STUDY
feminist theology?" My response is usually: when I was a student, feminist
theology or studies in religion did not exist. That is why a new field of study

needed to be invented. This question from students, however, does not just reveal how far we have come in the past thirty years; it also demonstrates historical forgetfulness. This forgetfulness can be dangerous, though, if it assumes that the feminist struggle for wo/men's theological authority is over and won. An e-mail I recently received from a student tells us otherwise: "I am having a really hard time in school—not with the work or anything, just being a feminist every day, reminding people of basic stuff (things like 'man' is not 'inclusive') and having people roll their eyes, or having professors refer to my critique as 'violent' and 'aggressive.' I come home exhausted and frustrated, and I often cry."

Such an experience of alienation is fueled by both the allegedly value-neutral antifeminist rhetoric of liberal institutions and by the strident antifeminist rhetoric of the Christian Right. For instance, in her book entitled *Ungodly Rage*, Donna Steichen calls Catholic feminists "enemies of G*d, of life, of nature, of the normal" and concludes her antifeminist diatribe in a prophetic mode threatening:

> In its ultimate manifestation, religious feminism is an anarchic madness. Most secular society has moved past it to different enthusiasms. . . . Even Gloria Steinem is talking more about the New Age 'journey within' than about feminism these days. But in the Church, feminism is still at a fever peak. Catholic feminists are like Gadarene swine, plunging off a cliff into the sea. Eventually, like all religious revolutionaries, they will dash themselves to destruction against the rock of the Church.[1]

Steichen calls her attempts to sort out the different Catholic feminist groups and to track the major leaders of the movement "a task unworthy of the efforts involved" and likens it to "untangling a knot of vipers." This is one way of writing the history of religious feminism. Another way of conceptualizing the history of feminist theology and religious studies is that of tracing the family tree. In the context of the European Society of Wo/men Scholars in Theology and Religion (ESWTR), feminist scholars have initiated a "history of feminist theology project" in several European countries. But to my knowledge such an initiative has been lacking in North America until now, although feminist theology in my view has its birthplace here. Thus, I am grateful to my colleague, Professor Ann Braude, who has taken up my suggestion and, with this conference, initiated such a historiographical project.

While we have several right-wing accounts of the history of feminist theology, to my knowledge there has yet to be written a critical and comprehensive history of feminist movements in the fields of theology and religion. I hope this conference will not only begin such a historiographical work, but also will celebrate the anniversary of two of the originating events of feminist theology and religious wo/men's studies in 1972: the conference called "Women Doing Theology" at Grailville, and the inauguration of the Women and Religion section at the American Academy of Religion.[2] We also commemorate in this year the one-hundredth anniversary of Elizabeth Cady Stanton's death.

Feminist historians tell us that it is part and parcel of the power of patriarchy (or as I would say kyriarchy) to eradicate wo/men's historical accomplishments, to trivialize our theoretical visions, or to co-opt our revolutionary work for "elite malestream" ends, so that every other generation not only has to reinvent the wheel, but also becomes tempted to collaborate in historical romanticization, rejection, forgetfulness, or trivialization. As a result, the history of feminist theology and studies in religion is often written in a progressivist mode. It is conceptualized either as one of progress—from intellectually naïve beginnings to the theoretical heights of postmodern post-feminism—or it is written as one of decline—in the beginning there was a vibrant women's movement whereas now feminism is being co-opted by the academy and the church. Or sometimes it is even caricatured as the bickering, squabbling, and infighting of smaller and smaller groups, whose relevance to larger society is increasingly tenuous.

In the 1970s, so another story goes, White middle-class western wo/men had a monopoly on feminism and articulated feminist theology in the interests of elite White wo/men only, whereas in the 1980s wo/men of color assumed power and unseated White feminist theology with womanist, mujerista, or Third World wo/men's theology. In the 1990s, postcolonial feminists proved that all feminist theology has been White, western, and obsolete. However, such progressivist replacement tales are not only misleading and prejudicial, but also do not square with the actual historical situation of feminism in the academy and in religious institutions (a situation that is still very precarious), nor do they square with the theoretical conceptualization and intention of most feminist work in the 1970s.

Most important, such a progressivist conceptualization of feminist history overlooks the fact that the wo/men's liberation movement emerged in the context of the free speech, civil rights, Third/Fourth World liberation, and the antiwar movements of the 1960s. Both the first and second waves of the wo/men's movement were able to emerge because of coinciding social and civil rights movements including the abolitionist, workers, Black power, postcolonial, peace, indigenous peoples or First Nations movements. These social movements engendered the growing awareness that wo/men as a group, or in earlier terms as a "caste," were discriminated against and oppressed because they were wo/men. In my own experience, the existence of a wo/men's movement was crucially important for articulating my theological self-identity in a new and different way.

Instead of conceptualizing the history of feminist theology and religious studies in terms of intellectual progress or displacement of the less pure with the "more correct," I, for one, would prefer to see our feminist history written as an ongoing intellectual struggle between so-called value-free hegemonic, elite-White-male religious scholarship that we ourselves have internalized, on one hand, and, on the other hand, a radical democratic, intellectually variegated, and engaged feminist movement for change comprised of feminist ministers, scholars, and professionals who speak from a multiplicity of cultural-political locations and socioreligious persuasions.

This conference gives us the opportunity to start our explorations in good feminist fashion with critically reflected personal experience, rather than by asking for the development of a theoretical conceptualization of how to chronicle the practices and accomplishments of feminist theology and studies in religion. This is appropriate insofar as feminist theology has problematized its methods but has continued to insist on beginning its work with a systemic analysis and reflection on feminist "yeah-yeah," "aha," or breakthrough experiences that challenge internalized ideologies of domination or the cultural religious ideal of femininity or of the "White lady" that have become "commonsense knowledge." While I have always had a more skeptical attitude to the "yeah, yeah" experience, I favor the "aha" experience and theologized it as a moment of metanoia, a turning around and moving into new directions.

Thirty years ago, in 1971 when I attended my first annual meeting of the American Academy of Religion and the Society of Biblical Literature in Atlanta, I heard by accident about a meeting of wo/men scholars whom Carol Christ had called together for founding the Women's Caucus Religious Studies and the Wo/men's Studies in Religion section.[3] Since I was one of only a handful of biblical scholars present at the meeting and was willing to serve, I was elected with Carol as first co-chair of the caucus, although I had just immigrated to the United States in the fall of 1970.

Another pivotal event took place in the summer of 1972, when a historic meeting was organized in Grailville, Ohio, by Clare Randall, general secretary of the National Council of Churches and members of the Grail. Approximately seventy-five women, Jews and Christians, Protestants and Catholics, ordained ministers and academic theologians had been brought together by the National Council of Churches and the Grail, an international Catholic ecumenical wo/men's group, for a workshop called "Women Doing Theology." This workshop proved to be one of the birthplaces of feminist theology, which has profoundly changed theology and churches. I was privileged to be invited to this gathering as a co-chair of the Women's Caucus Religious Studies.

These two events turned out to be decisive not only for me personally, but more important for the development of feminist studies in religion and feminist thea/ology.[4] Both of these articulations of feminist religious thought, feminist thea/ology and feminist religious studies, are important; they are distinct but not exclusive of each other, since many of us have been involved in both feminist thea/o/logical and cultural feminist studies in religion.[5] In my experience, the 1971 Atlanta meeting and the 1972 Grailville conference were important originary moments for the articulation of both feminist thea/ological and feminist cultural religious studies in the United States.

At the same time, it must be pointed out that neither the workshop at Grailville nor the AAR/SBL Women's Caucus chose to call their theoretical reflection and practical work "feminist." While the self-designation "feminist" was controverted from the outset, Carol Christ used it in 1974 as a designation for the New York Area Feminist Scholars in Religion. Historically, it is important to trace such self-designations, which reclaimed the power of naming. Whereas Gustavo Gutierrez is rightly credited for being the "father" of liberation theology and it is known that Carol Christ later introduced the variegation "feminist thealogy," it is not clear who coined the expression "feminist theology."[6] More research needs to be done here, since any genealogy of naming and origins is not only a question of historical memory, but always also a question of definition and power.

It should be obvious by now that in my understanding, "theology" is an umbrella term for reflection and inquiry done from within a religious commitment and community, rather than a dogmatic confessional theological subdiscipline. As a student in Germany, I had experienced theological studies not as doctrinal and limiting, but rather as opening up perspectives and understandings that had not been accessible to me through religious instruction and catechism. Hence, I was quite comfortable in calling myself a theologian.

Although in my first dissertation I had problematized the exclusion of wo/men from ministry and the ideological production of theology while challenging the masculine genderization of theology (and religious studies) as a systemic corruption of the theological frameworks and problematics of religious studies, I had worked in isolation and not yet given a proper name to my work. Only the wo/men's movement in society and church and its theoretical expressions in feminist and women's studies have enabled me to recognize that I articulate theology differently and conceptualize my discourse as a critical feminist theology of liberation.

I had come to the Women's Caucus meeting in 1971 and to the Grailville conference in 1972 with a "raised consciousness" and a critical understanding of the so-called woman question. Since I had published a book on ministries of wo/men in the church in 1964 and had written my doctoral dissertation on the radical democratic theological notion of the "priesthood of believers," I was conscious that understanding and undoing the exclusion of wo/men from the leadership of the church would require a critical questioning not only of the role of wo/men, but also of how theology and church leadership were articulated.

My first book on the ministries of women in the church was written in 1962 and submitted as a licentiate thesis in practical theology in 1963. In that book I anticipated (though sometimes in a rather unsophisticated way) several methodological issues that would later become decisive in the development of feminist and liberation theologies. The first of these issues has to do with the starting point of theological reflection: just as most feminist liberation theology today argues that theologizing must start with a systemic reflection on experience, so my thesis sought to legitimate theologically my own experience. Although so-called lay theology as a selective study of theology was well established in Germany, I was the first woman in Würzburg to enroll for the full program in theology that students for the Roman Catholic priesthood were required to take. My choice to study as a woman for the equivalent of the M.Div. degree, however, was severely challenged by the progressive theology that found its way into the documents of the Second Vatican Council.

Catholic theologians such as Karl Rahner, Johann Auer, Yves Congar, José Comblin, Cardinal Suenens, and others argued that the mission of the clergy, nuns, and brothers was to the church, whereas the mission of the laity was to the world. Consequently, in my licentiate thesis, I sought to clarify theologically whether I had missed my religious calling as a member of the laity because I was a wo/man who had no interest in joining a religious order nor was able to become ordained, yet had decided to undertake the full course of theological studies and to become a professional theologian.

The second methodological issue that connects my earlier work to my articulation of a critical feminist theology of liberation in my later work has to do with hermeneutical questions: just as malestream liberation theology insisted in the late 1960s and 1970s that theology begins with the praxis of the people of G*d—scrutinizing, evaluating, and rearticulating theology in light of this praxis—so my thesis attempted to articulate such a correspondence of theory and practice. In it I sought to show that the new progressive ecclesiology, to which I otherwise subscribed, did not correspond to the actual pastoral praxis of the Roman Catholic Church. The discrepancy between theory and praxis that I wanted to highlight was elucidated by the fact that wo/men who were not members of orders and who certainly did not belong to the clergy were working full time as professional ministers within the institutional Catholic Church in Germany. Although my thesis adopted the traditional framework that begins by discussing theory and then seeks to "apply" it to pastoral practice, its aim was quite the opposite. I argued for a reformulation of ecclesiology so that it could do justice to the actual practice of the churches.

The third issue that my earlier and later work of a critical feminist theology of liberation both share has to do with questions about the structural character of oppression. At the outset, I was less interested in the special role of wo/men or in articulating a feminine essence than in articulating a radical democratic theology of church and ministry in which the ecclesial rights and responsibility of all the people of G*d were foundational. At this point, however, I still worked with a hierarchical model of church. For instance, although I was well aware of the negative connotation that the word "lay" assumed in contrast to the designation "cleric," I nevertheless argued that the meaning of the word should be understood positively as referring to the people of G*d and Christian "brotherhood" rather than to the uneducated, uncouth, vulgar masses. Ironically, I sought to argue for a participatory model of church by pointing to the de facto clerical status of professional wo/men ministers in the churches.

Not surprisingly, when the book was published, it read like an argument for wo/men's ordination even though I was not interested in the clericalization of wo/men, but in the declericalization of the church. Believing that wo/men's ordination would amount to the clerical co-optation of wo/men, I argued that Roman Catholic wo/men must demand to be ordained first to the fullness of the priesthood and jurisdictional power of bishop, before accepting ordination to the lower ranks of the hierarchy. Only in this way, I contended, would wo/men's gifts be able to engender structural change in the church. A similar contradictory strategy has been pursued until very recently by the Women's Ordination Conference (WOC) in the United States. From its beginnings WOC has insisted on the ordination of women but into a *different renewed* church and priestly ministry.

A fourth issue that runs through both my early and later work has to do with gaining a more critical understanding of gender. In my research and writing, I became more and more critical of the dominant "theology of Woman" and its impact on the ministry of wo/men in the church. In the process, I became aware that the new, somewhat romantic theology of the "eternal feminine," which had replaced the traditional theological assumption of wo/men's inferiority and sinfulness, was buttressed by the all-pervasive cultural ideology of woman's nature and her biological/essential difference from man. Although I rejected this cultural ideology of the feminine and argued that the scientific understanding of the world and of wo/men would change when looked at from the perspective of wo/men, I lacked a comprehensive theoretical framework to articulate such a different perspective. Though I knew and partially accepted Simone de Beauvoir's existentialist analysis, which Mary Daly subsequently used as a theoretical foundation for her book *The Church and the Second Sex*, I was groping for a more constructive approach, one that could contribute to my vision of church and its mission to the world.

Since I was always ill at ease with the enthusiastic praise of women's essential difference and special nature as epistemological ground for feminist theology that was advocated in early feminist works in the United States, I was delighted to discover Simone de Beauvoir's work *The Second Sex* and enthusiastic about Elisabeth Gössmann's small book *Das Bild der Frau heute* (*The Image of Women Today*), which appeared in 1962. Because I was not able to find an alternative theoretical framework that would correspond to my own self-understanding as an intellectual wo/man in the malestream academic literature of the day, I was ripe for the wo/men's liberation movement that had its first stirrings in Germany among students in the late 1960s, but was not yet vocal in 1962–1963, especially in theological studies. The Grailville discussions, rituals, and meetings of wo/men from different social and religious locations were exhilarating and empowering. The "Women Doing Theology" conference at Grailville not only deepened these insights but also revealed their confessional embeddedness. Grailville taught me that the wo/men's movement was ecumenical and interreligious and, hence, feminist theology must be articulated not only in the interest of one's own particular group of wo/men, but in the interest of all wo/men. Since our vision is limited by the particular location where we do our work, it always needs to strive for "concrete universality," that at one and the same time insists on being rooted in one's particular community and points out how its truth claims contribute to universal well-being.

Some of the discussions at Grailville, however, made me impatient because of their sometimes anti-intellectual stance and their negative evaluation of contemporary theology, which I had experienced as positive during the Second Vatican Council. In contrast to many of the participants, I was reared in the progressive theology of Karl Rahner, Hans Küng, and Johann Baptist Metz, which was open to modernity or, in the theological language of the time, "open to the world." This differed from the neo-orthodox Protestant theology that was critical of modernity and that many of the Grailville participants had encountered in their studies.

Yet not only this difference in theological and confessional culture, but also the often essentialist romantic understanding of "Woman," gave me pause. I recall that I was very uneasy with the claims of essential difference between women and men and of "women's special nature" advocated by some at Grailville and in other emerging feminist discourses. Such a kind of reevaluation of the feminine and woman inspired the claim that wo/men will do a different theology because we are female and speak in a different voice. For whatever reasons, and I could mention many, I have never been successfully socialized into the cultural standards of femininity and therefore have never subscribed but rather rebelled against its regime. When I wrote my book on ministries of women in the church, I was very frustrated because I could not find any theological frameworks that would correspond to my experience of questioning this hegemonic discourse on femininity.

Since then I have called this discourse of woman's difference the discourse of "the (White) Lady," which determines the feminine identity not only of middle- and upper-class White wo/men but also the identity of all women. Like theology, however, most of the academic literature at the time propagated the cultural framework that insisted on feminine values and virtues culminating in either physical or spiritual motherhood. In order to be able to deconstruct critically the hegemonic understanding of femininity and the theology of woman that was then all-pervasive in Roman Catholic theology and has since then been advocated by Pope Paul VI and John Paul II, I desperately looked to the malestream literature in political science, psychology, legal studies, literary studies, and sociology for a different theorization of wo/men's nature and role. As in the case of theologians, though, political scientists, sociologists, and anthropologists have defined woman's nature in terms of nurturing and motherhood and construed it as inferior, complementary, or religiously superior to men.

What I found new and exciting at Grailville and elsewhere was to encounter for the first time a group of wo/men who claimed the "doing of theology" as their birthright, who reflected on their negative experiences of feminine socialization and role determination and then set out to change the situation. It was the experience of a wo/men's liberation movement that validated my own personal experience and perspective. In so doing it enabled me to understand myself as an intellectual "doing theology" with focus on, and in the interest of, wo/men as my very own people. The criterion for evaluating such a different theology was not orthodoxy, doctrinal systematics, or academic standards, but its ability to change the religious structures engendering and legitimating wo/men's second-class citizenship in religion and the academy, as well as its vision to transform theological and religious mind-sets of self-alienation and indoctrination.

This experience of the wo/men's movement in religion empowered me to reconceptualize my own self-understanding as a theologian. Although I had struggled to be admitted as the first woman in my university to study the full course of theology and to graduate with the equivalent of an M.Div. degree, I did not understand myself as a theologian who would shape the discipline of theology and its study. I had studied theology in order to mediate the theology of the "fathers"—Karl Rahner, Yves Congar, Hans Küng, Johann Baptist Metz—in its progressive malestream form to the people either through pastoral work or through teaching at the university. Yet I did not (and could not) understand myself as a theologian who would chart a different way of doing theology and would do so explicitly in the interest of wo/men as the people of G*d who have been excluded by ecclesiastical law and academic custom from professional theology. I could imagine that one day I would be pope. But I could not envision in the 1960s that one day I would be a feminist theologian, just as I could not then imagine what it would be like to work with a computer.

Decisive for my future work were not only the critical discussions at Grailville, the Wo/man's Caucus, and the AAR Women and Religion section, but also a sabbatical at Union Theological Seminary in New York in 1974. I enthusiastically participated in the New York Area Feminist Scholars in Religion group, which again was called into being by Carol Christ. These experiences helped me to begin to articulate my own theoretical feminist theological framework, though I did not quite have the courage to voice my theoretical disagreements because of the strong "yeah, yeah" ethos of the group. Members of this group, foremost among them Judith Plaskow, Beverly Wildung Harrison, Sheila Collins, Nelle Morton, Letty Russell, Anne Barstow, and Carol Christ herself, have decisively shaped feminist studies in religion.

In the period between 1972 and 1976, I wrote articles in four areas whose basic theoretical approaches I have sought to develop over the years.

The first and most important in this area, "Feminist Theology as a Critical Theology of Liberation," seeks to articulate my own feminist perspective and theoretical framework. In "Women Studies and the Teaching of Religion,"[7] I shared my teaching experience whereas in the German article "Für eine befreite und befreiende Theologie" ("For a Liberated and Liberating Theology") I discussed the institutional situation of wo/men in theology and religious studies. While many critical analyses of church structures existed, hardly any critical work had been done with regard to academic structures and institutions. Simply the presence of wo/men students and scholars in seminaries and universities, I argued, will not vouch for the transformation of theology and academy. For a liberated and liberating theology to emerge, the academy and its institutional practices must be transformed in terms of a critical feminist theology of liberation.

In "Feminist Theology as a Critical Theology of Liberation," I sought to articulate a theoretical feminist framework—not in terms of gender/femininity or sexual difference, but in terms of the oppression and emancipation of the nonperson (Gustavo Gutierrez) or the subaltern (Gayatri Spivak), the majority of whom are wo/men and children dependent on wo/men.[8] This theoretical framework, developed in conjunction with the critical theory of Jürgen Habermas as well as liberation theology, shaped my future work. Yet while I have learned much from critical theory, political theology, and liberation theology, I have nevertheless always maintained that feminists cannot simply take over the theoretical frameworks of the "masters" or the "godfathers," to use a religious term, because they are formulated without taking wo/men into account.[9]

Feminist theory has amply shown that all theoretical frameworks are masculine-gendered or, to use an older but still-valuable term, they are "androcentric." Yet these theories are not just androcentric, but they are kyriocentric (from the Greek *kyrios* meaning "lord/master/father/husband") because they are shaped by the experience and questions of White, elite, educated western (clergy)men. Consequently, feminists cannot simply take over malestream theoretical frameworks. We must scrutinize them to determine whether they allow for the theorization of feminist questions and experiences. In contrast to much of poststructuralist and postmodern feminist theology, my own work has never subscribed to one single theory or one hegemonic method. Instead, I have always used various theoretical approaches for articulating a critical feminist approach.

For example, in order to think through the problem of grammatically interpreting androcentric texts that claim to function in an inclusive generic way, one cannot limit oneself to a linguistic positivist epistemological framework. One has to take the insights of hermeneutics, critical theory, and ideological criticism into account. In other words, I do not understand theories and methods as closed intellectual systems, but as ways of seeing and investigating, as strategies for exploring and thinking through practical issues and theoretical problems so that I can combine and utilize them in a new process of investigation.

I was concerned with a different writing of early Christian history in a second type of essay, such as the German "Die Rolle der Frau in der urchristlichen Bewegung" ("Women in the Early Christian Movement")[10] or "Wo/men in the Pauline and Pre-Pauline Churches" and especially "Women in Early Christianity: Methodological Considerations." Here I took the first methodological steps toward my later book *In Memory of Her*.[11] In order to move away from the "study *about* woman," I argued, one must place wo/men as historical agents into the center of attention and reconceptualize early Christian history in such a way that it becomes the history of wo/men and men.

In doing so, it is not sufficient simply to study the historical sources about women, to take the "add woman and stir" approach, and produce a history of women. Rather it is necessary to reconceptualize early Christian history and see whether our sources would still allow us to write a feminist history of early Christianity. This proposal was articulated in conversation not only with the "Social World of Early Christianity" studies, which had adopted Ernst Troeltsch's interpretive scheme of "love patriarchalism," but also with the newly emerging feminist theoretical literature inquiring as to how to write wo/men back into history and how to conceptualize history in feminist terms. The hermeneutical and theoretical reflections on how to break the historical silences created by androcentric texts and make wo/men visible as historical agents in early Christianity inaugurate feminist biblical studies is a new field of inquiry.

The third type of essay opened up the hermeneutical direction in my feminist work.[12] During my time at Union, Letty Russell invited me to participate in the Task Force on Sexism in the Bible chaired by Valerie Russell, who was the assistant to the president of the United Church of Christ, and coordinated by Emily Gibbes, who was the executive of the Division of Education and Ministry of the National Council of Churches. After two years of work, the task force produced a guide to nonsexist biblical interpretation, *The Liberating Word*, which Letty Russell edited.[13] Over and against an apologetic hermeneutical approach focusing on the "positive" texts about "women in" or on depatriarchalizing the Bible, I argued in my chapter, "Interpreting Patriarchal Traditions," that feminist interpretation must pay as much—if not more—attention to the patriarchal texts inscribed in Christian scriptures and must not seek to explain them away.[14] I have called this approach a "critical feminist hermeneutics of liberation," although a critical feminist biblical interpretation is not concerned simply with understanding biblical texts but with changing biblical discourses.

Recognizing the rhetorical character of feminist historical and theological arguments, I have sought in the 1990s to theoretically explicate and rename my feminist historical and hermeneutical approach as a critical rhetoric and ethic. To make this theoretical reflection available to a wider readership, I have elaborated it in my book *Wisdom Ways* and detailed seven key interpretive strategies in a rhetorically conceived critical "dance of interpretation."

Although I understand my task primarily as working in the academy, I have reason to believe that my ministerial students will be able to work at the grassroots level with what they have learned in my classes. For instance, my feminist "dance of interpretation" has been used not only in many Bible study groups for consciousness raising but also in working with low-income, underliterate wo/men who are learning to read not just the Bible but also the newspaper as though their lives depended on it.

Representative of the fourth type of work is my essay "Feminist Spirituality, Christian Identity and the Catholic Vision," which reflects on my socioreligious positionality as a Christian Catholic theologian and names the special group of people to whom I feel myself most accountable.[15] It would go too far to detail here my involvement in articulating and shaping the strategies of the Catholic wo/men's movement except to mention my work with WOC, Wo/men-Church, WATER (Women's Alliance for Theology and Ritual), and international groups. By getting involved in movement politics and strategies, I was deterred from romanticizing feminist sisterhood. Recognizing the deep structural ecclesiastical division between so-called nun-women and so-called laywomen prevented me from idealizing the feminist community as a liberated exodus community.

Although feminist theories and theologies have forcefully indicted androcentric dualisms, we ourselves have also produced such dualistic "either/or" thinking. While feminist scholars have severely critiqued all types of dualism, our own discourses have more often constructed dualistic oppositions and focused on shortcomings among ourselves, rather than developing a robust culture of debate that can articulate strategies and theories for changing structures of domination in which we all remain enmeshed. Rather than developing powerful coalitions, we have often tended to seek for the impossible: political "innocence and purity."

In contrast to those who became involved in the women's movement in religious studies in the early 1970s, I had experienced religion and theology not as totally oppressive and completely alienating, but as challenging and intellectually exciting. Therefore, I never subscribed to the dualistic alternative that has permeated feminist discourses in religious studies and theology: either totally identify with church and theology, or denounce it and leave it completely behind. In such an essentializing gesture, religion and churches or synagogues are understood as totally patriarchal, and feminist wo/men are seen as liberated from kyriarchal mind-sets and ideologies.

This dualistic feminist "either/or" has been articulated at the onset with the biblical image of religion as "home" and that of "exodus" as leaving institutionalized religions. Wo/men who continue to define their identity in terms of institutionalized religion are like the daughters of the house. Whereas right-wing wo/men see the hierarchical church as their protective patriarchal home, the wo/men's ordination movements claim equal standing with their brothers in the home. However, both groups can do so only by overlooking the "domestic violence" wo/men in general and ordained wo/men in particular continue to suffer in hierarchical church institutions.

The other biblical image that has inspired feminists in religion has been the image of the "exodus." With the help of this image the wo/men's movement was understood as an exodus community freed from the slavery of ecclesiastical Egypt in order to move into the feminist promised land of liberated sisterhood, situated on the margins or in the "other world." Mary Daly marching out of Harvard's Memorial Church has come to symbolize this exodus of wo/men out of religion. Yet, as Carol Christ and especially Native American theologians have observed, the exodus tradition is a dangerous one because it engenders the conquest and occupation of foreign lands.[16]

While I have appreciated the power and strategy of both images, I have not subscribed to either of them because of their essentialist either/or tendencies. Because I had experienced Catholicism not just as limiting and oppressive but also as emancipatory, I did not share in the exodus impulse to reject biblical religion in general and Catholicism in particular as inherently sexist and destructive of wo/men's authority and self. Nor did I think wo/men could be "at home" in an institution that had excluded them from its leadership for centuries. Instead of arguing for an exodus from the church or an apologetic defense of it as home, a third alternative seemed necessary.

My way of dealing with such either/or alternatives has not only been to say "both and," but also "neither/nor, but different." "*Neither/nor, but different*" implies that one needs first to deconstruct dualistic opposites by identifying their function in a complex kyriarchal system of multiple oppressions. Only after such a thorough deconstruction of both binary poles can a different reconstruction be attempted. Since neither the discourse of "home" nor that of "exodus" to the margins can provide a satisfactory organizing metaphor, I searched for a third image that would share in both but be neither and different. So I proposed the radical democratic notion of *ekklesia of wo/men*, which can be translated as the "congress of Wo/men" or "wo/men-church" as an alternative image that could articulate the wo/men's movement and feminist theology as a variegated, contentious, and conflictive emancipatory radical democratic movement with organized religions as sites of feminist debates and struggles for change.

Although from the very beginning I was critical of the cultural and theological conceptualization of feminist theology as a "theology of woman" in terms of femininity, gender, and sexual difference, I nevertheless worked for some time with the theoretical framework of patriarchy, which was defined in dualistic gender terms and understood as the domination of all men over all women. As an immigrant resident alien, I was all too aware of the divisions and prejudices among wo/men, but I nevertheless had cast my lot with the wo/men's liberation movement in academy and church. Two challenges to the dualistic conceptualization of patriarchy that came from the women's movement in the mid-1970s stand out in my memory as having moved my thinking away from such a dualistic conceptualization of gender oppression and given me the courage to search for an intellectual framework that could encompass my negative experiences with wo/men.

The first challenge came at a public lecture when a wo/man in the audience suggested that I develop a notion of patriarchy that would include her experience as an African American woman who did not understand herself as primarily oppressed by Black men, but much more so by the racism of White men *and* women. Her challenge made immediate sense to me because I myself had argued for quite some time that my own experience as a woman scholar was determined not just by my gender but also by the fact that I was a university professor and a resident alien immigrant, speaking with a German accent. While immigrant wo/men from Europe do not face the same or even similar oppressions as immigrant wo/men of color do, I argued, we nevertheless experience some discrimination as foreigners. Hence the need arose for a category of analysis that could conceptualize such shifting experiences of identity.

The second challenge also materialized in the late 1970s from a telephone call of a feminist journalist whose name I do not recall, asking what feminist scholars had to say about the biblical texts that continued to preach the subordination of women, texts that fueled the rhetoric of the Moral Majority. I remember answering quite smugly that scholarship had long recognized that these so-called household code texts were "time conditioned," and therefore not normative for Christians. But after her phone call, I began to work again on these texts only to discover that malestream scholarship had begun to see them in a new light, as texts espousing neo-Aristotelian antide-mocratic political philosophy, albeit without explicitly reflecting on the theo-logical and cultural implications of this shift in interpretation.[17] Again, my theoretical work set out to respond to the need of the women's movement for clarification of these texts. This theoretical development also brought the recognition that androcentric dualism, which at the time was almost univer-sally understood as the root of oppression, was an ideology that was engen-dered by a pyramidal system of structured oppressions and has developed in critical opposition to the ideal of democracy.[18] I first elaborated this research into the complex structuring of patriarchy in antiquity at a conference in Hawaii in 1978 and systematized it in the early 1980s. I waited until the early 1990s to rename patriarchy *kyriarchy*.

Over the years I have been involved in feminist explorations and meetings that sought to develop new institutional ways of doing theology. During my sabbatical in New York, Judith Plaskow and I began to talk on and off about founding a feminist theological journal. Since publications, journals, and books are very important institutional means for academic theologians, we wanted to give women scholars in religion the possibility of publishing their feminist research. Such a refereed journal was to provide a forum for develop-ing and discussing feminist studies in religion as an intellectual discipline that remained rooted in the women's liberation movement in society and religion. We felt the need for such an ecumenical, interreligious, and interdisciplinary journal because at that time, established theological journals were not keen on publishing feminist research. Moreover, leading feminist journals were, by and large, not interested in research on religion. Hence Judith and I pooled our financial resources and our professional contacts, and the first issue of the *Journal of Feminist Studies in Religion* was published in 1985, the same year in which the first issue on feminist theology in *Concilium* appeared.

Concilium, an international Roman Catholic journal that has little influ-ence in the United States, was founded to keep alive and develop the theo-logical visions of the Second Vatican Council. It is published six times annually in seven languages. I had been elected to the editorial board as the first wo/man scholar and joined it in 1978 with the goal of promoting femi-nist theology and wo/men's presence. After intense debate, the international foundation and editorial board of *Concilium* decided in the early 1980s to re-structure its twelve sections, which represented traditional theological disci-plines, and to establish two "extraordinary" new sections: Liberation/Third

World Theologies and Feminist Theology. Sister Mary Collins, O.S.B., professor of liturgy at the Catholic University of America, and I were appointed coeditors and prepared the introductory issue, "Women: Invisible in Church and Theology."

Whereas the *Journal of Feminist Studies in Religion* has adopted an interreligious, academic feminist studies approach, the feminist theology issue of *Concilium* strives to articulate a critical feminist liberation theology for an international audience within a "progressive" Catholic theological framework. The framework and approach of a critical feminist liberation theology required a different methodological approach from that of traditional theology. In contrast to a method of systematic theology that follows the canon of doctrinal topics such as Christology, ecclesiology, discussing Bible and tradition before moving to contemporary official church teaching and practical theology, such a critical feminist approach begins with women's experience and focuses on problem areas that are critically explored using a feminist systemic analysis and a critical constructive theological option. Over the years Mary Collins, Ann Carr, Shawn Copeland, Kwok Pui-Lan (as guest editor), and Maria Pilar Aquino have collaborated with me to make the feminist issue one of the best-received issues of *Concilium*. In Spain, Italy, and Latin America, for some time the issue was the only available feminist resource in religion. However, whereas the JFSR operates financially on a shoestring in order to preserve its feminist independence, the fate of feminist theology in *Concilium* is controlled by an institutional structure that requires consistent struggle for the intellectual integrity of the feminist issue, a struggle that may be lost.

A third kind of movement work that has been more or less successful has been my work for institutionalizing feminist theological education. After the first ordination conference in 1974, Sister Helen Wright constituted a task force on theological education that met for several years. Our discussions laid the groundwork for the Wo/men's Theological Center, which, under the leadership of Francine Cardman, was initiated in Cambridge, Massachusetts.

Some of us, among them Mary Collins and I, had proposed a satellite model of feminist theological education based on the consciousness-raising process of the wo/men's movement, and envisioned local feminist study groups that would come together periodically on a regional basis to work with a trained feminist theologian as a resource person. Rather than uprooting wo/men and bringing them to a theological school or center, such a model would have sustained a feminist movement for change by creating a network of feminist study groups all across the United States and the world. At the time, I tried to persuade sisters in positions of leadership in religious education to make available congregational funds for such a theological institute that would have been open to all wo/men, but would have especially attracted sisters and Catholic wo/men who constituted the major summer school population in Catholic universities such as Notre Dame. Yet I did not meet with success. Because of the communication possibilities of the Internet, today such a model could be realized much more easily, if financial and institutional backing could be found.

More successful was a different venture, which is also now threatened by budget cuts. When after almost fifteen years of teaching I moved from the University of Notre Dame to the Episcopal Divinity School (EDS) in Cambridge, Massachusetts, I did so not just because of personal reasons but also because the dean of EDS, the Reverend Dr. Harvey Guthrie, had persuaded me that the school would provide a conducive environment for my feminist theological work. He was convinced that the challenge facing the church was not just wo/men's ordination, but feminist theology. For this reason, EDS seemed the ideal place to work for establishing a Resource Center for Feminist Liberation Ministry and Theology. My colleague Katie G. Cannon suggested that we name the center the Pauli Murray Center. My proposal for such a center stated:

> The center should be dedicated to the education of future feminist ministers and to the articulation and exploration of feminist theology and ministry. To my knowledge no such center exists to date in this country. There are community-based and movement-based feminist theological centers but none within the context of a traditional theological educational institution. Since Christian religion and church have been involved—consciously or not—in the legitimation and continuation of patriarchal oppression, it becomes necessary in a disciplined way to explore the patriarchal elements and functions of ecclesial ministry and theology. EDS therefore could make a great contribution to the wider church and its feminist praxis of theology and ministry with the establishment of such a resource center. The work of the center would consist in offering the M.A. and D.Min. degrees in the area of feminist liberation ministry and theology, in initiating research, bibliographic documentation, and a wide range of publications, in sponsoring conferences and continuing education events, and in serving as a resource center for feminist theology and ministry.

My proposal went on to spell out the institutional conditions and implications for the creation of such a center. My colleagues, however, did not believe that it was feasible to engage in such a bold venture, but decided to
focus on an important part of the proposal, the implementation of a doctor of
ministry program and, at a second stage, that of an M.A. program and degree
in feminist liberation theology and ministry as a part of the established
D.Min. and M.A. programs.

At Harvard Divinity School, I have pursued this dream of institutionalizing feminist theological education in a different way by working to establish a
Wo/men's Studies Department or a Feminist Studies Center that could integrate the Wo/men's Studies in Religion Program and the doctoral programs
in religion, gender and culture, as well as develop a feminist studies concentration at the M.A. level and a research program in feminist religious studies
and ministerial leadership. However, my dream has remained just that, a
dream! Since according to the gospels no prophet is recognized in her own
hometown, I have shifted my energies away from Harvard to Bahia, Brazil,
where together with Professor Lieve Troch, I have worked over the past four
years on theological education at the invitation of Yámi, the feminist leadership group of Instituto de Educação Teológico da Bahia. This dream includes
the organization of an International Forum of Feminist Scholars and Educators in Religion, who are committed to a feminist thea/ological vision and
variegated movement.

I have focused here on my own experience and spoken of my work in
such detail because I wanted to contradict the growing trend of periodizing
and of classifying the history of feminist theology in terms of a modernist
model of progress from nontheoretical experiential beginnings to the heights
of postmodern feminist theory. From the very beginning, feminist scholars in
religion have produced variegated theoretical discourses and developed fruitful new methods, strategies, and approaches. We have begun to change the
academic field of theology and religious studies because we were rooted in
and responsible to a variegated wo/men's movement for change, although
this movement often did not take notice of us. Feminist theology and biblical
studies, nevertheless, has matured into a rich and exciting intellectual field of
study, and I am grateful to have been part of this historic development. However, we must not forget that the institutional and theoretical inroads we have
made are very fragile, and can easily be wiped out if the gains of the first generation of feminist scholars in religion are not further institutionalized in

feminist terms. We need a national and transnational foundation or organization of Feminist Studies in Religion that is supported by and responsible to the variegated grassroots wo/men's movements, in order to survive and change in society and religion.

NOTES

1. Donna Steichen, *Ungodly Rage: The Hidden Face of Catholic Feminism* (San Francisco: Ignatius Press, 1991), 398. For biblical studies, see the attempt of Cullen Murphy, *The Word According to Eve. Women and the Bible in Ancient Times and Our Own* (Boston: Houghton Mifflin Co, 1998).

2. A similar section in the Society for Biblical Literature, entitled "Wo/men in the Biblical World," was introduced only in the 1980s.

3. See Christ's works *Diving Deep and Surfacing, The Laughter of Aphrodite,* and the two pathbreaking collections *Womanspirit Rising* and *Weaving the Visions,* which she edited with Judith Plaskow.

4. The section on Women and Religion was initiated in 1973 and has been crucial for the development of the field. See Judith Plaskow and Joan Arnold, eds., *Women and Religion* (Missoula, Mon.: Scholars Press, 1974).

5. Thea/o/legein is derived from the Grk. feminine *thea* (Goddess) and the masculine form *theos* (God) and *legein* meaning "to speak." Thea/o/logy in the proper sense is therefore speaking about the Divine. I use "theology" whenever I refer to a professional discipline and institution.

6. The work of Hedwig Meyer-Wilmes, *Rebellion auf der Grenze. Ortsbestimmung feministischer Theologie* (Freiburg: Herder Verlag, 1990; has also appeared in English translation) provides a substantive intellectual historiography of the development of German feminist theology. Karin Volkwein, *Der Traum einer gemeinsamen Sprache. Feministische Theologie in den USA der siebziger Jahre* (Mainz: Matthias Grünewald, 1999) is such a work but is not translated into English and written from a German perspective about American feminist theology. Without question American feminist thea/ology has greatly influenced feminist theology in Germany and Europe, but we need a work that is a substantive account of the development of feminist thea/ology and studies in religion written by those who have shaped its history.

7. Elisabeth Schüssler Fiorenza, "Women's Studies and the Teaching of Religion," *Occasional Papers on Catholic Higher Education* 1 (1975): 26–30. "Für eine befreite und befreiende Theologie. Theologinnen und Feministische Theologie in den USA," *Konzilium* 8 (1978): 287–294.

8. "Feminist Theology as a Critical Theology of Liberation." *Theological Studies* 36 (1975): 606–626; reprinted in *Woman: New Dimensions,* ed. W. Burghardt (New York: Paulist Press, 1977), 19–50.

9. See my remark in the introduction of this article in Elisabeth Schüssler Fiorenza, *Discipleship of Equals: a Critical Feminist Ekklesia-Logy of Liberation* (New York: Crossroad, 1993).

10. Elisabeth Schüssler Fiorenza, "Die Rolle der Frau in der urchristlichen Bewegung," *Konzilium* 7 (1976): 3–9; "Women in the Pre-Pauline and Pauline

Churches," *Union Seminary Quarterly Review* 33 (1978): 153–166; "The Apostleship of Women in Early Christianity" and "The Twelve," in *Women Priests: A Catholic Commentary to the Vatican Statement on the Ordination of Women*, ed. A. and L. Swidler (New York: Paulist Press, 1977), 135–140; "Women in Early Christianity: Methodological Considerations," in *Critical History and Biblical Faith in NT Perspectives*, ed. T. J. Ryan (Villanova, Penn.: CTS Annual Publication, 1979), 30–58.

11. Elisabeth Schüssler Fiorenza, *In Memory of Her: A Feminist Theological Reconstruction of Christian Origins* (New York: Crossroad, 1983; 10th anniversary ed., 1994).

12. Elisabeth Schüssler Fiorenza, "Understanding God's Revealed Word," *Catholic Charismatic* (1977): 4–10.

13. See Elisabeth Schüssler Fiorenza, "Interpreting Patriarchal Traditions of the Bible," in *The Liberating Word*, ed. L. Russell (Philadelphia: Westminster, 1976), 39–61. As far as I remember, my use of feminist and my hermeneutical proposal were edited out. I had a similar experience when publishing my article "Word, Spirit, and Power: Women in Early Christian Communities," in *Women of the Spirit*, ed. R. R. Ruether and E. McLaughlin (New York: Simon and Schuster, 1979), 29–70. Because one of the editors objected to my hermeneutical proposal, my ending was rewritten "because of stylistic reasons."

14. My books *Discipleship of Equals: A Critical Feminist Ekklesia-logy of Liberation* (New York: Crossroad, 1993); *Jesus: Miriam's Child, Sophia's Prophet: Critical Issues in Feminist Christology* (New York: Continuum, 1994); *Sharing Her Word: Feminist Biblical Interpretation in Context* (Boston: Beacon, 1998); *Wisdom Ways: Introducing Feminist Biblical Interpretation* (Maryknoll, N.Y.: Orbis, 2001) have sought to refine this critical feminist hermeneutical approach.

15. Elisabeth Schüssler Fiorenza, "Feminist Spirituality, Christian Identity and the Catholic Vision." *NICM Journal* 1 (1976): 29–34, reprinted in *Womanspirit Rising*, ed. C. Christ and J. Plaskow (New York: Harper & Row, 1979).

16. See, for example, Robert Allan Warrior, "Canaanites, Cowboys and Indians: Deliverance, Conquest and Liberation Theology Today," *Christianity and Crisis* (September 11, 1989): 261–264.

17. For literature see Elisabeth Schüssler Fiorenza, *In Memory of Her; Bread Not Stone: The Challenge of Feminist Biblical Interpretation* (Boston: Beacon, 1985, 10th anniversary ed., 1995); and *But She Said: Feminist Practices of Biblical Interpretation* (Boston: Beacon, 1992).

18. For further discussion see Elisabeth Schüssler Fiorenza, *Rhetoric and Ethic: The Politics of Biblical Studies* (Minneapolis, Minn.: Fortress, 1999).

TEN

Margaret M. Toscano

1976 Feminist awakening while studying at Brigham Young
    University
1984 "Missing Rib" speech asserts women's right to Mormon
    priesthood
2000 Excommunicated from LDS Church for feminist activism

ON A VISIT TO SALT LAKE CITY A FEW YEARS AGO, GLORIA STEINHAM
quipped that the LDS Church had probably created more feminists than she

ever had. Certainly this was true in my case: my Mormon experience, particularly at the church's conservative Brigham Young University, opened my eyes to the problem of being a woman. Personally, I had no objections to being one. Growing up, I liked dresses, pantyhose, makeup, high heels (and still do). I was good at sewing and cooking and looked forward to marriage and a family. But I had two problems: I was smart in school, and I was not good at pretending to be something I wasn't—qualities that became obstacles to finding a husband at BYU, touted as the most fertile matchmaking ground for LDS youth.

Like most young Mormon women, I had been trained to put motherhood before career. In fact, I had no career plans at all when I entered BYU in the fall of 1967. But I was intellectually ambitious and very curious. I chose an undergraduate English major with a history minor. I also took the required religion courses, mostly glorified Sunday school classes replete with whitewashed church history and dogmatic theology. But in these classes, I took very seriously the required reading of the scriptures and foundational Mormon documents. I quickly discovered that there was much more in these texts than I had ever heard from the pulpit. I found, in fact, outright contradictions between the two. These religious texts began to stir in me something I had never felt in church meetings. I caught a religious fervor that perhaps can only be experienced in one's teens or twenties. I began to feel longings to connect with God and a desire to be like the visionaries who filled the scriptures.

But I had a problem: I was female. In contrast, all the best spiritual role models from the Bible and Mormon scriptures were male. And their service to God was linked with prophetic or priestly power. But my tradition affirmed that only men could be ordained. Priesthood was for men, and motherhood was for women. And yet I saw something besides these church teachings in the scriptural texts. There priesthood was presented not primarily as a church office but as spirituality, love, light, and knowledge; it was about bringing salvation and hope to others. What could be so wrong about a woman wanting these things? Yet my culture seemed to say that God preferred men. My sex, which I had always seen as a blessing, was really a curse. All women were Eve, cursed of God. I had arrived at a crisis of faith.

This happened as I was finishing my B.A. in English. I was still not married, so I decided to press on toward a master's degree in classical languages, with the eventual goal of pursuing through ancient languages my interest in biblical studies. I was preoccupied with finding out if women had always been second-class citizens in God's kingdom. They certainly were at BYU, where all university leadership positions in the 1970s were held by men, both as religious and academic authorities. As a graduate student, I saw all of my fellow, male graduates mentored into prestigious Ph.D. programs elsewhere, while no one seemed to see me as a serious candidate for an academic career. But I began to see myself differently. I was teaching Latin and Greek, and I was good at it. The academic life suited me. This success led to a full-time adjunct position at BYU. This, however, only intensified my crisis of faith. On the career totem pole, I was at the bottom, despite open acknowledgment of my dedication and talent. In the church as well, I was subordinate to and controlled by men, even when their knowledge and devotion were notably less.

Then two events occurred that moved me beyond crisis to a transformation. The first happened when I was allowed to participate in the LDS temple ritual (what Mormons call "receiving one's endowments"). Mormons usually are not allowed to take part in this ceremony unless they are either about to leave on a mission or about to get married. I was not about to do either, but I talked my bishop into giving me the necessary ecclesiastical recommend required to participate.[1] The LDS Church emphasizes the culmination of the temple ritual, the marriage and sealing that binds families together forever, but this is only one element of the temple ceremonies. The longest ceremony is an initiation ritual drama in which Adam and Eve (representing each man and woman) take a cosmic journey through several stages of existence. As this drama unfolds, each initiate in the audience is invested with pieces of ceremonial garb, including the sacred undergarment, that together constitute what are called "the robes of the holy priesthood."[2] Women are clothed in these robes exactly as are the men. As this occurs, women are told they are being prepared to become queens and priestesses, while the men are told they are being prepared to be kings and priests. In this ceremony women officiate for women and men officiate for men. Of course all this occurs under male leadership. But I had been trained to read a text. And I could clearly see that here was something I had never seen outside the temple. Here women acted as priestesses to initiate other women while wearing priestly clothing. This knowledge changed me. I knew on a deep level that in the temple I was given a gift. I had been invested or endowed with priesthood. This came to me in a flood of spiritual insight where I felt God's love overflowing the rigid boundaries prescribed by corporate Mormonism. God loved and honored women even if church leaders did not.

The second transformation resulted more from a process than an event. At about this time, I began digging into Mormon history and theology. I discovered that Mormon women had more power, spiritual standing, and visibility in the nineteenth century than in the twentieth. While reading the sermons of Brigham Young, I found this statement: "the man that honors his Priesthood, the woman that honors her Priesthood, will receive an everlasting inheritance in the kingdom of God."[3] This was heady stuff. A number of my male friends who collected Mormon historical documents began feeding me whatever they found about nineteenth-century Mormon women. I learned that these women exercised spiritual gifts, participated in faith healings by the laying on of hands (a ritual only male priesthood holders are allowed to perform in the church today), and enjoyed more autonomy and respect than modern Mormon women. Eliza R. Snow, plural wife of Joseph Smith and later Brigham Young, had been called a prophetess and high priestess; and her poems and sermons were influential in the church. Early Mormon women controlled their own organization and money, were among the first to receive the right to vote, were avid suffragists, had ties to Susan B. Anthony and Elizabeth Cady Stanton, and published their own newspaper where they wrote ardently about women's rights.[4]

In the midst of these discoveries, I had a moment of awakening. It took place at a 1975 BYU assembly during a speech given by English professor Elouise Bell entitled "The Implications of Feminism for Brigham Young University" (a speech that would never be allowed today).[5] In it Elouise argued that feminism was not inimical to the mission of the church, that our pioneer foremothers had pointed the way for us, and that BYU should strive for more equality in their treatment of women in scholarships, admissions, career planning, and the presentation of knowledge itself. I was electrified. Here was another Mormon woman whose issues were my issues. She had given them a name: feminism—a name that until this time had seemed foreign, something for non-Mormon women who didn't like men. But there on the spot I knew that I, too, was a feminist. I felt linked to the cause.

DEVELOPING A FEMINIST THEOLOGY

My dedication to feminism took the form of developing a broad feminist Mormon theology. I wished to show that at its roots Mormonism was not only compatible with feminism but that Mormon history, scripture, and foundational texts contained some of the strongest arguments for women sharing equal power with men that could be found in any religion. From my own experience I knew that LDS women and men could see the sexist problem only if they saw it in the context of their own faith. Nevertheless, my interest in theology and scholarship led me to borrow from feminist theologians of other traditions: Virginia Mollenkott, Judith Plaskow, Rosemary Radford Ruether, Elisabeth Schüssler Fiorenza, Carol Christ, Blu Greenberg, Letty Russell. All of these women showed me how to reinterpret religious texts, how to question interpretive foundations, how to recontextualize evidence, and how to call power structures into question. I also began discovering feminist work done by other Mormon women, mostly women's history, such as the seminal 1976 book, *Mormon Sisters*, edited by Claudia Bushman and containing articles by Laurel Thatcher Ulrich, Judy Dushku, Jill Mulvay Derr, and Maureen Ursenbach Beecher, among others.[6] I discovered publications like the magazine *Exponent II*, started in the late 1970s by a group of Boston women and still publishing articles that provide an important support for Mormon women exploring gender issues through personal essay.

My own research remained theological because I was interested in uncovering the theoretical framework that supported male power in the LDS Church. I did not think women could ever have a voice in the church unless it could be shown that women's full participation and leadership were in harmony with basic Mormon tenets. This work resulted in my first paper: "The Missing Rib: The Forgotten Place of Queens and Priestesses in the Establishment of Zion." I presented it at the annual Sunstone Symposium in August of 1984 while I was pregnant with my youngest daughter. (Yes, by that time I had married and had four daughters in five years—slowing me down a little.) The Sunstone Foundation is one of a few Mormon venues not controlled by the LDS Church hierarchy. At Sunstone it is possible to freely discuss and publish on Mormon theology, history, and social issues. In "The Missing Rib" I examined the speeches of Joseph Smith given in 1842 in Nauvoo, Illinois, at the founding of the Female Relief Society, the still-extant women's organization of the LDS Church. Joseph Smith, in these speeches given on several occasions, made the stunning announcement to the women present that "part of the priesthood belongs to them," that he wanted to show them "how they will come into possession of the privileges . . . and gifts of the priesthood," and that he was going to make them into "a kingdom of priests."[7] My paper showed how the first Mormon prophet included women in a priesthood council and was expanding their leadership role before his death. The women who received these blessings from him continued in this tradition in Utah. But after they died, the knowledge of these things faded. My paper caused quite a stir. Though others had been reclaiming Mormon women's history, no one had yet stated quite so boldly or foolhardily that Mormon women had a legitimate right to priesthood.

This was the first of a long series of papers I wrote examining aspects of Mormon theology from a feminist perspective. Many of these were published in *Strangers in Paradox: Explorations in Mormon Theology,* a book I coauthored with my husband, Paul.[8] Other papers were published in the few independent Mormon journals.[9] In these articles I explored not only woman and the priesthood, but also the early and now virtually forbidden Mormon revelation of God the Mother. Joseph Smith, before his death, gave this revelation; and it was referenced later in a hymn written by Eliza R. Snow.[10] One lyric reads: "In the heavens are parents single? No, the thought makes reason stare. Truth is reason, truth eternal, tells me I've a Mother there."[11] Women's priesthood and a female deity were, in my mind, doctrines essential for women's equality; and foundational Mormon texts provided the framework and justification for both. While these two doctrines have been the focus of the majority of my Mormon feminist work, in recent years I have been more interested in questions of representation and identity, as shown by my essay "If I Hate My Mother, Can I Love the Heavenly Mother? Personal Identity, Parental Relationships, and Perceptions of God."[12] Influenced by contemporary theories of gender, I have come to believe that women's subordination is not simply a matter of male-dominated institutional structures but of underlying symbolic and cultural patterns, relationships, and perceptions. Women's roles and status in society cannot fully change until the categories "man" and "woman" are fully deconstructed and reconstructed.[13]

CONNECTING WITH OTHER MORMON FEMINISTS

For me personally, one important result of my work from 1984 onward was that it began connecting me with other Mormon feminists. To this point, most of my intellectual friendships had been with men, and I had felt isolated from other women. Speaking and writing caused me to network with like-minded women, and as a result I began developing many feminist friendships, especially through women's retreats. At one such retreat in 1984, a few of us started a feminist monthly study/book group, which we called the "Redemptive Cooking Club." In sharing actual food as well as intellectual and spiritual food, we were both playing with the stereotype of women as responsible for food production and at the same time asserting the necessity of redeeming what had traditionally been deemed second class through an association with women. We were interested in a brand of feminism that married the body and the spirit, the heavens and the earth, the political and the personal, the pragmatic and the idealist, the mystical and the mundane, the bitch and the saint. We wanted to balance polarities as well as critique them. While the Redemptive Cooking Club lost and gained members over time, it remained intact as a group for about fifteen years and served as a vital emotional support as well as a stimulus to creative feminist work.[14]

FEMINIST ACTIVISM

After the defeat of the Equal Rights Amendment (which occurred in part due to the opposition mounted by the LDS Church) and after the much-publicized excommunication of Sonia Johnson in 1980 for her founding work in Mormons for ERA, Mormon feminism went underground for most of the 1980s. Private women's retreats during this period proliferated and served as an important source of support, empowerment, and consciousness raising. Then in 1988 some of us made another foray into the public arena. Two friends, Kelli Frame and Karen Erickson Christ, who were disturbed about women's second-class status in the LDS Church, felt that what we needed was a public forum for discussing women's issues. They had read articles by me and other Mormon feminists and believed that if mainstream Mormon women could just hear some of these ideas, they would awaken to gender problems in their lives and want things to change. So Karen and Kelli approached me, and the three of us decided to launch the group as the Mormon Women's Forum because we wanted to create a venue for discourse on women's issues that could include Mormon women with different perspectives. We held our first meeting in a rented hotel conference room (paid for by Kelli), where Karen read a speech written with Kelli about women's subordination and I addressed the effects of women's exclusion from priesthood and leadership in the church. It was perhaps a rather strong beginning. Some of Karen's conservative friends attended from her LDS ward (that's a local Mormon congregation). They later told her they were especially offended by my "ferocious" feminist approach. Very quickly the group became a feminist one, attended only by those who felt in some way alienated from the mainstream. The first two or three years were very exciting. We discussed all sorts of issues: women and priesthood, God the Mother, abortion, Sonia Johnson, women's history, spiritual gifts, lesbian identity, sexual and domestic abuse, body image, women and the law in Utah, and so on. Often 200 women attended these meetings. We started a small publication that was more radical than any that had gone before. Hopes ran high that we could make a difference.

TROUBLE WITH THE CHURCH

This was not to be. Two factors deflated the power of the forum: internal conflict, which I understand is common in such groups; and increasing pressure from the church hierarchy that discouraged women from participating if they wished to maintain membership in the church.[15] I was one of the first to feel consequences from this threat. In 1989, after participating in a debate about women and the priesthood that received local television news coverage in Salt Lake City, the classes I was scheduled to teach for the upcoming semester at BYU were suddenly and without explanation dropped. Over the next seven years, the church increasingly pressured women to disassociate from feminism. To be labeled "feminist" was to be labeled "anti-Mormon." Beginning in 1993, a crush of church tribunals was convened to deprive many women of their church membership for their feminist activism. Lynne Knavel Whitesides, Lavina Fielding Anderson, Maxine Hanks, and Janice Allred, all of whom had been involved in the forum and had written and published feminist works, were among the high-profile feminists excommunicated at this time.[16] Cecilia Konchar Farr and Gail Houston, two avowed feminist faculty members at BYU, were each denied tenure (Cecilia in 1993, Gail in 1996), even though they were both devout church members and qualified scholars. My husband, Paul, was also excommunicated in 1993 for challenging the church's authoritarianism, criticizing ecclesiastical and spiritual abuse, critiquing the leaders' fascination with power and money and their departure from the core Christian message that empowers the downtrodden and imparts grace to all.[17] The fact that he had supported the forum and identified with feminism did not help his position in the church either.

MY EXCOMMUNICATION

Common among those excommunicated by the LDS Church was the high visibility of their criticism of church policy and practice. The church is extremely sensitive about its image and easily threatened by any negative assessments. I was also threatened with church action in 1993, although I was not finally brought to trial or excommunicated until the year 2000. What initially brought me into the church leaders' crosshairs was the public nature of my discussions of women's right to the priesthood and the importance of the Mormon concept of the Mother God. The Mormon hierarchy wants to project an image of the church as a happy and contented extended family of well-adjusted nuclear families headed by men and served by women completely satisfied with their roles as wives and mothers. The men who excommunicated me felt that I had misused my membership by publicly discussing issues they might cause members to lose faith in the leadership and discredit this idealized family image that church leaders believe is one of Mormonism's principal appeals to prospective members. The specific event that instigated the church's action against me started with an invitation to speak at the controversial feminist BYU club known as VOICE in the summer of 1993. To a group of about forty students, mostly women, I presented a slide show entitled "Images of the Female Body: Human and Divine"—a piece that explores iconography and artwork as a source for women's spirituality and the body as the focal point for discovering the divine female. A summary of my piece, along with my picture, appeared the next day in the student newspaper, which is always distributed to the top leaders at LDS Church headquarters in Salt Lake City forty-five miles away.

Later I learned from my local church leader, stake president Kerry Heinz (a leader over a large area of ten to twelve congregations), that one of the Twelve Apostles, Boyd K. Packer, saw the article and contacted him to ask, "Can't you control that woman?" President Heinz was not supposed to tell me that he had been instructed by Packer to bring action against me because the general leadership of the church wants to maintain the impression that they have no involvement in trying individuals for their church membership. Church policy states that such matters are to be handled solely by the local leaders who know the members personally and therefore have more of a basis for fair judgment. Also, since evidence or confession is supposed to be the basis for any action, it is obviously a kangaroo court if the outcome has been determined before any evidence is produced or heard. If high leaders are directing the proceedings and outcome, then it is already prejudged. In addition, denying any involvement in the excommunication of intellectuals and feminists keeps the leaders at the top above reproach; it leaves the dirty work to those below them in the church hierarchy.[18]

Since I was one of the first feminists to be threatened with excommunication in 1993, why did it take the church seven years finally to bring me before a disciplinary council?[19] I believe there are four main reasons:

1. My husband purposely drew the fire away from me and onto himself. Since I am part of an old Mormon family of eight generations in the church and he is a convert, he felt excommunication would be more damaging to me. Also, since his personality is more abrasive than mine, he was a psychologically more satisfying target for the stake president than I was.

2. Once Paul was excommunicated, publicity went wild in the local and national news. I don't believe President Heinz wanted to draw more attention to himself by pursuing my case; he was already embarrassed that his name had appeared in print.

3. Because the church is so patriarchal, there was the feeling for a time that I had somehow been taken care of through action against my husband.

4. After two years we moved to another stake in Salt Lake, and it took the church bureaucracy some time to organize its case against me and to find a local leader who was willing to act.

Although I had been estranged from the church for years because of its harsh treatment of many of my friends and family, I decided to attend my church court on the night of November 30, 2000. It took place at a local chapel in a conference room on a Thursday evening from 7:00 to 10:30 P.M. When the men on the tribunal asked me why I had come when I was inactive in the organization, I gave them three reasons:

1. Mormonism was my heritage and I felt compelled to defend my rights as a member of the group.

2. I did not want them to cut me off without having to face me and see what kind of a person I was.

3. I wished the church could be a more open and loving community and hoped they would act in this way. I felt, however, that they wouldn't. And they didn't.

It was a kangaroo court from first to last. Church doctrine requires disciplinary councils to be fair, with witnesses, rules, and people to support the accused. But none of this was applied in my case. As a lone woman I faced sixteen men, all part of the ecclesiastical structure of the local region. None of them knew me. All owed allegiance to the stake president. The charge against me was apostasy, now defined at the highest level of the church as public opposition to the church and/or its leaders or teaching as church doctrine what is not church doctrine when corrected by a leader. I pleaded innocent to both, asserting that I had never opposed the church nor claimed my personal beliefs to be official church doctrine. Moreover, I believed my work to be faith-promoting. Many women had told me my writings had helped them stay in the church and provided them with spiritual hope.

Stake president Dale Blake, who acted as prosecuting attorney, judge, and jury, produced as evidence against me a letter sent from Kerry Heinz, my stake president of seven years earlier, in which he had forbidden me to write, publish, speak, or discuss anything to do with church history or doctrine in any setting. If I disobeyed, I was told that I would have church action taken against me. The head of the tribunal asked me whether I had disobeyed this order. I replied that I had said seven years earlier that I would not obey the order because it was neither just nor authoritative and because to do so would promote unhealthy authoritarianism and corrode the spirituality of the church community.

The court ignored my admission and proceeded to show by reference to my many speeches and writings that I had not heeded the order. I was therefore an apostate simply for disobeying my leader's order not to speak or write. In the process, the court also tried to show the dangerous content of my speeches. When I attempted to defend myself by suggesting that my ideas were in line with many LDS scriptures and prophetic texts, the stake president harshly interrupted me midsentence, saying "We will not allow you to lecture us. And you may not use that kind of argument again." I was never allowed to fully answer the many accusations. At the end of the trial, I was given a few moments to make a final statement. I knew they would not let me defend myself by an appeal on doctrinal grounds, so I made a quick and impassioned plea for freedom of speech. (Freedom or free agency, ironically, is a pillar of Mormon doctrine, and the U.S. Constitution is considered an inspired document.) Freedom of belief, I told them, was the heart of spiritual growth. Can't we disagree about doctrine and yet still love each other? Can't we treat each other with respect even when we disagree? This got to them. Suddenly they were on the defensive. They all affirmed their belief in freedom. But, they said, I had gone too far. There had to be limits. They sent me out of the room for thirty minutes while they deliberated. Then I was brought back for sentencing. The stake president told me they had been impressed with me: I was both intelligent and respectful—so nice really. But they had to excommunicate me to protect the "purity" of the church, and I could not return to the church until I had publicly renounced all of my "pernicious" doctrine and repaired all the damage they claimed I had done to people's testimonies of the church.

AFTERMATH: FAITH & FEMINISM

How do I feel about my excommunication? I have to agree with my husband's description that it was a little like being gang-raped by the Care Bears. It was violence done with politeness and a smile. Anyone who watched the television coverage of the 2002 Winter Olympics in Salt Lake City, sometimes called the "Mormon Olympics," knows that the Mormons are known for being friendly and nice. Culturally Mormons are trained not to be confrontational. And yet there is a shadow behind the sunny appearance. The male leaders who cut me off from the church all wanted to shake my hand and tell me that they cared about me as I left to go home at the end of my trial. It was rather bizarre considering that an excommunicated member, according to Mormon doctrine, is eternally barred from heaven or celestial association with other worthy family members or saints. In this life, an excommunicated Mormon is barred from participating in any kind of worship or church meeting anywhere in the world.[20] Unlike Protestant denominations, since the LDS Church organization is centralized and universal, being excommunicated means there is nowhere else to go to remain part of the faith. And since members are trained never to question the actions of their leaders, it means being considered a sinner by active family and friends who should sympathize in no way with the excommunicated. It means being cut off from family rituals and community ties. Since even Mormon funerals are considered church meetings, my husband recently was forbidden to speak at the funeral of a very dear friend. The same will apply to me when my mother dies. And since both of us are alumni of BYU, our alma mater, too, must shun us. To be an excommunicated Mormon is to be labeled dangerous and outcast.

NOTES

1. In order to receive a temple recommend, an LDS member must undergo a confidential interview with her bishop (a local leader who presides over a congregation of about 400 to 600 people), in which she is questioned about her activity in and financial contributions to the LDS Church, her sexual purity, her honesty, and her obedience to church leaders.

2. For a discussion of the function of priesthood garments in LDS culture, see Colleen McDannell, "Mormon Garments: Sacred Clothing and the Body," in *Material Christianity: Religion and Popular Culture in America* (New Haven, Conn.: Yale University Press, 1995), 198–221. For a general discussion of the Mormon temple ritual, see Margaret Toscano, "Rending the Veil" and "The Mormon Endowment," in Toscano and Paul Toscano, *Strangers in Paradox: Explorations in Mormon Theology* (Salt Lake City, Utah: Signature Books, 1990), 265–291.

3. Brigham Young, *Journal of Discourses* 17 (1966): 119; reprint of 1855 ed.

4. Two important books that document Mormon nineteenth-century women's history and status are: Claudia L. Bushman, ed., *Mormon Sisters: Women in Early Utah*, new ed. (Logan: Utah State University Press, 1997); Carol Cornwall Madsen, ed., *Battle for the Ballot: Essays on Women Suffrage in Utah* (Logan: Utah State University Press, 1997).

5. Elouise Bell, "The Implications of Feminism for Brigham Young University," *Brigham Young University Studies* 16 (Summer 1976).

6. Claudia L. Bushman, ed., *Mormon Sisters: Women in Early Utah* (Salt Lake City, Utah: Olympus, 1976).

7. *Women's Exponent* 7, no. 3 (July 1, 1878): 18; Scott H. Faulring, ed., *An American Prophet's Record: The Diaries and Journals of Joseph Smith* (Salt Lake City, Utah: Signature Books, 1987), 244; Andrew F. Ehat and Lyndon W. Cook, eds., *The Words of Joseph Smith* (Provo, Utah: Religious Studies Center, Brigham Young University, 1980), 110.

8. Toscano and Paul Toscano, *Strangers in Paradox*. I had three reasons for writing my feminist theology with my husband: (1) one of my purposes was to create a theology of equality where men's and women's voices and perspectives are balanced; (2) I did not want women's issues to be seen as tangential, something apart from and therefore subordinate to general theological issues; and (3) I probably would not have gotten my work published at this time without my husband's influence. This last reason is a commentary on the subtle sexism found in the Mormon intellectual and scholarly community, which has always been better in theory than in practice on gender equality.

9. The three main journals receptive to such feminist work have been: *Dialogue: A Journal of Mormon Thought, Mormon Women's Forum; An LDS Feminist Quarterly;* and *Sunstone*.

10. There is some question as to whether the doctrine of a Mormon Mother God originates with Joseph Smith or Eliza R. Snow. For a discussion of the evidence, see Linda P. Wilcox, "The Mormon Concept of a Mother in Heaven," in *Women and Authority: Re-emerging Mormon Feminism*, ed. Maxine Hanks (Salt Lake City, Utah: Signature Books, 1992), 4–6.

11. This hymn, entitled "O My Father" in the current LDS hymnal, was originally called "Invocation, or the Eternal Father and Mother." While this is still an official church hymn (and therefore canonical on a certain level) and also extremely popular among church members, there is a growing tendency among members to feel hesitant to talk about their "Heavenly Mother." This is most likely due to the fact that feminists like me have been censored for emphasizing her importance. In a 2002 Sunstone Symposium paper (in my possession), Doe Daughtrey suggests that the current LDS desire to be considered part of mainstream American Christianity may be another reason for eliminating discourse about a female god. The fear is that a doctrine of a Heavenly Mother smacks too much of polytheism, which has been a common attack against the LDS Church from Evangelical Christians.

12. Margaret Toscano, "If I Hate My Mother, Can I Love the Heavenly Mother? Personal Identity, Parental Relationships, and Perceptions of God," *Dialogue* 31, no. 4 (Winter 1998): 31–51. Currently I am working on representation and desire in official images of women in LDS publications.

13. My essay "Put on Your Strength O Daughters of Zion: Claiming Priesthood and Knowing the Mother" in *Women and Authority* is an attempt to bring such theories to bear in exploring women's priesthood and female divinity.

14. I am deeply indebted to the following women for their love, sense of humor intelligence, and stimulating conversation and for their willingness to listen to my ideas and respond to my papers in their initial stages: Lynne Whitesides, Julie Nichols, J. R. Card, Kathy Ray, Deborah Hunt, Alda Jones, Joyce Cox, Bonnie Alvord Merrill, Ellen Toscano, Janice Allred, Barbara Haugsoen, Vicki Voros, Vickie Stewart Eastman, Ann Wilde, Deborah Rossiter, Ginger, Sue Hidley, Marti Jones, Martha Pierce, Lynette Catherall, and Muffy Milner.

15. There has never been official membership in the Mormon Women's Forum, which is a registered nonprofit organization. Anyone could come to meetings or subscribe to the publication. We eventually had a mailing list of about 2,000 interested people, mostly in the United States and mostly women. The members of the organizing and editorial board changed over time, with as many as twenty and as little as two at one low period. The internal conflict seemed to come from four factors: (1) It was very difficult to create a structure with shared but organized power. At first we had no offices or leadership positions to avoid hierarchy. But as more women worked on the board, some naturally took charge so we could get things done. And then they were accused of being power hungry, which was both true and untrue. (2) Because the group tried to be both a support group and an activist group, personal issues often got in the way of business. (3) Since some women were more in the spotlight and others did more grunt work, there was some resentment about various roles. (4) The fact that the forum became a scapegoat for all the church's fears about women's power meant that the women in the group often felt personally attacked, which made it difficult to avoid paranoia and turning against each other.

16. Lynne, Lavina, and Maxine were part of a group of six intellectuals and femi-
    nists all brought to trial during September of 1993 and thus called "the Sep-
    tember Six" in the widespread and international news coverage of these events.
    (The other three were the historian D. Michael Quinn, biblical scholar Avra-
    ham Gileadi, and social critic and attorney Paul Toscano—my husband.)
    Lynne was actually disfellowshipped, which is a somewhat lesser punishment
    than excommunication, although it has had the same effect in her case. Janice
    Allred, who happens to be my sister, was excommunicated in 1995 for refusing
    to discontinue publishing and speaking about the Heavenly Mother (see her
    God the Mother and Other Essays, published in 1997 by Signature Books). Janice
    is currently the president of the Mormon Women's Forum, and Lynne was the
    president of the forum at the time of her church court. Lavina, an editor and
    historian, was excommunicated for her ongoing documentation and publish-
    ing of cases of ecclesiastical abuse (in *Mormon Case Reports*). Maxine edited the
    important collection of feminist essays, *Women and Authority: Re-emerging
    Mormon Feminism.*

17. Paul's speeches on these subjects were written over a fifteen-year period (from
    1979 to 1994) and published in *The Sanctity of Dissent* (Salt Lake City, Utah:
    Signature Books, 1994).

18. All "worthy" male members of the LDS Church receive the priesthood at the
    age of twelve. Although the Mormon priesthood is, in general, a lay priest-
    hood without special training or monetary compensation, all leaders on the
    general level in Salt Lake City who work for the church full time are given
    salaries. The LDS Church is headed by a three-man First Presidency, with a
    president/prophet and his two counselors. Next comes the Quorum of the
    Twelve Apostles, the body out of which is drawn the next president on the
    basis of seniority when the old president dies. The next level of this complex
    hierarchy is several Quorums of Seventies who are in charge of managing the
    general regions of the church. The local areas are divided into stakes (about
    ten to twelve congregations), governed by stake presidents and their high
    council. Each local congregation is headed by a bishop and his two counselors.
    Since all decisions for the church on any level are made by male priesthood
    leaders, it is easy to see why feminists are concerned about priesthood and
    women's lack of a voice or a vote.

19. Church tribunals, which used to be called "church courts," are now called
    "disciplinary councils." Some have argued that this change of name is the
    church's way of moving away from the idea that these "courts" are under the
    obligation to act according to American ideas of civil justice.

20. Officially an excommunicant can attend meetings, but he or she is not allowed
    to speak or comment or participate in any activities or rituals.

ELEVEN

Riffat Hassan

1976 Professor of Religion, University of Louisville
1995 Author, *Women's Rights and Islam*
1999 Founder, International Network for the Rights of Female Victims of Violence in Pakistan

MY LIFE JOURNEY BEGAN IN LAHORE. PEOPLE FROM LAHORE OFTEN say with love and pride, "Lahore is Lahore," meaning thereby that the city is matchless and that there is no place like it in the world. The place where one is born and spends one's childhood always has a special place in one's heart and one's memories, and for me, also, "Lahore is Lahore," the place I always return to in my dreams.

Lahore is an old "Mughal" city with the famed Shalimar Gardens and many celebrated monuments made of red sandstone with marble ornamentation. Lahore was once a walled city surrounded by a moat. Now the thirty-foot brick wall and the moat have been replaced, except in the north, by a garden. A circular road around the rampart gives access to the Old City by thirteen gates. Some relics of the past remain but few except visitors have much interest in them. For all their profession of love for their city, the people of Lahore have made few visible efforts to maintain the city's historic and cultural heritage, and over the decades the Old City has decayed in much the same way as many old city centers in this country have.

The house where I was born—68 Temple Road—was not situated in the Old City but in a historic neighborhood with a well-known "temple." I was the fifth child and third daughter of Syed Feroze Hassan, my father, and Daisy Dilara, my mother, both of whom came from Lahore's "oldest" families. My father's family had a long tradition of service to the government (and was, therefore, regarded as highly respectable), and my mother's family had a long history of commitment to the creative arts (and was, therefore, regarded as rather eccentric).

The foundations of the house in which I was born were weakened by earthquakes, and so, in the 1960s, when I was studying in England, my father had the old house demolished and a new one built in its place. But it is the old house—the house in which I had spent the first seventeen years of my life—that I remember whenever I think of my early years. The old house stood facing a *galee* (narrow street) that culminated in our *kothee* (bungalow). On both sides of the galee were houses (each called a *makaan*) lined up right next to each other with no empty spaces between them and no front or back-yard (although they had inner courtyards).

All societies have their own sets of prejudices and discriminations. The cult of elitism developed by educated Muslims of the Indian-Pakistan subcontinent—largely under British influence—required the erection of serious psychological barriers not only between people who lived in cities and those who lived in villages, but also between those who lived in kothees and those who lived in makaans. The distinction between the kothee dwellers and the makaan dwellers has never been one of pure economics but of birth and "culture."

That in many ways my siblings and I were privileged children is evident. We were born into an upper-class *Saiyyad* family. Saiyyads, who are descendants of the Prophet Muhammad, are considered the highest "caste" of Muslims even though Islam is supposed to have done away with the caste system. We lived in a spacious kothee, had a fancy automobile and a household full of servants, and were educated at the best English-language schools established by the British.

But though generally children who lived in kothees did not play with children who lived in makaans, this rule did not apply to us. This was largely due to the fact that my father—universally referred to as *Shah Sahib* or *Shahji* (titles of respect given to a Saiyyad)—though a bureaucrat trained in the tradition of British civil service, was regarded as the patriarch of the neighborhood, and his house was always an "open" house.

With so many obvious advantages, why was my early life so full of shadows? The major reason for my troubled childhood was undoubtedly the deep differences and conflict between my parents. Not only did they have diametrically opposing philosophies of life but also radical incompatibility of temperament and character. In many ways my father was traditional and conventional and my mother a nonconformist to tradition and convention.

Through most of my life I hated my father's traditionalism, because I understood it almost exclusively in terms of his belief in sex roles and his conviction that it was best for girls to be married at age sixteen to someone who had been picked out for them by the parents. It took me a long time to see that in some ways my father's traditionalism had been pure gold. He truly believed in taking care of people in need, relatives and strangers alike. Kind and compassionate, he took pleasure in solving other people's problems, whether they were personal, professional, or social. Anybody could call on him at any hour, and he would receive the caller with courtesy and grace.

What made my mother very unusual in a traditional society, and in my father's house, was her rejection of the hallowed cult of women's inferiority and submissiveness to men. Pre-Islamic Arabs had buried their daughters alive because they had regarded daughters not only as economic liabilities but also as potential hazards to the honor of the men in the tribe. Islam notwithstanding, the attitude of Muslims toward daughters has remained very similar to that of their nomadic forebears. Against this, my mother, who was a gifted poet with a brilliant mind, believed strongly in women's autonomy and independence.

Long before I began to understand the complexities and ambiguities of the Muslim value system, I knew that my mother would not win in any popularity contest vis-à-vis my father. She had a protected place in society because she was the daughter of the outstanding and creative artist-poet, playwright, and scholar, Hakim Ahmad Shuja'—who had also been a highly regarded educator and bureaucrat—and was my father's wife, but in her own person she was viewed as a dangerous deviant. The fact that she was fiercely independent in some ways and believed—like Nietzsche—in the will to power, which can make people ruthless, did not help to improve her image in many eyes. However, to me, all through my childhood, my mother was a savior figure who protected me from being sacrificed on the altar of blind conventionalism. And my father, who was admired and loved by so many, seemed to me through most of my early life to be a figure of dread, representing customary morality in a society that demanded that female children be discriminated against from the moment of birth.

Physical and verbal violence did not characterize the relationship between my parents, but there was no disguising the fact that they had deep-seated resentments against one another that manifested themselves in all kinds of destructive ways. As a child I often wondered why they continued to live together. Now I understand the reasons that made it imperative for them to live under one roof—they both came from "old" families to whom divorce was anathema, and they had nine children to raise. But the one roof under which we all lived could not be called a "home," if one defines this term as a place of love, warmth, and security. Our home was a rough sea where tempests raged incessantly. I could deal with the unremitting hostility that pervaded the atmosphere only by becoming a recluse.

I believe that it was because I withdrew from an outer to an inner reality that I was able to survive the seemingly unending crises and calamities to which I was exposed. A hypersensitive, painfully shy, and profoundly lonely child, I hated the ugliness that surrounded me and retreated to a world made up of a child's prayers, dreams, and wishful thinking. In this world I found three things that have sustained me through the heartbreaks and hardships of my life: an unwavering belief in a just and loving God, the art of writing poetry, and a deep love of books. Unable to relate at a deep personal level to either of my parents—such dialogue, I see now, is virtually impossible in Muslim culture, in which human beings relate to each other mainly in terms of their "function" or roles and not in terms of who they are as persons—I learned to talk to my Creator and Preserver, who at all times seemed very close. I often asked God to reveal to me the purpose of my life and to help me fulfill this purpose. Perhaps this was a strange prayer for a child. But I believed then, as I believe now, that God had put me on earth for a reason and that there was something that God wanted me to do.

Alone in my inner world I discovered that, like my mother and grandfather, I could write poetry almost effortlessly. This gave me great happiness and hope. I felt as if this were a gift from God given to me so that I could create a world free of shadows, of hate, bitterness, and pain. Writing was my chief mode of communication during my childhood, and I wrote much. By the time I was seventeen years old, two volumes of my poems, short stories, and articles had been published.

Most of my childhood I spent alone, writing and reading. I was a star pupil in my class from the beginning to the end of my scholastic career and won many honors and awards. But as a child what I craved was not success but love and peace around me and within me. I was a superachiever almost against my will. Toward the end of my high school career I became resentful of my own success, which my family members hardly seemed to notice, let alone to celebrate. I thought that if I failed they might pay some attention to me. Had it not been for a teacher who cared for me, I might have acted out my bitter, rebellious feelings, but I did not, and in future years I was very grateful that I had not wrecked a record career. I learned very early in life that there is no necessary connection between success and happiness, but I have also come to know that though many bright women are afraid to succeed, lack of success is not likely to lead to an enhancement of happiness, and I could not have found what I craved through underachieving.

My struggle as an "activist feminist" began in the twelfth year of my life. Until then, for the most part, I had lived in an inner sanctuary. But before I had turned twelve, the reality of the external world suddenly seemed to close in on me, threatening to destroy my place of refuge. My second sister was married off at sixteen to a man with a lot of money and very little education. She had tried to resist the arranged marriage but ultimately had succumbed—as most girls do—to the manipulations by means of which vulnerable and wavering girls are blackmailed into acquiescence in the name of family "honor." Witnessing what happened to her, I experienced total panic. I realized with acute shock that I was the next in line. Four years later the same ritual would be reenacted, and this time I would be the sacrificial victim unless I found a way to fight my father's, and my society's, rigid conventionalism. At twelve I had not yet learned how to fight. I had not wanted to learn to fight. I simply wanted to be left alone in my dream world where I could write my poems and read my books . . . but I knew then, as I know now, that if one is born female in a patriarchal society in which girls are regarded as objects to be given and taken, one has no option but to fight. And so I learned to fight, and the fight continues to this day, though many battles have been won and lost. Battle-weary beyond words, I pray for the dawning of the day when women like myself will not have to spend their entire lifetime fighting for justice and freedom, but I also pray for strength to continue the fight until the last of my sisters has been freed from darkness and death into light and life.

My father, who had not seemed to like me much when I was a little girl hiding in my room, liked me even less when I appeared to become an impossible teenage rebel who disregarded his wishes. For instance, when I was twelve he wanted me to withdraw from the coeducational school where I studied and enroll in an all-girls' school. Thinking with the mind of a twelve-year-old, I believed that if I said yes to him once, I would always have to say yes to him. Therefore, I refused to comply with his desire and said that if I was forced to leave the school where I had studied for a number of years (and where my brothers still studied), I would not go to another school. My father did not force me to leave, but he upbraided my mother constantly for spoiling and misguiding me. From the time that I was twelve until I went abroad to England at age seventeen, my father never stopped being upset with me over the fact that I studied with boys. But he never reprimanded me directly—perhaps because, during most of that time, he and I were not even on speaking terms with one another.

I learned through those tense, silence-filled years how dreadful cold war is and how through the coldness of its silence it may inflict deeper injury than the angriest of words. Looking back, I am stricken with sorrow that the world in which we lived made it impossible for my father and me to talk to one another for so long. Perhaps if we could have communicated directly we could have resolved some of our differences, or even learned to build a personal relationship with one another; but in Muslim societies fathers and daughters seldom talk to one another as peers or persons until the daughters have left the father's household and become part of another household. I, who have been looking for a father all my life, never knew my own until the last year of his life when he had become so weak and ailing that he cried when his children came and cried when they left. Not until then did I know for sure that he cared about me and wanted to see me happy, regardless of how he had disapproved of me through my growing-up years. We had so little time to get to know each other, but I am grateful that I was reconciled to him before he died. Such reconciliation does not, and cannot, of course, make up for a lifetime of deprivation, but at least it makes it possible for me to weep for my father and for what we missed.

While being alienated from my father left a deep imprint on my life, my intense and strange relationship with my mother left an even deeper one. For much of my life my mother was the most important person in my life. Feeling as I did that I lived in an arena of gladiators, I regarded my mother as my sole protector after God, and depended on her for my emotional survival. Certainly my mother gave me the opportunity to become a "person." Perhaps my particular tragedy lay in the fact that my mother regarded me as her Derby-winning horse who would actualize all her dreams of glory. Perceiving me as the most single-minded of her children, my mother believed that I had what it took to do what she wanted to do in her life. Much of what I am today is due to my mother's schooling, but I could never become the Nietzschean superwoman she wanted me to be.

In my society there are many stories of how a mother's love is superior to all other kinds of love because it is "unconditional." As a child I wanted so much to believe this, but I could not since I heard my mother say repeatedly to me, "I do not love you, I love your qualities." Her words, which were meant to affirm my "qualities," made me feel very sad and lonely. I could not receive my mother's love simply because I was her child. I could receive her approval only if I proved myself worthy. As a child my mother's attitude toward me often made me very melancholy, but as an adolescent it made me very angry. Part of this anger, which stayed with me for a long time, was directed at myself because I could not break loose of my mother's control over me. Regardless of how strongly I wished to resist her emotional manipulation, when confronted by her immensely powerful personality I felt myself relapsing into a state of juvenile behavior in which I would begin to react to her instead of acting as an autonomous person. It took some devastating experiences finally to sever the chains that bound the little girl in me to my mother's power and to liberate me from the burden of living out her fantasies instead of being able to live my own life.

Free of the bondage, I sought to reestablish the bond. Though I could never "dialogue" with my mother, I remained bound to her in love and duty. I was with her at the time of her sudden death in 1991 and was able to spend some hours sitting by her as she lay, beautiful and serene, in her final repose. Gazing silently at the most extraordinary human being I had ever known, I told her all the things I did not have a chance to tell her when she was alive. That time together was exceedingly precious not only because I could pay homage to my mother for her indomitable spirit reflected in her steadfastness of purpose, courage, and refusal to give up in the face of insuperable odds, but also because I could wash away all the antagonisms that had existed between us with my tears. I believe that in the hour of death my mother listened to me and understood my silent words better than she ever did my spoken words, and this comforts me as I carry forward the legacy of women's struggle that she bequeathed to me.

At age seventeen, after standing first among the 24,000 students who took the intermediate examination in the Punjab, I was allowed to go to England for higher studies. I had expected my father to oppose the idea of my studying abroad, but he did not. One reason for his letting me go was to remove me from my mother's sphere of influence. But my academic success, which brought much "honor" to the family, could also have influenced his decision.

My seven years at St. Mary's College, University of Durham, England, were full of homesickness and hard studying. After three years I graduated with joint honors in English Literature and Philosophy, and then, at age twenty-four, I became a Doctor of Philosophy specializing in the philosophy of Allama Muhammad Iqbal, the spiritual founder of Pakistan, whose work I had loved and admired since childhood. However, when I returned home after finishing my studies abroad, I found that I was alienated from both my mother and father in fundamental ways.

It is not possible for me to narrate even a summary of what happened during the next phase of my life within the scope of this paper. All I can say is that during this time I experienced some of the most important events of my life—marriage, motherhood, and divorce; self-exile from my beloved homeland; and death, first of my father in 1970 and then of my two most dearly loved brothers in 1974. The imprint left on my heart, mind, and soul of these events was deeper than words can convey. What sustained me during the darkest and most difficult days of my life was my faith in God and my child, who has been God's greatest gift to me. I named my daughter Mehrunnisa Mujahida. *Mehr* refers to "love" and "the sun," and *Mehrunnisa* refers to one who is a symbol of love and sunshine among women. *Mujahida* refers to a woman who engages in *jihad* or struggle in the cause of God.

Certainly the most important relationship of my life has been with my daughter, who has been, from the moment of her birth, "the light of my eyes and the joy of my heart," as easterners say. I could not have withstood the ordeals of my life without her, even though raising her single-handedly in the face of multifaceted adversities has been a most difficult task. But when I look at her today I feel immeasurably comforted and strengthened. Exceptionally sensitive, she has a radiant personality yet is able to empathize deeply with those who suffer.

Experientially I have always known what it means to be a Muslim woman, but it was not until the fall of 1974 that I began my career as a "feminist" theologian in a rather strange way when, in the midst of a very difficult period of my life, I moved with my very young child to Stillwater, Oklahoma. I had a Ph.D. but very few survival skills when my search for a job that could support me and my child after the collapse of a marriage in which I had invested a lot brought me to a small university town in which I knew no one. Here I was asked to be the faculty advisor to the Muslim Students Association (MSA) chapter at Oklahoma State University (OSU), where I had been appointed a Visiting Assistant Professor in Religion and Humanities. The MSA was a North American association, which had chapters in many colleges and universities in the United States and Canada.

The membership of the MSA chapter at OSU consisted entirely of Arab men largely from Saudi Arabia, Kuwait, and the Gulf area. These men were so patriarchal in their mind-set that they did not allow women to become members of the association. However, there was a rule at OSU according to which every student chapter had to have a faculty advisor and that year I happened to be the only Muslim faculty member on campus. This is how I came to be the faculty advisor to this group of Arab men who made it clear to me from the outset that they were not too thrilled at the prospect of working with a woman.

The MSA chapter at OSU had a tradition of having an annual seminar in the fall of each year. It was customary for the faculty advisor to make one of the introductory presentations on the theme of the seminar. However, I was asked by the organizers of the MSA seminar to speak on the subject of women in Islam. I knew that this was not the topic of that year's seminar. I also felt that I had been asked to speak on this subject because in the opinion of the MSA organizers, I was not competent to talk on any other subject pertaining to Islam, even though I taught Islamic studies. I resented what the assigning of a subject meant. Furthermore, I was not much interested in the subject of women in Islam at that time.

Despite my reservations I accepted the invitation for two reasons.

1. I knew that being asked to address an all-male, largely Arab Muslim group that excluded women even from being a part of the audience (though many of the male Arabs had wives who helped them in organizing the event) and who thought that hearing the voice of a woman unrelated to them was *haram* (forbidden) was itself a breakthrough.

2. I was so tired of hearing Muslim men pontificate on the position, status, or role of women in Islam, while it was totally inconceivable any woman could presume to talk about the position, status, or role of men in Islam.

After accepting the invitation, I began to think about what I was going to talk about. I knew that the MSA organizers wanted me to focus on the traditional roles of Muslim women as "good" wives and mothers—a subject on which hundreds of books, brochures, and articles have been written. I thought that it was time to look at the subject of women in Islam from a different—a nonpatriarchal—perspective. I had read the Qur'an many times and used it as a textbook in the courses I teach on Islam, but until then I had not done a systematic study of the Qur'anic passages relating to women. I decided to undertake this study as a preparation for my presentation. At that time I had no idea that this study would change the course of my life.

At what time my "academic" study of women in Islam became simultaneously an Odyssean venture in self-understanding I do not know. Perhaps it was when I realized the impact on my own life of the so-called Islamic ideas and attitudes toward girls and women. Soon after I began my research I became aware of the glaring discrepancy between normative Islam and Muslim practice. But "enlightenment" does not always lead to "endless bliss." The more I saw that justice and compassion formed the core of Qur'anic teachings regarding women, the more anguished and angry I felt seeing the injustices and inhumanity to which a large number of Muslim women are subjected in actual life. I began to feel strongly that it was my duty—as a part of the microscopic minority of educated Muslim women—to do as much consciousness raising regarding the situation of Muslim women as I could. The journey that began in Stillwater, a small town that lived up to its name, has been an arduous one. It has taken me far and wide in pursuit of my quest. When I remember the stormy seas and rocky roads I have traversed, it seems like the journey has been a long one. But when I think of my sisters who, despite being the largest "minority" in the world—more than half of the 1.3 billion-strong Muslims *ummah* (community)—remain for the most part nameless, faceless, and voiceless, I know that there is no end to the journey in sight. In 1974 when this journey began, I had no idea where it was going to take me or how drastically the world of Islam would change in the next ten years.

Between 1974 and 1983 the major focus of my research was on interpreting the Qur'anic passages relating to women from a nonpatriarchal perspective. In 1979, while I participated in an ongoing "trialogue" of Jewish, Christian, and Muslim scholars (under the sponsorship of the Kennedy Institute of Ethics in Washington, DC) who were exploring women-related issues in the three "Abrahamic" faith-traditions, I wrote a monograph entitled *Women in the Qur'an*. In this study I did a systematic analysis of those passages of the Qur'an that related to women in various contexts—for example, female infanticide, attitudes toward girl children, birth control and abortion, the creation of woman and the story of the "Fall," marriage and divorce, polygamy, motherhood, segregation and "veiling" of women, women's economic rights, women and inheritance, women as witnesses to contracts, and women's "reward" in the afterlife. In particular, I focused attention on those passages that were regarded as definitive in the context of woman-man relationships and on which the alleged superiority of men to women largely rested. On the basis of my research I became convinced that though several Qur'anic texts had often been used to legitimize discrimination toward women, an unbiased reading of the Qur'an clearly affirmed the equality of men and women. In fact, recognizing the fact that women have traditionally been victimized and oppressed in various ways, the Qur'an puts a central emphasis on safeguarding their rights.

Between 1974 and 1983 I presented my research findings at various conferences and meetings, underscoring the need to critique the negative ideas and attitudes toward girls and women widely prevalent in Muslim culture in the light of normative Islamic teachings embodied in the Qur'an and the life of the Prophet of Islam. During the same time, however, the gap between theory and practice appeared to widen with the onset of "Islamization"—a process whereby the governments of predominantly Muslim countries, including Pakistan, began to impose so-called Islamic laws on their already largely Muslim populations.

In order to understand the powerful impetus to "Islamize" Muslim societies and why "Islamization" has focused so heavily on women and the imposition of so-called Islamic punishments, in my judgment it is important to know that of all the challenges confronting the Muslim world, perhaps the greatest is that of modernity. Muslims, in general, tend to think of "modernity" in two ways: (a) as "modernization," which is equated with science, technology, and material progress; and (b) as "westernization," which is associated with promiscuity and all kinds of social problems ranging from the breakup of marriages to the falling apart of communities. While "modernization" is considered highly desirable, "westernization" is considered equally *un*desirable. Generally speaking, an emancipated Muslim woman is seen by many Muslims as a symbol not of "modernization" but of "westernization." This is so because she appears to be in violation of what traditional societies consider to be a necessary barrier between "private space" (i.e., the home) where women belong and "public space" (i.e., the rest of the world), which belongs to men. The presence of women in men's space is considered to be highly dangerous for—as a popular *hadith* (the sayings attributed to the Prophet Muhammad) states—whenever a man and a woman are alone, "ash-Shaitan" (the Satan) is bound to be there. In today's Muslim world, due to the pressure of political and socioeconomic realities, a significant number of women may be seen in "public space." Caretakers of Muslim traditionalism feel gravely threatened by this phenomenon, which they consider to be an onslaught of "westernization" under the guise of "modernization." They believe that it is necessary to put women back in their "space" (which also designates their "place" of subservience and subordination to men) if "the integrity of the Islamic way of life" is to be preserved.

Though I have lived in the United States since 1972, I have maintained close ties with Pakistan and have frequently visited Lahore, my city of origin, during the summer break from my university teaching obligations. In 1983–1984, however, I got the opportunity to spend almost two years in Pakistan. I had a sabbatical leave of absence and research fellowships from the National Endowment for the Humanities (NEH) and the American Associa-

tion of University Women (AAUW) to do research on the Qur'anic texts pertaining to the relationship between Muslims and the *Ahl al-Kitab* (Jews and
Christians). This period was one in which many women in Pakistan had been
jolted out of their dogmatic slumber (in Kantian terms) by the enactment,
under the directives of the military ruler General Muhammad Zia ul Haq, of
laws such as the Hadud Ordinance (1979), according to which women's testimony was declared to be inadmissible in "Hadd" crimes, which included rape.
In 1983 two other antiwomen laws—the Law of Evidence and the Law of
Qisas and Diyat, or "blood money" (which were promulgated subsequently)—
were being debated, accompanied by increased violence toward women and a
deluge of antiwomen literature, which swept across the country.

Upon my arrival at Lahore in the spring of 1983, I could see that powerful forces—including those of military authoritarianism and religious
conservatism—were determined to reduce the status of women systematically—
virtually mathematically—to one-half or less than that of men. Reflecting
on the scene I witnessed with increasing anxiety and alarm, I asked myself
how it was possible for laws that were archaic, unjust and un-Islamic to be
implemented in a society that professed a passionate commitment to both
modernity and Islam. The answer to my question was so obvious that I was
startled that it had not struck me before. Pakistani society (or any other
Muslim society, for that matter) could enact or accept laws that specified
that women were less than men because in patriarchal Muslim culture it is
regarded as a self-evident truth by almost all men and women that women
are inferior to men. In this culture anyone who argues in favor of women's
equality with men is likely to be confronted, immediately and with force,
by a mass of what is described as "irrefutable evidence" taken from the
Qur'an, hadith, and Sunnah to "prove" that men are "above" women.
Among the arguments cited in this context, the following are perhaps the
most popular: according to the Qur'an, man are *qawwamun* (generally
translated as "rulers" or "managers") in relation to women; a man's share
in inheritance is twice that of a woman; the witness of one man is equal to
that of two women; according to the Prophet, women are deficient both in
prayer (due to menstruation) and in intellect (due to a woman's witness
counting for less than a man's).

Since in 1983–1984 I was (in all probability) the only Muslim woman in the
country who had been engaged in a systematic study of women's issues from a
nonpatriarchal theological perspective, I was approached numerous times by

women leaders (including the members of the Pakistan Commission on the Status of Women, before whom I gave my testimony in May 1984) to state what my research findings were and if they could be used to improve the situation of women in Pakistani society. I was urged by a number of women activists who were mobilizing and leading women's protests in a country under martial law to help them refute the arguments, which were being used against them, on a case-by-case or point-by-point basis. I was eager to help. I did not think that the best strategy for stemming the tide of antiwomen legislation was simply to respond to each argument that was being used to deprive women of their human—as well as Islamic—rights. I knew on the basis of my research that behind and below these arguments were others, and no sooner would one line of attack be eliminated than another would be set up in its place. What had to be done, first and foremost, in my opinion, was to examine the theological ground in which all the antiwomen arguments were rooted to see if, indeed, a case could be made for asserting that from the point of view of normative Islam, men and women were *essentially* equal, despite biological and other differences.

As a result of further study and deliberation I came to perceive that in the Islamic, as well as in the Jewish and Christian, tradition, there are three theological assumptions on which the superstructure of men's alleged superiority to women has been erected. These three assumptions are:

1. God's primary creation is man, not woman, since woman is believed to have been created from man's rib, hence is derivative and secondary ontologically.
2. Woman, not man, was the primary agent of what is generally referred to as "man's Fall," or man's expulsion from the Garden of Eden; hence "all daughters of Eve" are to be regarded with hatred, suspicion, and contempt.
3. Woman was created not only *from* man but also *for* man, which makes her existence merely instrumental and not fundamental.

The three theological questions to which the above assumptions may appropriately be regarded as answers are:

1. How was woman created?
2. Was woman responsible for the "Fall" of man?
3. Why was woman created?

The research I have done on these questions since 1984 has been incorporated in a number of published and unpublished writings. The draft of a book entitled *Equal Before Allah: The Issue of Woman-Man Creation in the Islamic Tradition*, which I began in Pakistan in 1984, was revised during the year I spent as a research associate in the Women's Studies in Religion Program at Harvard Divinity School (1986–1987). Some parts of this book have been published in the form of articles. In many of my writings I have presented compelling evidence to show that the Qur'anic text does not support the above-mentioned foundational theological assumptions, which—in fact—are contrary to the teachings of normative Islam.

While I have continued to pursue my theological research on issues relating to women in Islam, I have been increasingly engaged, since 1983, in sharing my research findings with diverse groups of Muslim women and youths in many countries. Believing that knowledge is power, I have endeavored, through extensive travel and participation in a large number of educational meetings, to disseminate, particularly among Muslim girls and women, the positive outcome of my study of the sources of normative Islam.

In the decade of the 1990s, when women's rights were the major focus of international discourse on human rights, I had the opportunity to be a major spokesperson for "liberal" or "progressive" Islam at the international conferences sponsored by the United Nations at Cairo (1994), Copenhagen (1995), Beijing (1995), and Istanbul (1996). Presenting the findings of my research over two decades, I urged Muslim women to claim the rights granted to them by God. Paramount among these rights is the right to acquire knowledge, which is so strongly emphasized by the Qur'an.

The United Nations Conference on Population and Development (ICPD) held in Cairo, Egypt, in September 1994 was an extremely important landmark in raising global consciousness with regard to some of the most intimate and intricate issues pertaining to women's lives as well as human sexuality and relationships that have ever been discussed at an international forum. One of the fundamental issues underlying the deliberations of the Cairo conference was that of the "ownership" of a woman's body. Women's identification with body rather than with mind and spirit is a common characteristic of the dualistic thinking that pervades many religious, cultural, and philosophical traditions. Ironically, however, though women have traditionally been identified with body, they have not been seen as "owners" of their bodies, and the issue of who controls women's bodies—men, the state, the church, the community, or women—has never been decided in favor of women in patriarchal cultures. The great breakthrough of the Cairo conference was the fact that Muslim women forcefully challenged the traditional viewpoint not only with regard to women's identification with body, but also with regard to the assumption that women are not "owners" of their bodies.

After the Cairo conference at which I had made nine presentations, I was given a grant by the Ford Foundation office in Cairo to do a series of workshops in the Middle East on issues that Muslim women needed to focus on at the United Nations Fourth World Conference, which was to be held at Beijing, China, in September 1995. The resource papers that I wrote for these workshops (held in Cairo, Jordan, Tunisia and Pakistan) were later compiled into a monograph entitled *Women's Rights and Islam: From the I.C.P.D. to Beijing*.[1]

Having successfully challenged age-old definitions of womanhood imposed on them by patriarchal cultures, women were confronted by a new challenge as they journeyed from Cairo to Beijing. This challenge was to shift from the reactive mind-set of those who are subjected to systematic discrimination and made to feel powerless to the proactive mind-set of those who have a strong sense of personal identity, autonomy, and efficacy as makers of their own lives. I hoped, as I went to China with thousands of others, that women in general, and Muslim women in particular, would be able to build on the hard-won gains of the ICPD and begin to speak of themselves as full and autonomous human beings who have not only a body but also a mind and a spirit.

Unfortunately, however, what happened at Beijing was a reversal, almost a betrayal, of the promise that had been seen and felt at Cairo. Instead of engaging in a critical dialogue on the existential situation of the majority of Muslim women in the world (who generally share three characteristics—they are poor, illiterate, and live in a village), the spokespersons of the most visible Muslim groups at the nongovernmental forum in China denied that these women had any serious problems that needed to be addressed. Instead of confronting the indisputable fact that Muslim culture, like other patriarchal cultures, is pervaded by antiwomen biases, which have a negative impact on every aspect of a woman's life, these spokespersons not only defended, but glorified, whatever goes under the name of Islam in traditional Muslim societies. As the conference in China drew to a close, it seemed that the hope of a paradigm shift from reactive to proactive thinking that had come to birth at Cairo was likely—like female children in pre-Islamic Arabia—to be buried alive.

For "liberal" Muslims there were important lessons to be learned from the experiences at Cairo and Beijing. Paramount among them was the need to understand the role of religion and culture in Muslim societies and communities and the discrepancy between the norms or ideals of Islam's primary sources and Muslim practice with regard to women and women-related issues. A deep analysis of Muslim history, particularly of modern times, and the political, economic, social, and psychological factors that have had a formative influence on Muslim consciousness was also required.

That "liberal" Muslims in general had not done the hard work required to make a compelling case in support of a "liberal" or "progressive" approach to understanding Islam was apparent at Beijing. Perhaps like many other "liberals" they had assumed that what they had to say was inherently so "reasonable" or "rational" that it could be regarded as self-evident, requiring no corroborative data. But what the conferences at Cairo and Beijing have demonstrated is that the greatest impact is made by those who have done their homework best.

So much that was so significant and so complex happened at the ICPD and the Fourth UN Conference on Women that historians and other analysts will reflect on, and write about, the events in these landmark conferences for a long time. From these recollections and reflections will come a better understanding of what happened at Cairo and Beijing, which, in turn, will provide guidance for the future. But while the work of critical inquiry and analysis goes on, the historic process of which these conferences were a part also continues. The challenge that confronts us today, both individually and collectively, is how to participate, as creatively and constructively as possible, in the shaping of this process.

My personal response to the challenge was to develop programs on Muslim women's empowerment and self-actualization that could be implemented in specific Muslim societies or communities. The first of these programs that focused on Pakistan and selected areas of India was funded by the United Nations Population Fund (January 1997–February 1998). In the summer of 1998, the Women and Development Division of the Foreign Ministry of the Government of the Netherlands began the implementation of a program that focused on the empowerment of Muslim women in the Netherlands as well as in six other participating Asian and African countries. I was the principal researcher for this program (1998–2000) and was involved in its teaching and training activities as well as in developing a curriculum on Muslim ethics that could be used both in educational institutions as well as in community-based workshops. In the summer of 1999 I also conducted a short project funded by the Center for Population and Development Activities in Washington, D.C., which focused on the life stories of exceptional Muslim girls and women in the city of Lucknow in Uttar Pradesh, India.

In January 1999 the BBC aired, in England, a documentary entitled "Murder in Purdah" about so-called honor killings of girls and women in Pakistan. On February 15 and 16, 1999, ABC's *Nightline* presented the same documentary with the title "A Matter of Honor," adding two commentators who answered questions asked by Forrest Sawyer, the presenter of the program. I was one of the commentators, and responded to the question about why men were killing their wives, sisters, and daughters in the name of "honor" by stating that such crimes had nothing to do with the teachings of Islam but had to be seen in the context of patriarchal culture. In this male-centered, male-dominated culture, men's "honor" was regarded as irreplaceable while women's lives were held to be of little worth. To many persons in this culture, men had proprietary rights over women, who were regarded as possessions.

While I expressed my concern about the erosion of women's rights in Pakistan, particularly in the wake of "Islamization" (and "Talibanization"), I did not agree with the presenter's view that the situation was utterly bleak and hopeless. I said that in my travels across the Muslim world I had seen a paradigm-shift taking place, particularly at the grassroots level among Muslim women and youths toward a different understanding of Islam. This new understanding of Islam was centered on affirming human rights and women's rights. I concluded by saying that the changes I had seen in the last twenty-five years made me believe that a process of internal empowerment was under way and that my optimism about the future was not rooted in naive idealism.

Following the showing of the *Nightline* program, I received a large number of messages by e-mail, telephone, fax, and letters from a variety of women and men in the United States. Two important sentiments that were common to these messages were a strong sense of outrage that vulnerable girls and women were being subjected to so much brutality and violence in Pakistan and a keen desire to do something about this state of affairs. Responding to these messages, I took the initiative of setting up a network to be called the International Network for the Rights of Female Victims of Violence in Pakistan (INRFVVP). This network, which became incorporated as a tax-exempt organization in 1999, now has members in many countries. Even with very scarce financial resources it has been an effective voice in highlighting the issue of violence against girls and women in Pakistan and in other Muslim countries and communities. More information about the INR-FVVP can be obtained from its website (www.inrfvvp.org).

A new struggle has become the focal point of my life in the aftermath of September 11, when more attention has been focused on Islam and Muslims than perhaps at any other point in modern history. Much of this attention—particularly in the case of mainstream U.S. television channels—has been negative, not only with regard to those who committed the criminal acts, but also with regard to Islam and Muslims/Arabs at large.

The September 11 assaults on the United States have been condemned strongly by the global community, including a large number of Muslims from all walks of life, ranging from leaders of Muslim countries to ordinary people. However, the crisis was perceived—and described—from the outset in terms that polarized the world into two absolutely opposed camps. The worldview that became dominant in the discourse of both the American administration and media was symbolized by expressions such as "us versus them," "either you are with us or you are against us," and "good versus evil." The dualistic thinking that permeated this discourse seemed, at times, to be cosmic in magnitude. It appeared as if the so-called clash of civilizations between the West and the world of Islam posited by Samuel Huntington had indeed come to pass.[2]

However one interprets the fateful events of September 11, 2001, one thing is clear: the world changed forever on that day. There is now no going back to the situation that existed prior to that day. We cannot go back—we can only go forward. This poses a serious challenge both for (non-Muslim) westerners and for Muslims. How and on what basis are we going to create a new world order in the aftermath of what happened on September 11, 2001? Is it possible to "depolarize" the world and to build a bridge between the West and the world of Islam?

At a meeting of an organization called Women in Networking (WIN) held in Milan, Italy, a couple of weeks after September 11, I was asked to propose a plan of action for depolarizing the world and building bridges between conflicting parties. Some of the participants pledged their commitment to follow through on my suggestions. This collective endeavor has led to the birth of Women Engaging in Bridge-Building (WEBB), an international network of women—and men—that aims to set up centers in as many countries as it can. The first bridge that members of WEBB have undertaken to build is between Muslims and non-Muslims. In pursuance of this goal, WEBB is holding its premier conference, entitled "Islam and Diversity: Bridging the Gap," in Ottawa, Canada, in June 2003. It is a wonderful thing that this conference is being sponsored by many Canadian parliamentarians and other persons of vision who want to promote a culture of peace through knowledge and dialogue. More information about WEBB and its activities can be obtained from its website (www.webb-international.org).

My life's *jihad* goes on—from struggle to struggle to struggle. But I want to end this fragment by celebrating the spirit that keeps women living and striving in the face of endless trials and tribulations, dangers and death. This poem, which I wrote during a life-threatening crisis, epitomizes not only my personal journey but that of many of my sisters here and elsewhere.

I am a woman
with the eternal heart
of a woman
who, like Othello,
loved not wisely
but too well.

I am a woman
with the eternal heart
of a woman
living in a world
in which the rules
are made by men—
and where men can
break all the rules
and yet be gods
saviors and saints
martyrs and heroes
but where if women
break the rules
made by men
broken by men

they cannot live
without being shamed
slandered and abused
beaten and hurt
scourged and stoned
burned and buried
alive and damned.

I am a woman
with the eternal heart
of a woman
born to love
living in a world
in which when men
love—they are called
princes and knights
poets and mystics
or at the worst—perhaps—lunatics;
but when women love
then love becomes
a mortal sin
for which they must
give up their life—
for when a woman
is guilty of
a mortal sin
—the sin of loving—
then she must die
so that the jealous
god of love
may be at peace.

I am a woman
with the eternal heart
of a woman
living in a world
in which there are

a number of men
and also some women
who cannot love;
and since love is
what makes us human
and gives us life
these men and women
are callous and cold,
cruel and cowardly
though they wear
the masks of sages
and madonnas
and cherubs;
and they are always
ready to strike
my eternal heart
because I dare
to live and love.

I am a woman
with the eternal heart
of a woman
who has endured
so many births
and so many deaths
so that the seed
of life and love
may not be
destroyed by those
who in the name
of god of love
who does not love
want to create
a loveless world
a lifeless world
full of tombs
where one cannot hear

the sound of life—
the laughter of
a little child
warm from the womb
who wants to live
and wants to love
and to whom
an eternal—
hearted woman
is what god should be.

I am a woman
with the eternal heart
of a woman
the bearer of life
the nurturer of life
the protector of life
I can give life
because I am not
afraid of pain
for I know that love
is always pain
even joyful love
is ringed with pain
and no one can love
who cannot embrace
with heart and soul
the pain of living
the pain of loving.

I am a woman
with the eternal heart
of a woman
and I can suffer
again and again
the pain of loving
men and women

who do not love
who will tear
my heart and soul
to little shreds
and who will put
my life-carrying body
upon death's bed
in order to
placate a god
who says he is
the god of love
but who abhors
both life and love
and who demands
a sacrifice
—my sacrifice—
and says that I
must slaughtered be
just like an animal
helpless and trapped
whose blood is spilled
so that the sins
of those who kill
may be forgiven.

I am a woman
with the eternal heart
of a woman
and though I may be
tormented and abandoned
dishonored and disowned
scourged and flogged
stoned and burned
and buried alive
I will never
be a martyr
I will never

be a victim
I will never
be a loser
I will always
be a survivor
I will always
be a winner
I will always
be triumphant
for though I go
I will return
and though I die
I will live again
forever and forever
for I am a woman
with the eternal heart
of a woman
and since my heart
is made of love
and love is eternal
embodied in creation
leading to resurrection
though all else will burn
with the funeral pyre
in the flames of the fire
my eternal heart
will never to ashes turn
and like a phoenix I will rise again
and like a phoenix I will be reborn.

NOTES

1. Riffat Hassan, *Women's Rights and Islam: From the I.C.P.D. to Beijing* (Lahore: 1995).
2. Samuel P. Huntington, *The Clash of Civilizations* (Cambridge, Mass.: Harvard University, John M. Olin Institute for Strategic Studies, 1993).

TWELVE

Vicki Noble

1970 Awakened to feminism by reading Kate Millet's *Sexual Politics*

1976 Shamanic healing crisis leads to Motherpeace Tarot

1998 Develops Buddhist Dakini practice for women

PART I: DESCENT AND INITIATION

Religion was minimal in my Iowa upbringing. My family's weekly outings to attend the local Presbyterian church were mainly linked, in my mind, with me and my two younger sisters getting to wear our Sunday best outfits with little matching shoes and purses. Sunday school was a social event, a place where other kids hung out. Friends seemed to have more interesting religions, like my best girlfriend in fourth grade. I went with her to Catholic mass, where they dipped their fingers in holy water, chanted in Latin, genuflected, and knelt at the front of the church to receive a communion made of *real* red wine. A Jewish boyfriend in junior high school took me to visit his temple services, also more exotic than my own pallid Protestant experience.

In high school we moved to a small college town not far from the University of Iowa. Under that refreshing influence, I committed my first act of individual protest: I went across the street from the Presbyterian church of my parents to join the more liberal Methodist church on my own. I also had one good teacher in high school who encouraged my literary inclinations. I remember painstakingly making my way through every word every month of my subscription to *Harper's Magazine*—reading articles by such luminaries as Jean-Paul Sartre, for whom I was utterly unprepared, but fascinated anyway.

My academic aspirations were high, and I was accepted into the liberal arts college of my choice. Unfortunately my parents couldn't see the value of spending so much money for something as ephemeral as an education (for a girl!), and I was given my choice of colleges from among the state schools. As a freshman at the University of Iowa in the fall of 1965, I found myself speechless in honors seminars where upper-class students discussed highbrow ideas like the "death of God" under the tutelage of erudite international professors who spoke the language of the intellect. They had us read the entire Old Testament under the rubric of ancient literature. I pledged a sorority, which deactivated me at the end of my freshman year when I got pregnant (like four other members of my pledge class) and "had to" get married to a senior on the cheerleading squad who was in ROTC. We lived in married student housing (quanset huts) on campus, until he graduated and we were assigned to the Pease Air Force Base in Portsmouth, New Hampshire. At nineteen, I had my first baby in the teaching hospital in Iowa City under the direction of an enthusiastic male resident who called having my choice of anesthetic natural childbirth.

The marriage brought on my first real existential crisis, as I came to understand within the first year that I had made a horrible mistake in choosing someone who was supposed to be my partner for life, but whom I did not actually know or love. When I arrived at the SAC base, I was presented with a small hardbound booklet entitled "Mrs. Lieutenant," which purported to

teach me the values under which I would need to conduct myself as an officer's wife.[1] I experienced my first primitive awareness of being "karmically
trapped" by my own choices in life. There seemed to be no way out of my situation: I could leave my husband, but without any marketable skills and with
(by 1968) two small children, what would I do and where would I go? Back
home to my father's house seemed a terrible alternative, so I toughed it out,
promising myself that when a door opened for me, I would walk through it.

I entertained myself studying the Sunday *New York Times* every week and
reading all the best-sellers on its weekly list—the base library kept a standing
order for me and just sent the books over as they came in. I sewed intricate
little outfits for my small daughters and utilized the base's day care center
while I studied old English at the University of New Hampshire nearby. And
when my husband was sent to Vietnam in 1969, I went home to Iowa, where
I witnessed for the first time with a shock my father's alcoholism and my parents' hopeless marriage. I sought out my old friend, the Methodist minister,
for help and tried to intervene but without success.

I share all of this in order to try to establish a palpable sense of the intellectual flatness and emotional bewilderment that I was wrapped in at this
confusing moment just before my first taste of spiritual liberation. I want to
somehow conjure up what it was like to be so split in my consciousness during a time when the whole fabric of our society was splitting wide open. In
1969 at my parents' Iowa home, my mother and I watched Seymour Hersch
on the Dick Cavett morning show, as he unveiled the horrors of the Mi Lai
Massacre. While my mother insisted that "they couldn't have done that,
Vicki, and if they did, it must have been for a good reason," the revelation
haunted me and changed me forever.

At the Air Force Academy in Colorado Springs (our next plum assignment) in the early spring of 1971, I received Kate Millett's *Sexual Politics* from
the library.[2] Reading it was an epiphany. Everything I had ever felt or thought
seemed to rearrange itself within the framework of the brilliant intellectual
container she provided, and for the first time I truly knew myself—I had
found my own authority. Just having the book on my coffee table was an act of
rebellion, and I began to thrive. I tried briefly to get my husband to make a
"marriage contract," based on other writings by women in the feminist movement, and then giving up on that, I wrote a letter to the local newspaper asking if there were any "women's liberation" groups in Colorado Springs. When
some professor's wives from a local college answered my letter, I went to my

first consciousness-raising group. Within three months I had come out as a lesbian and filed for divorce, and within a year I was back in college on a full scholarship, where I would soon create the first interdisciplinary women's studies major at Colorado College.

There is one day I recall that most vividly sums up the tremendously liberating force of feminism in my life. It was the morning after Halloween, and I had stayed out all night at a women's liberation function where I had my first sexual experience with a woman. I was driving home at dawn to what I assumed would be a frightening showdown with my husband. Instead of feeling fear, however, I felt unusually expanded—what I now know to be an altered state—and what I noticed that morning as I drove was the sparkling, almost glittering clarity of the sunlight against the blue sky and the rays of light falling on beautiful Pike's Peak overlooking Colorado Springs. It was my first direct religious experience, and I knew I was free.

The five years I spent in Colorado Springs as a single mother and women's liberation activist were very juicy. My daughters went to a community school where feminist friends were the teachers, and my life was caught up in direct action and public speaking. When I visited a women's circle at UC Irvine in southern California where they were learning to look at their own bodies with speculums and cure their yeast infections with yogurt, I brought home a dozen plastic speculums and introduced the self-help concept to my consciousness-raising group. From then on we were a women's health organization. With a religious fervor I joined marches, wrote mission statements (even cowrote a women's self-health handbook called *Circle One*, widely used by feminist clinics around the country), and spoke on conference panels for the reproductive rights of women everywhere.[3] When in 1973 the Supreme Court made abortion legal, we opened our own feminist gynecological clinic in Colorado Springs that continued for ten years after I left. I got Lonnie Barbach to come from Berkeley and train us in "preorgasmic" counseling groups, which became my specialty. I had male and female lovers as I wished, sometimes at the same time, and it seemed that we had broken the mold in terms of old outworn patterns.

PART II: SHAMANISM AND THE GODDESS (1976)

The shadow inside all of this freedom was my health. I think of those times and see myself speaking on women's health panels with a cigarette hanging out of my mouth. My diet was mostly chocolate, and I almost never slept. Chronic tension headaches required me to ingest larger and more potent prescription pills over the years to subdue the pain, until by 1976 when I left Colorado Springs for Berkeley—with my partner Karen Vogel and my pre-pubescent daughters—I was terribly ill and couldn't figure out why. Once again my inner conflict built to a breaking point, and I not only threw my prescription drugs down the toilet, but all of western medicine as well. I have written elsewhere (*Shakti Woman: Feeling Our Fire, Healing Our World*) of my "shamanic healing crisis" and the healing that came spontaneously to me through dreams, visions, herbal medicine, nutritious food, and the practice of yoga, which has remained for me a lifelong path.[4] In the first psychic reading I ever had, a clairvoyant told me that when I got feminism, I thought it was the whole thing—but that in fact, I had barely cracked the door, which was now opening into dimensions I had never known possible.

I had direct experiences of reincarnation, I dreamed what would happen in advance of events, and once I even wrote a check out for groceries before the clerk had told me the total. I got the "heat that heals" in my hands and catalyzed spontaneous recoveries for myself, my family, and other people. One spectacular visionary experience plunged me into a sustained state of bliss while crystal clear images flashed on the wall—as if being projected onto a screen—of Amazons, Goddesses, griffins, and words that appeared first in a strange unrecognizable script and then dissolved into English so I could read them: "heal," "Helena," "hell no," and "heal all." I taught an original form, which I named "Lunar Yoga," to mostly women students in Berkeley for several years, while Karen and I developed and self-published the round feminist Motherpeace Tarot deck, which has now sold 200,000 copies, and I later wrote three accompanying texts that are still in print.[5] Motherpeace has a devotional following of women from around the world. We became part of the Goddess community in the Bay area, practicing our private devotion to the Mother Goddess and performing public rituals and ceremonies in women's spirituality. (As a legal minister in California, I also perform marriages, funerals, and so on.)

After Karen and I split up in 1981, I married Jonathan Tenney for eight years, an astrologer and the father of my seventeen-year-old son, Aaron Eagle, who has Down syndrome and is the subject of my 1994 book, *Down Is Up for Aaron Eagle*.[6] I ran a popular school for women in shamanistic healing in Oakland during the late 1980s, published a magazine called *SnakePower: A Journal of Contemporary Female Shamanism*, and in 1991 wrote my handbook for women healers called *Shakti Woman: Feeling Our Fire, Healing Our World (The New Female Shamanism)*. For almost a decade I traveled internationally, teaching and speaking to women about Motherpeace, healing, the Dark Goddess, and the shamanistic energies that I believe to be natural to our biology. I still lead groups of women on tours to ancient, sacred sites where we perform rituals and revision an ancient way of life that was peaceful and matristic.

Although we certainly would never have used the term ourselves, I am part of the contemporary group of independent feminist scholars defined by those in the academy as "essentialist," due to our belief in a particular value and way of life that emerges organically from being female. Instead of throwing out biology, we are taking it back. Instead of being defined by sex, we are reclaiming it. In my original research I show how this lunar, female-centered approach is typical of ancient worldwide shamanism, and my book, *The Double Goddess: Women Sharing Power*, frames this concept under the rubric of female sovereignty—including the governing of society.[7] I have taught as an adjunct professor in two master's degree programs in women's spirituality since their inception at California Institute for Integral Studies (CIIS) and New College in San Francisco.

PART III: BUDDHIST PRACTICE AND THE DHARMA (PRESENT)

When not teaching, writing books, or traveling, I have made my living for more than twenty years by seeing private clients for Motherpeace astrology, shamanistic healing, bodywork, and the study and practice of "tantric" sexuality. Since 1980 I have also been a practicing Tibetan Buddhist, using chanting, visualization, and other magical practices to transform my life and my health. I used Mayumi Oda's image of the Black Dakini on the front cover of my book *Shakti Woman*. For almost twenty years I was in and out of Buddhist institutions, unable to find a home (a *sangha*) due to the pervasive and largely unconscious male domination of most centers that were established in the West. Not only the male lamas have been biased against women, but the White men who, until recently, ran most of the Buddhist organizations intentionally barred the door to women being anything other than secret "consorts" or helping in the kitchen. Nowadays this trend seems happily to be reversing, as most centers are now run by women, and as younger Tibetan lamas open to the presence of equally gifted female practitioners and teachers. Biographies of famous yoginis have been translated into English, like that of Yeshe Tsogyel (the female founder of Tibetan Buddhism who hid the "mind treasures" for people like me and Karen to discover in later reincarnations, as we did with Motherpeace).

In 1997 I had what in shamanistic language is called a Big Dream. I dreamed that a volcano erupted on the top of my head leaving a dime-size hole, out of which a Tibetan *stupa* emerged made of wedding cake frosting. In Tibetan Buddhism such a protuberance from the top of one's head is called an *usnisa* and points to the state of enlightened wisdom. In the vivid and powerful dream, I was leaving a large building where I had been teaching my students—wishing that they would join me, but accepting that they were busy with their own agendas—in order to stand in line with my son Aaron Eagle, waiting to speak to a lama. I particularly noted how nice it was to be with Aaron, who lacks the self-conscious aggressiveness of ego and is therefore more spacious than most people. When I got to talk to the lama, he ignored me completely because of my being a woman. But I leaned over and pointed to my stupa, at which point he snapped into action. It seemed in the dream that certain protocols in Tibetan Buddhism would naturally overrule more limited personal prejudices.

Later in that same year, 1997, I was invited to travel in Russia to visit museums and speak with archaeologists who have been unearthing Amazon graves near the Volga River for the last fifty years. I noticed that many of the "priestesses" were buried with a bent knee, also typical of the Tibetan Buddhist icon of the *dakini*, or "sky-walking woman." Pursuing this very intuitive connection—which seemed a long shot at best—has filled the better part of my last five years of scholarly endeavor, while my public career went through a nasty crash-and-burn phase as a result of changing fashions in the culture. Just as the publishing industry was going very bland and my editor at Random House told me point blank to "take the Goddess and the kundalini" out of my work in order for her to sell it, I decided instead to leave Berkeley and act on my deeper longings to be more quiet and live in the country. In desperation, I pulled the plug on my active community involvement in the Bay area and moved to the mountains near Santa Cruz. There I do mostly private teaching and counseling, adapting Tibetan Buddhist dakini practices for the women students and clients. The dakinis are icons of untamed female freedom, and the mandala practice is a method for concretely transforming your life. The agenda is a feminist one—that of becoming the subject at the center of your life, instead of the object of someone else's reality.

When I got to my cabin in the woods, it was as though I was ship-wrecked and thrown up on some foreign shore. I had no money, and seri-ously needed healing. The fact that I couldn't sell a book or even get a magazine article published was very discouraging, and I had to be vigilant in order not to sink into debilitating depression and despair. I realized that if my Buddhist practices were any good at all, then they should be able to help me through such a dark transition period. I began to do my dakini practices in earnest, for the first time daily, and with intent. My forest cottage is heated by a woodstove and it gets below freezing, so I had to learn to chop wood and build a fire—all good training for a "witch in the woods," as my one of my students called me.

I take daily walks in the hills and do my practices. I have glorious unin-terrupted periods of quiet in which I am able to contemplate and experience direct connection with the forces of nature. In the midst of our current cul-tural focus on war, fear, and global mayhem, I am finding the peace and tranquility that I believe are necessary for any of us to change the ingrained patterns of aggression and hostility—in ourselves internally, as well as in the world outside us. I have two new books coming out next year (2003) from a small press in Vermont, Inner Traditions, and they seem to love my work just as it is (full of Goddess and kundalini!). Students from across the coun-try come and spend several days in my home on private tutorials; I give them a practice text in English, a formal transmission, and facilitate the creation of a collage of the dakini mandala that they take home to support their daily practice.

Salient to the 1997 dream I had is the fact that my magical house is one mile up the road from Pema Osel Ling, the well-known Vajrayana school of Tibetan Buddhism. I can hear the lamas blowing the Tibetan horns when they do ceremonies. Aaron Eagle and I have started going there to participate in retreats, where he attends what he calls "Buddha camp," and I learn com-plicated chanting and visualization practices to the Black Wrathful Dakini, Thröma, in the company of many Tibetan lamas (even a woman now and then) and serious Vajrayana practitioners with their bells and drums.

Recently I have made a profound connection with a young, radical lama who is free from the constraints of doctrine and orthodoxy. Tulku Thubten Rinpoche sanctions and encourages my work with the dakini practices that

I'm adapting for my western women students who are mostly not Buddhist. He and I have begun to collaborate on several writing projects, which we hope will culminate in a book about the "wild women," the "crazy yogis," the Black Dakini, and the contemporary feminist movement.

NOTES

1. Mary Preston Gross, "Mrs. Lieutenant" (Chutuota, Fla.: Beau Lac, 1968).
2. Kate Millett, *Sexual Politics* (Garden City, N.Y.: Doubleday, 1970).
3. Elizabeth L. Campbell and Vicki Ziegler, eds., *Circle One: A Women's Beginning Guide to Self Health and Sexuality*, 2nd ed. (Colorado Springs, Colo.: Circle One, 1975).
4. Vicki Noble, *Shakti Woman: Feeling Our Fire, Healing Our World* (San Francisco: HarperSanFrancisco, 1991).
5. Motherpeace Tarot Cards by Karen Vogel, illustrated by Vicki Noble (Stamford, Conn.: US Games Systems, 1997); Vicki Noble, *Motherpeace* (New York: Harper & Row, 1983); Vicki Noble, *Ritual Practices with the Motherpeace Tarot*, 2nd ed. (n.l.: Inner Traditions Intle Ltd., 2003); Vicki Noble, *Making Ritual with Motherpeace Cards: Multi-Cultural, Women-Centered Practices for Spiritual Growth* (n.l.: Three Rivers Press, 1998. See also Vicki Noble and Jonathan Tenney, *Motherpeace Tarot Playbook* (n.l.: Wingbow Press, 1987).
6. Vicki Noble, *Down Is Up for Aaron Eagle* (San Francisco: Harper Collins, 1993).
7. Vicki Noble, *The Double Goddess: Women Sharing Power* (Rochester, Vt.: Bear & Co., 2003).

THIRTEEN

Charlotte Bunch

1966 President, University Christian Movement
1974 Cofounder, *Quest: A Feminist Quarterly*
1989 Founder, Center for Women's Global Leadership, Rutgers University

I THINK I REPRESENT MANY OF THE WOMEN WHO ARE NOT IN THIS room or this book—women for whom religion played an important part in our path to feminism, but who left the institutional church because of our disappointment in its responses to our feminist challenges. My story is more about how religion influenced and led me to feminism than it is about feminism within religion. The Methodist church, and particularly the Methodist Student Movement (MSM), played an important role in putting me onto the path of feminism. It was also the vehicle through which I discovered the world. It provided a political and caring community that helped me to express my first sense of politics and shaped my responses to injustice in the world. It trained me in many ways, as a woman, to lead and to stand up for my principles. And then it abandoned me when I tried to do so in areas not to its liking and in places where the institution did not want to go. I think, with a lot of variations, this is the story of many feminists in relation to religion.

I started my own particular journey in the 1950s in a small dusty working-class town called Artesia, New Mexico. Or perhaps it really started before I was born when my idealistic parents decided in the 1930s that they were going to be medical missionaries to China. But World War II and my father's asthma put an end to that dream, and they became something more like domestic missionaries instead—moving my family to a remote rural area called little West Texas because they needed a doctor there. My parents were pillars of the local Methodist church and active in civic affairs in Artesia. Our house was also the local hot spot for visiting foreign students and people who passed through from around the world, whether missionaries or Rotarians.

My mother was an unconsciously feminist housewife, trained as a social worker, who clearly enjoyed her civic activities more than housework. She was the first woman to be elected president of the local school board, and was often the lone vote for things like spending money on classroom equipment rather than on the football team. Both of my parents taught us to stand up for our principles and that you can disagree with and be different from the people around you without necessarily being alienated from them. Yet while my parents were involved in local issues, traveled throughout the United States, and cared deeply about the state of the world, they did not have a sharp or ideologically defined politics. Our home in the 1950s was activist in temperament and deeply imbued with Christian social justice values but somewhat apolitical.

My childhood was one of mixed messages about what it meant to be female, but the imperative to be a responsible active citizen was never in doubt. In that small-town atmosphere, the only role models that excited me, in terms of what women could do, were the missionaries. I could listen for hours to the women (and men) who came to our local church and showed slides of foreign countries and talked about going around the world and doing things. They were my ideals of how to be a "good" female and still have adventure in your life. And I was looking for adventure. My hometown was a pretty boring place, and I wanted to travel; I wanted to see the world. My inquisitive nature and desire to explore the world were encouraged by my parents, and I was rarely told that I should not do certain things because I was female. Yet something was missing. There was little discussion of what I wanted to be when I grew up, while there was much hand-wringing about my brother's future. I had a strong desire to do something meaningful and keenly felt the family imperative to be active, but no one seemed to think it important that I shape that into a career. There was pressure to perform well in school and to get a good education, but what I was supposed to do with that remained fuzzy. So, my first decision about my career was to be a missionary or later, at least its secular equivalent, a social worker.

THE STUDENT CHRISTIAN MOVEMENT
AND THE YWCA

In 1962, when I left home bound for college at Duke University in Durham, North Carolina, I was restless and searching for something that I did not know how to name. It was through the student Christian movement in the 1960s—the YWCA and the Methodist Student Movement in particular—that I was able to transform my vague ideals into a life as a political activist. I was lucky to arrive in the South just as the Black civil rights movement was transforming the political and cultural landscape. While I pursued my studies at Duke, it was the movement, as mediated by the student Christian movement, that gave me my political education. In that process I learned a great deal about another way of understanding religion that was heavily influenced by both the Black church in the South and by the global ecumenical movement of the era that was strongly influencing campus ministries around the United States. These blended into a spiritual vision of a politically engaged, interracial, ecumenical community that excited many of us in the 1960s as a way to give expression to our religious impulses and to give meaning to our lives.

Making the Methodist Student Center at Duke my first home away from home was a natural step for me when I entered a college where I knew no one and was seeking a familiar place to find friends. The timing could not have been better. This was a place of intellectual and political ferment at the time where existentialist theology intermingled with discussion of world events like the Bay of Pigs, and simultaneously practical plans were made for participating in local and state civil rights demonstrations. As part of this community, I got up the nerve to go on my first demonstration—an interracial pray-in outside one of the local segregated churches in Durham. Gradually, through my involvement with the MSM, I became more involved in civil rights in the South but also learned about racism and poverty in the North through a spring break study tour to New York City and then a summer working in an inner-city project for children sponsored by the Methodist Deaconess Home in Philadelphia.

I soon became a MSM activist leader, elected president of the MSM of North Carolina in my sophomore year and going onto the National Council of the MSM in the summer of 1964. At my first council meeting, we agonized over the dangers of a Goldwater presidency, while also seeing the limitations of Lyndon Johnson, and finally voted to endorse Johnson with the slogan of the day, "Part of the Way with LBJ." It was the first time the MSM Council had made an explicitly political endorsement, and we called on the church to do likewise. Our move was met with considerable displeasure among many in the church hierarchy, but we felt it was an important dialogue and were supported by others there as well.

My vacations and weekends (and sometimes school days) became filled with activities like going to the Selma-to-Montgomery voting rights march as a part of the MSM delegation and local antiwar pickets at the Durham post office. At national and then international conferences, I met Christians engaged in social justice struggles from around the world, ranging from South Africans working against apartheid to Eastern Europeans involved in Christian-Marxist dialogues and Latin American liberation theology adherents. Throughout most of the tumultuous 1960s, the Student Christian Movement was the ecumenical and political community though which I processed almost everything, and through it I came to see religion as being about community and working for justice.

I was also active locally in the campus YWCA at Duke, and it too helped to shape my developing politics and particularly my nascent feminism. In the MSM I was a female leader, but it was in the YWCA that we talked about our lives as women and what it meant to imagine careers as politically active women. I was also lucky to be at a woman's undergraduate college at Duke that operated within a coeducational university. I therefore had the experience simultaneously of a women's college that encouraged women's leadership and where we did many things like the YWCA only as women, and at the same time, we were engaged in coed activities as well. This combination enabled me to have more confidence as I went out into the world. Religion was an important part of this for me, because it gave me a feeling that I was rooted in something strong, something deep with values, and that I was part of a community.

I see both subtle and direct influences in how this related to my growing feminism. The first most explicit feminist message I remember was the campus YWCA director giving us hardbound copies of the *Feminine Mystique* to read over the summer of 1963, soon after it was published.[1] We were undergraduates and most of us were becoming political, so we read it and then said, "Okay, that's what we're *not* going to do." But the real feminist education came more in the ways that we began to experience our leadership as women. I was encouraged as a woman to take leadership in both the YWCA and at the MSM. Maybe the Methodist Student Movement didn't have enough active men at the time—I don't remember that well, but I felt that there was a lot of support for me. There were also other female students taking leadership in these arenas so I did not feel isolated or that I had to be the exception, and there were at least a handful of important active career women on the staff of some campus ministries, like Jeanne Audrey Powers, and in the headquarters of the national Methodist church, like Peggy Billings and Ruth Harris, who were role models for us.

Thus, while I was a student I was given a great opportunity to discover the world, to learn about myself as a leader, and I didn't feel many obstacles as a female to that. But when I graduated from college and began to move away from the cocoon of the student world into more adult engagement with the church hierarchy, I began to realize how male they were and how few women were allowed to move into the more powerful positions. After my college graduation in the summer of 1966, I became the first national president of the University Christian Movement (UCM), a radical three-year utopian experiment in ecumenical Christian life that included faculty as well as students. In that capacity, I participated in a number of activities with the National and World Council of Churches as well as with the hierarchies of the Protestant denominations and discovered their entrenched patriarchal nature. I was tolerated as the voice of the "youth," but the more I had to work with these hierarchies, the fewer females there were around. I could feel the difference although I still could not name it.

I was also the UCM representative in many secular left groups, like meetings of the Anti-war Mobilization Committee and other coalitions. Here again I found myself one of the few women there. I felt patronized by the men of the left, both as a woman and as a Christian. But they usually wanted my access to the church constituency and/or its money, so they also tolerated my presence as a female leader. But soon after my presidency of the UCM ended, I went to work at the Institute for Policy Studies (IPS), a left-wing think tank in Washington, D.C. This was my first real job after college, and I discovered that those male chauvinist things that you read about really did happen, like when you say something and nobody responds, and then ten minutes later a man says the same thing and they all comment on his brilliance. I guess this was my first full frontal experience of the male-dominated world.

When this started to happen to me at IPS, I wasn't ready to take it. Unlike some of the women who hadn't had the opportunities that the church had given me for leadership, I was surprised and did not accept this treatment. The YWCA and the student Christian movement had trained me to lead and taken me into the world, so when I left college and went into the male-dominated adult world, I really wasn't prepared to step back and be invisible. I don't think I had a feminist notion of it at first, I simply wasn't willing to accept that treatment. So when other women at IPS, particularly Marilyn Salzman Webb, suggested that we start a women's group, I was ready. And I was ready to fight for women's liberation, precisely because it gave me the same sense of outrage over injustice that the Methodist Student Movement had taught me about racism and American imperialism and other injustices in the world.

FEMINISM AND COMING OUT IN THE WORLD

I became involved in the women's liberation movement very quickly in 1968. I took with me all of my church community experiences of organizing as well as a lot of national and some international connections. I tended to assume that many of the people I had worked with would also want to go in these new directions, and some did. For example, when the Washington, D.C., Women's Liberation Movement decided to organize the first national women's liberation movement conference at Thanksgiving of 1968, I con-

vinced the staff of *Motive Magazine*, an avant-garde Methodist church student magazine with which I had worked for many years, to send a staff person
and devote a special issue to women's issues.[2] In March of 1969 they put out a
special issue on the women's liberation movement that I coedited with the
young woman they sent from their staff to the conference. Sixty thousand
copies sold out in two months, and it was soon adapted for publication as a
book, *The New Women* by Bobbs-Merrill.[3] *Motive* got more letters to the editor responding to this issue, both pro and con, than any other issue in its entire thirty-year history. And the church started to withdraw support from the
magazine. I began to learn hard lessons about church institutions and the
power they wield when they are not prepared to follow the leadership of their
staff or of those they have nurtured to lead.

For a couple of years, I continued to operate with one foot in the secular
world and one foot in the Christian community. I cannot remember how
many women's caucuses I was part of forming in both the new left and church
groups, but that was a time when women felt the need to meet separately and
caucus to try to change each institution to respond more to our concerns and
lives. I was part of conversations that later became the Campus Ministry
Women's Caucus and on the Executive Committee of the World Student
Christian Federation, where we started a women's project to publish articles
about women's rights from around the world. We had a rather naive belief
that if everybody just knew about women's oppression, they would of course
see that it needed to end. I remember being at the mimeograph machine
cranking out more copies of *Why Women's Liberation* with the dedication of a
true believer who thought that if we could just get everybody in the country
to read this, they would agree.[4]

Most of the first articles that I wrote about women's liberation were for
church-related publications, because that was still how I saw myself. Those
were still my people. And that was still where I felt I could speak and be
heard. But the more the feminist movement grew, the more radical our interpretation and analysis of patriarchy became, and the more we saw how
deeply rooted it was in religious institutions. Many of us grew impatient
with the church's persistent male domination and its slowness in responding
to women's demands for change. I found myself moving inexorably farther
and farther into the secular world and away from the church, which seemed
to me then to not be able to keep up with the imperatives of the revolutions
of the day.

In 1971 I began to explore questions of sexuality, and I came out as a lesbian. I still naively believed that if we wrote articles explaining the need for lesbian and gay rights from a feminist perspective that this was going to be okay with most people. I wrote a letter to my old friends in the church about coming out and how this was a logical expression of my feminism and my justice commitments; a handful wrote back, some of them very touching letters, but most of them didn't reply. My last institutional activity with the church was to edit one of the final two issues of *Motive Magazine*, which were dedicated to lesbian and to gay civil rights. These were the last issues because the church had withdrawn support from the magazine, and it was clear to the editors that the magazine could not survive independently. The staff of the magazine, some of whom had been in the closet and were just coming out themselves, agreed to dedicate the last issues, to use the last of their church resources, to seek to put forward an understanding of lesbian and gay liberation.

This really was the point at which I finally ended my institutional life with the church. I realized that I could not be part of a religion or institution that labeled me as a sinner or saw me as unworthy of being a minister, as a second-class citizen. Fortunately I didn't have a job that depended in any way on the church. I worked in a secular institution, IPS, which had come to accept feminism as one of its mandates as a progressive institution, even if not something it fully embraced, and where conversation about gay and lesbian liberation could at least happen. So I decided that I did not need (or want) the church anymore, if I could not be viewed there as an equal. They had taught me all my life to stand up for my principles and had trained me to lead and to take my life seriously, but as I took my calling and my sexuality seriously, the church was no longer there for me and it no longer provided a context for my life's work. I had a terrible sense of being abandoned, but it followed several years of disappointment in the institution's responses to feminism, so it in some ways it was also a relief to stop trying to make myself fit into that institution. I realized that in spite of my deep history there, the places where I was leading were no longer acceptable to the institution. It could not go there with me, and I could no longer go where I needed to go with it.

While the institutional parting was complete, at the same time there was still a community of people, and especially of women, that I knew from all those years of working within the student Christian movement with whom I still shared a bond. Some of them remained friends and continued to support me personally, and many of them supported each other in various efforts to bring feminist changes in the institution. In my work as part of the secular women's movement over the next three decades, I have continued to see progressives working in the context of the church as one of the important allies for feminism. I am glad that other women have not given up on changing the church, and these feminists are the embodiment of the continuation of that journey of feminism in relation to religion. Especially in this time when political movements around the world have claimed the name of religion for an antifeminist agenda, for an anti–human rights agenda, in this country as well as elsewhere, it is more important than ever that feminists not concede religion to that narrow perspective. We must continue to challenge their narrow views of religion for their political agenda and to claim the religious impulse as part of our vision that a different world is possible.

Finally, let me add that having had a strong background in religion has been a source of personal strength for me even in secular movements. I think it gives me—I don't even have the right words for it—but I feel that it gives me a depth and ability to continue struggling and to see my work as part of a broader picture. I have continued some of the spirit of those days in the 1960s into my work on feminism and human rights. I continue to feel the need to search for a values-based politics, for a politics that bases itself explicitly in principles. Perhaps that's part of why I became interested in trying to bring feminism and human rights together, because I felt that human rights were also about a struggle to create a politics based in ethics, a politics based in a vision of justice and not just power struggles. It is also a politics based in hope, a vision that a different world is possible and that community is a critical part of building that different world. These are all lessons that I learned from my religious activism and have tried to bring into my feminist activism.

At the Center for Women's Global Leadership, for example, we have a leadership development program for women's rights activists from around the world, and I realize that part of what I have been trying to do is to recreate for them what I gained from my activism with the World Student Christian Federation and the Student Christian Movement. These experiences gave me a chance to interact across national, ethnic, racial, and other divisions, a chance to engage with people around the world who cared about something in common and to build trust and community for working together. That religious vision of an engaged community has continued to influence my life. I feel that my work today on feminism and human rights is in continuity with the struggle I began in the 1960s to find a values-based politics that can give hope and vision for a better life for all—in community and with respect for our incredible human diversity.

NOTES

1. Betty Friedan, *The Feminine Mystique* (New York: Norton, 1963).
2. *Motive Magazine* was published in thirty-two volumes from February 1941 to Winter 1972.
3. *The New Women; A Motive Anthology on Women's Liberation*, ed. Joanne Cooke, Charlotte Bunch-Weeks, and Robin Morgan (Indianapolis: Bobbs-Merrill, 1970).
4. Marlene Dixon, *Why Women's Liberation* (San Francisco: San Francisco Bay Area Radical Education Project, 1970).

FOURTEEN

Judith Plaskow

1969 Became a feminist while studying for Ph.D. at Yale
1981 Cofounder, B'not Esh, Jewish feminist spirituality
   collective
1990 Author, *Standing Again at Sinai*

I BECAME A FEMINIST IN THE FALL OF 1969. THAT WAS MY SECOND
year as a graduate student in religious studies at Yale, and the year Yale admitted women to the undergraduate college. When the *New York Times* ran a

front-page story on the entry of women, and Yale prepared for women's education by hiring a gynecologist and putting full-length mirrors in the bathrooms, two graduate students called an open meeting to discuss how it was that we had been at Yale for eighty years and no one had noticed.[1] I went to the meeting out of curiosity and found myself in a room with about fifty other women. Very few of us were feminists; I certainly wasn't. The fact that we were at Yale indicated that doors had been opened to us, and probably most of us assumed that they were open to any woman who was "good enough." The combination of suspicion, dismissal, surveillance, and condescending courtliness we met at Yale was something most of us had never before experienced. We began meeting weekly and talking about our lives, at Yale and outside it. We called ourselves the Yale Women's Alliance, and, as I recall, we spent roughly half our time on consciousness raising and half on activist issues connected to life at the university.

The process of our meetings that fall was life-changing for me. As I began to connect my personal history with my new understandings of women's socialization and social roles, my whole way of looking at the world began to shift. Since I was a graduate student in religious studies, it was hard *not* to apply my new feminist insights to religion. Carol Christ was one of the other women at the initial gathering of the Yale Women's Alliance, and we fairly quickly began to relate our growing feminist awareness to our studies in theology. We began to *notice*, for example, that we had never been assigned a single book or article by a woman. We began to *notice* the dreadful things about women said by virtually every theologian we were studying. When Carol wrote a short seminar paper on Karl Barth connecting his statement that women are ontologically subordinate to men with his hierarchical understanding of God and creation, it helped launch both of us on our way to becoming feminist theologians. We eagerly read Mary Daly's *The Church and the Second Sex*, invited Rosemary Ruether to speak at Yale, and somehow discovered Valerie Saiving's feminist critique from 1960.[2] The result of these explorations for me was that, in the spring of 1972, despite the opposition or nonsupport of almost everyone on the faculty, I decided to write a feminist dissertation. I wanted to root Saiving's theological critique in a nonbiological understanding of women's experience. I wrote on two Protestant theologians, Reinhold Niebuhr and Paul Tillich, because I was studying Protestant theology. I didn't think theology was central enough to Judaism that a feminist dissertation on Jewish theology would contribute to religious change.

My choice to write a feminist thesis—I think perhaps the second in religious studies in the United States, after Rita Gross'—marked the beginning of my involvement in the creation of women's studies in religion.[3] In the summer of 1972 I attended the conference "Women Exploring Theology" at Grailville. There I met Elisabeth Schüssler Fiorenza and began another friendship that was to have an important impact on my development as a feminist scholar. And there I first experienced the power of women doing theology together. The wonderful small group I participated in that week tried to capture the significance of feminist community by exploring consciousness raising as a religious experience and then talking about the relationship between Eve and Lilith as a paradigm of sisterhood. Though I was scarcely aware of it at the time, my writing "The Coming of Lilith" at Grailville represented my first incorporation of Jewish modes of thinking into my attempts to theologize.[4]

In the fall of 1972 I became co-chair with Joan Arnold Romero of the Women and Religion Group of the American Academy of Religion, during the second and third years of its existence. We followed Mary Daly as chair, and I will never forget the excitement of those early sessions as we squeezed into rooms far too small to contain either the numbers or the energy of those who gathered, knowing we were off to explore uncharted continents. In 1973, the first year of the program, I was a research associate in women's studies at Harvard Divinity School (HDS). The associates weren't expected to teach that year but were given the job of transforming the HDS curriculum to reflect the emerging scholarship on women. I can't claim to have had much success in getting the theology department to change at the behest of a twenty-six-year-old graduate student, but my time at Harvard certainly forced me to articulate the challenge of feminist theology and provided me with another important experience of feminist community. Then, in 1974, I moved to New York and had the privilege of participating in the early conversations of the New York Area Feminist Scholars in Religion. It was there that I was first challenged by Goddess theology, heard Karen Brown's early work on voudou and Naomi Goldenberg's on dreams, and thrashed out issues in an emerging field with many remarkable women.

In the same period that I was becoming a feminist academic, I was undergoing a parallel, though in many ways more difficult, process of conscientization as a feminist Jew. Ironically, I discovered feminism at precisely a moment in my personal life when I was also exploring traditional Judaism. While I was attending the Yale Women's Alliance, I was spending Saturday mornings sitting in the back of a chapel, a nonmember of a minyan consisting mainly of male undergraduates. One Sabbath, as my new husband and I were standing outside the chapel chatting with a friend, a student came out and urged my husband to come in immediately to make the minyan. I suddenly realized that, though I had been attending services regularly for over a year and he was a relative newcomer, only his presence was relevant to the purpose for which we were gathered. That was an enormously important *click* moment for me. My experience that morning led me to develop a talk entitled "Can a Woman Be a Jew?" that I presented in a number of contexts in the early 1970s. My answer was an ambivalent yes. On one hand, of course women are Jews, Jews who have led rich and committed Jewish lives through the centuries. On the other hand, Judaism is a bit like color-blindness: women pass it on but don't often contract it. Excluded from public prayer and study, women are excluded from the heart and soul of traditional Judaism.

My conflicted relationship to Judaism in this period was reflected in the talk I gave at the first Jewish feminist conference in 1973. There I argued that the identity of Jewish feminists "lies somewhere in the conflict between being a woman and being a Jew and in the necessity of combining the two in as yet unknown ways. . . . We are here," I said—and I remember being interrupted by applause at this point—"because a secular movement for the liberation of women has made it imperative to raise certain Jewish issues now, because we will not let ourselves be defined as Jewish women in ways in which we cannot allow ourselves to be defined as women." I was speaking as someone who had discovered a new source of community and identity in feminism and who desperately wanted to find and help bring its energy and transformative insights into the Jewish community.

Throughout the 1970s, however, I felt stymied by this quest. I had difficulty finding either a worship community in which I felt comfortable or an ongoing context in which to explore Jewish feminist questions. I characterized my academic and Jewish feminist lives as developing on parallel tracks, because, in fact, there was a certain disconnection and even tension between them. By the mid-1970s I had wonderful group of feminist colleagues in the American Academy of Religion (AAR) with whom I had developed a fairly nuanced scholarly understanding of the role of women in western religion. We analyzed women's exclusion from public religious roles and the absence of women's experiences and perspectives from theology and religious symbolism. But we also realized that this exclusion was not the whole truth, that women had found ways to express ourselves religiously within and against traditional frameworks. In the Jewish context, however, the realities of women's subordination and exclusion were far more real to me than the ways we had carved—or might someday carve—a niche for ourselves within this patriarchal tradition.

Several pivotal events in the early 1980s led me in the direction of an integrated Jewish feminist identity that also changed my life as a scholar. First, in the summer of 1980, I decided to teach a course on Jewish feminist theology at the first National Havurah Summer Institute—essentially an adult-learning camp for countercultural Jews. It was my first opportunity to raise in a Jewish context the theological questions that most excited me, and, although I had no idea whether anyone would be interested in taking such a class, in fact several people came to the institute precisely because it was offered. The seriousness with which the women and two men present grappled with difficult theological questions gave me my first taste of Jewish feminist community. It was an incredibly exhilarating teaching experience, and a moment in which the separated aspects of my life began to come together.

Partly as a result of the excitement generated by a number of feminist courses at the institute, a group of women decided to create a space in which we could explore feminist issues in an ongoing and more focused way. In May of 1981 sixteen Jewish feminists gathered at the Grail Retreat Center in Cornwall-on-Hudson with the modest goal of reconfiguring Judaism in four days. That weekend became the founding meeting of B'not Esh (daughters of fire), a feminist spirituality collective that has been meeting annually ever since. I now had a Jewish context within which to explore feminist questions and attempt to create a feminist Judaism. B'not Esh was a space in which we could not only talk about feminism but could bring into being some of the changes that we hoped someday might be incorporated into the larger Jewish community.

B'not Esh was crucial in helping me to move from an angry sense of powerlessness to a vision of a transformed Judaism, but that change did not come swiftly or easily; nor was it due to B'not Esh alone. Rather, a confluence of factors moved me in a new direction. On the academic side, the publication of Elisabeth's *In Memory of Her* was a crucial turning point for me.[5] Reading the book for an AAR panel—I believe in 1983, when it first appeared—I found myself struggling mightily against its fundamental premises.

When Elisabeth argued that "the Christian past [is] women's own past" and that to assume that androcentric texts accurately depict reality is to collude in women's oppression, I repeatedly scrawled in the margins: how do you know this? Isn't this an enormous assumption, indeed an a priori commitment? At some point I realized I was resisting being thrust into a place of unaccustomed and frightening power. To accept the notion that religious history is the history of women is to have to move beyond nursing one's grievances to confront the huge task of reconstructing women's history and demanding that the Jewish community integrate women's experience into every aspect of communal life.

Coincident with my beginning to make this shift was my coming out as a lesbian. This huge step for me could have added more fodder to my anger at Judaism, in that it threw into bolder relief the relationship between its sexism and heterosexism. But, in fact, coming out freed me to claim my own power on the emotional and spiritual levels, just as *In Memory of Her* was encouraging me to do on the intellectual level. In part I attribute this effect to a deep connection among sexuality, embodiment, and creativity that I experienced powerfully at this point in my life. But also I think I discovered that, having walked through one closed door and survived, I could also walk through others.

A third pivotal event that occurred in 1983 is that, toward the end of our second retreat, B'not Esh resolved to stop seeking a common denominator in prayer that we would never be able to achieve. Instead of trying to reach consensus on how to worship together, we would empower individual women to take turns creating the liturgies that they wanted to experience, and we would agree to be present and try on things that might challenge our own proclivities and boundaries. This crucial decision ushered in many years of exciting liturgical experimentation. All of us began to appreciate the various, sometimes radical, ways in which we could incorporate our voices as women into the liturgy and still maintain ties to the deep structures of tradition.

It was the confluence of these events that enabled me to begin writing *Standing Again at Sinai* and, in doing so, to bring together the critical and constructive, academic, feminist, and Jewish feminist commitments in my life.[6] I was able to draw on many years of conversations with Christian and post-Christian colleagues in the academy, to articulate a feminist vision that went beyond Judaism, and still also feel that I was speaking out of and for a very particular Jewish feminist community. I never felt alone in working on *Standing Again at Sinai*. I experienced it as thoroughly grounded in and

emerging out of twenty years of feminist and Jewish feminist experimentation and writing in which I had participated along with many others.

As is perhaps clear from the silences in this account, I did not come to
this new place in my life and work because of any conviction that the core of
my tradition is sympathetic to the liberation of women. Indeed, I don't see
Jewish tradition primarily as a source of overarching values that can be ab-
stracted from certain texts and historical contexts, but rather as a huge and
often unwieldy bundle of texts, traditions, laws, practices, folkways, and so on
that constitute the past and establish the foundations for the future of the
Jewish people. Just as individuals continually reevaluate, select, and reorder
elements of our own personal histories as we move through our lives, so Jewish communities can sort, reconfigure, and add elements to the bundle, drawing on those parts of it that best serve our needs. The core of tradition is not
a given but a subject of fierce and ever-renewed debate over where Judaism
should be headed and who will have the power to decide.

It has been sobering to me in reflecting on my history to note how many
of the watershed events in my own feminist saga, and that of the academic
and Jewish communities in which I have participated, occurred in the 1970s
and 1980s. I have experienced the 1990s as a time of fragmentation and re-
confrontation with the question of what comes next. B'not Esh continues to
meet, but with less clarity of focus. Women's issues have been integrated into
the American Academy of Religion in ways that we could scarcely have imagined in the early 1970s, yet this had made it far more difficult to keep track of
new developments. I see in both the larger liberal Jewish community and
among many students an ignorance about history of feminism, a reluctance
to embrace the term, and a refighting of battles that we hoped we had laid to
rest twenty years ago.

Through all this, two things have remained constant for me. Shortly
after I finished my dissertation in the mid-1970s, I encountered a former
professor of mine at the AAR—a man who had always liked me but who was
perplexed by my interests. "What are you going to work on," he asked me,
"when you finish working on women?" "I'm never going to finish," I answered—and, of course, I have not. Within this fundamental commitment, I
also continue to hold onto the notion of women's power and responsibility to
shape the future of our religious traditions as part of the broader project of
repairing the world. Frail as this power seems at this frightening moment in
history, I am nonetheless grateful for the profound intellectual, spiritual, and

political adventure on which my feminism has propelled me. It is one I could never have imagined when I walked into the first meeting of the Yale Women's Alliance thirty-three years ago.

NOTES

1. William Borders, "Yale Going Coed Next September," *New York Times*, November 15, 1968.
2. Mary Daly, *The Church and the Second Sex* (New York: Harper & Row, 1968). Valerie Saiving, "The Human Situation: A Feminine View," in *Womanspirit Rising: A Feminist Reader in Religion*, ed. Carol P. Christ and Judith Plaskow (San Francisco: Harper & Row, 1979), 25–42.
3. Rita M. Gross, "Exclusion and Participation: The Role of Women in Aboriginal Australian Religions" Ph.D. diss., University of Chicago, 1975. Judith Plaskow, "Sex, Sin, and Grace: Women's Experience and the Theologies of Reinhold Niebuhr and Paul Tillich," Ph.D. diss., Yale University, 1975.
4. Judith Plaskow, "The Coming of Lilith: Toward a Feminist Theology," *Womanspirit Rising*, 198–209.
5. Elisabeth Schüssler Fiorenza, *In Memory of Her: A Feminist Theological Reconstruction of Christian Origins* (New York: Crossroads, 1983).
6. Judith Plaskow, *Standing Again at Sinai: Judaism from a Feminist Perspective* (San Francisco: Harper & Row, 1990).

FIFTEEN

Nadine Foley

1975 Coordinator, Women in Future Priesthood Now—A
    Call to Action
1986 Prioress, Adrian Dominican Congregation
1989 President, Leadership Conference of Women Religious

MY SHORT PRESENTATION THIS MORNING IS TO BE A REFLECTION
on the convergence of feminism and religion as I have experienced it in an
organization, the Adrian Dominican Congregation, a Catholic religious congregation of women whose ancestral home, or what we call, infelicitously
sometimes, the "motherhouse," is in Adrian, Michigan. I reflect upon this
confluence as a member for fifty-seven years now, as one who has taught in
secondary and higher educational institutions and in campus ministry over

the years, and as a former prioress of the congregation. In that latter capacity I was also elected to serve for three years on the leadership team of the Leadership Conference of Women Religious in the United States, the organization of the majority of leaders of congregations of "women religious," as we tend to call ourselves, in the United States. I was also during this same time elected to represent the United States as one of three delegates to the International Union of Superiors General, which met annually in Rome. So I've had a perspective on this whole area of women religious, "sisters" as we might be called, though some people call us "nuns," which is not completely accurate. These are all organizations affiliated within the Roman Catholic Church in one way or another and have given me both a national and an international perspective on women who are members of the organizations of what we call "religious life."

In speaking about feminism, I do not do so from any particular definition. What I have experienced in my congregation, and others nationally and internationally, is the phenomenon of what is often called, after Carol Christ and Judith Plaskow, "womanspirit rising," or the rise of feminine consciousness.[1] It was occurring over the years in my congregation and others as it did among women generally. For the most part members of our congregation were not reading the influential feminist writing of the 1950s and 1960s. Some did, of course, as I did, and we were able to say, "yes," as it reinforced our own experience.

I should point out that, in a congregation like mine whose members were educators and healthcare professionals, and who had institutions that belonged to us, we were a highly educated group. There were few in our congregation who did not have a master's degree unless they were new recruits. We were administrators in schools, hospitals, and institutions of higher education. Besides master's degrees we had many doctoral degrees, and in running our institutions we were interacting with all kinds of accrediting associations. In our education we were meeting people in other secular and Catholic universities. So we had a broad area of experience that was not particularly noticed by officials in the church. Yet it was extremely important as we entered into the process of renewal and into examining the "signs of the times." In the early years one area that we did not study for the most part was theology. That was considered to be the province of priests.

At the same time we had women overseas who were observing the colonialism and imperialism of our country and the effects they were having on poor people in the areas where they were. We also had women in inner cities in our own country who were seeing the effects of poverty stemming from national policies. All of that was going on during the same time that feminism was rising.

Official leaders in my church have sometimes suggested that women religious and other women in the church have been unduly influenced by "feminists." This is not a positive judgment. It suggests that the likes of us were willing dupes of misguided women. But this is not true. We were women caught in a patriarchal system replicated in the matriarchy of our religious congregations. And beneath the surface of what appeared to be a highly controlled and obedient workforce for the church, discontent was brewing. It was about to break forth and, interestingly enough, it was the official church itself that forced a geyserlike explosion. For after Vatican II (1962–1965) some directives were sent to all religious congregations:

1. They were to hold general chapters of renewal within three years of the notification.
2. In preparation they were to consult all the members.
3. They could alter some parts of their constitutions and engage in a designated period of experimentation.
4. They were to write new constitutions also within three years.

In religious communities and congregations such as mine, which is a so-called pontifical congregation, we then had to take those constitutions to Rome for approval.

The crucial directive was the second one, the one that affected a seachange in the religious life of women in the Catholic church, "Consult all the members." Members had not usually been widely consulted in preparation for general chapters, the legislative assemblies that occur on a regular basis in our congregations. They concentrated on election of congregation leaders. Otherwise they dealt with trivial things, at least in times past, like appropriate nightwear—pajamas or nightgowns—the time limit for being out of the convent in the evening, the distance one might travel from the convent without special permission, and so on.

So the directive from Rome was new. Things came to the surface that were never dreamed of—certainly not by those in Rome from whom the directives had come. I, who was in my forties at the time, like so many others, was able for the first time to have a forum in which to express my thoughts, feelings, and questions about our religious life, an important component of which was our identity as women in the church.

But before I continue I would like to recount some elements of my prior experience that informed my earlier life and had a bearing on how I participated in what we call "renewal."

I am the daughter of a woman, mother of eight children, who for her oldest daughter wanted everything of which she had been deprived. She had actually been prevented from going to high school, so she had only an eighth-grade education. She went to work to make it possible for me to have all that she had ever wanted for herself, particularly a college education.

I am the product of a small-town public coeducational school in the upper peninsula of Michigan where teachers took particular interest in their students and promoted them in every possible way. One of the things we had in our school, which was so remarkable and had so much influence on my life, was a speech program that started in seventh grade and went through twelfth. We had to do it all—declamations, orations, extemporaneous speaking, and debate. At the time, I didn't realize what an influence those experiences were going to have as time went on.

I went to a Catholic women's college, and there came under the influence of highly educated women, most with doctoral degrees, who represented hitherto unknown possibilities to me. In that environment I learned something very important: I learned how to be friends with women. And we had one priest professor of philosophy who had a constant theme: don't let anyone tell you that you can't learn or do something because you are a woman. This was in the 1940s, by the way.

We often think that sisters were educated totally in Catholic institutions. In the 1940s I had all women professors and all members of the congregation. They had degrees from Columbia University, from the University of Michigan, from Fribourg in Switzerland, from the University of Dublin in Ireland, and any number of other places besides Catholic universities.

I entered the Adrian Dominican Sisters after I had completed my college degree at a time when we had a strong, self-motivated, dynamic leader, Mother Mary Gerald Barry, who, while she imposed the usual disciplines of religious life at the time, was never an absolutist. She always made the practical decision over strict adherence to law. She almost never sought the advice of priests and bishops. And when she did, she often did not follow their advice. She sent out her sisters to accomplish new endeavors without telling them what to do or how to do it and so gave them an arena of freedom to achieve what she expected. And they did.

I think, particularly, of the twelve women, whose median age was about twenty-eight, who were sent to Barry College in Miami Shores in 1940 to bring a women's college into being. They had no predetermined plan to follow. They were left to their own devices. They succeeded. Unlike some congregations I know, we were not fitted into a unified mold of behavior. In recent times someone has said, "When you meet one Adrian Dominican, you have met one Adrian Dominican."

Yet my entrance into religious life involved me in a kind of schizophrenia. On one hand I was certain that my decision was God's will for me and I wanted to carry out all of the observances as perfectly as possible. But at the same time, interiorly, I questioned just about everything. I remember once asking the question of another woman in my group, "What does this prepare us for?" I was convinced that our formation program didn't prepare us for much. Our congregation had originated from a cloister in Regensburg, Germany, and we had some remnants of practices that made no sense.

I think of the observance of Good Friday, a day of great penance. We got up in the morning at five-thirty and had a whole series of practices and we didn't eat until eleven o'clock. We would all sit around the table and someone would come with a little tray to brush and crumb the table. We hadn't eaten a thing at this point. There was nothing there to crumb. I remember asking our director, "What is the meaning of this observance?" She became very upset with me because I am sure she didn't know but we did it anyway. It no doubt had significance in the cloister of Regensburg, but had been lost along the way. And that's just one of a number of peculiarities.

All of this, and more, was in my background at the close of Vatican II in 1965. I and so many more were reading the documents from the council with excitement. I read in particular, as did so many, the document entitled *The Church in the Modern World.*[2] We were impelled out of an inward-turning spirituality (if one can call it that) of recited prayers and observances to an outward movement in relationship that encompassed the world in which we lived. Our notion of religious experience and spirituality expanded. Many of our members were already there, but for many more there was a spiritual awakening. And the interesting thing about this development is that the impetus came to the congregation from the Vatican. As IHM Sister Margaret

Brennan once said, "We were nothing if not obedient." We did what they told us to do.

We Adrian Dominicans didn't get our new constitutions written within the required three years after the General Chapter of Renewal in which we were engaged in the summers from 1968 until 1970. We finally finished them in 1989. As one involved in writing our new constitutions, I was insistent that we claim an inner authority that derives from our identity as a charism, that is, a free grace, in and for the church. We were adopting for ourselves something always central in the original constitutions of the Dominican order to which I belong, the one written for the men of the order. They had a unique kind of democratic process, originated by the founder of the order in the thirteenth century, that had a series of interlocking relationships of governance. Some have even suggested that it was a model known to those who developed the democracy of our own country.

We felt that, while we had emerged from the enclosed nuns of the Dominican cloister in Regensburg, Germany, we had developed over the years a different kind of religious life in a ministerial tradition. So we were claiming that reality for ourselves when we wrote the constitutions. In another sense we were adopting the liberating kind of constitution written for the men of the order. Incidentally, the men of the order have never had to submit their constitutions for approval, as we women of the order are required to do.

We had some interesting conversations in Rome about our claim to inner authority. Actually, a close reading of how the official church is organized shows that we are not part of the hierarchical structure at all. There is an important document out of Vatican II, *The Dogmatic Constitution on the Church*, which says that the church consists of bishops, clergy, and laity.[3] We women religious are not bishops or clergy so it would seem that we are laity. Then there is the chapter on laity in the same document that says, "The laity are all those in the church who are neither clerics nor members of religious institutes." So I always maintain that we were aced out of the church, that is, out of the hierarchical church, and that's not a bad place to be.

I recall one incident in Rome as we sat at a table with Vatican representatives of the Congregation for Institutes of Religious Life and Societies of Apostolic Life who were examining our newly written constitutions. One of the men, an Irish Carmelite, said in a quizzical manner, "I notice that you use the word 'woman' frequently in this document." I replied that I did not think we had overused the word. His response was, "Well, you don't want to use words that are just a fad." Now, that's what we were dealing with. One can get angry at this kind of insensitivity, but it's scarcely worthy of a response.

"Spirituality" was not a term that many of us used in former days. I have always believed that we were schooled in an ethic, not in a spirituality. The observances of religious life were understood as what we had to do to "save our souls." And it often seemed to me that we were evaluated in terms of how we carried out what I would call the incidentals of our life in community, especially on how we carried out our part of the housekeeping in the convent. While I, and others, yearned for more personal time for reflection and contemplation, the demands of our ministries were often totally time-consuming. And yet we were an order of Dominicans whose motto is "to contemplate and to give to others the fruits of contemplation."

I was educated to the doctoral level in philosophy in the Aristotelian-Thomistic tradition. I am not sure just when I began to see that the dualisms in this train of thought no longer served. But in teaching theology at Barry College (now University) in the 1960s, I often had students ask questions that I blithely answered. I remember once presenting the difference between natural virtues and supernatural virtues as covered in our textbook.

A student asked, "How do I know if I am acting out of a natural virtue or a supernatural virtue?" I know that I muddled through some kind of response, but I knew, and I am sure that the student did, that it made no sense. I was beginning to realize that the answers were inadequate and perhaps meaningless. And during that time I had the experience of several of those flashes of insight we sometimes have that instantaneously changed my direction.

They occurred during a summer conference as I was listening to a priest professor who was an expert on this kind of philosophy. He was talking about the natural and supernatural virtues. He had a scientific background, and on the blackboard he had an intricate electrical circuit on which he was organizing the natural and supernatural virtues and showing how they related to one another. When he finished, a woman near me let out a great sigh of appreciation. But at the same time a young priest in the back of the room shouted out with vehemence, "And when you know all of that, what more do you know of yourself?" I resonated immediately with his question. How does such intellectualization relate to our personal experience? It was a moment of change for me.

This priest who asked the question, I remember, as we were walking among the grounds in the mountains of North Carolina, had a clipping, and he held it out to me and he said, "What do you think about this?" I looked at

it and saw that it was a picture of fully habited sisters with placards demon-
strating outside a dormitory at a Catholic university in Chicago. They were
protesting the university's racist policy of excluding African Americans from
the residences. I said, "That seems to be an inappropriate thing for sisters to
be doing." I was wearing the full habit of the Dominican order at the time,
and he pointed at me and said, "If you have the right to wear that, you have
the obligation to put it where the gospel is being contradicted." I knew in-
stantly that he was right.

It became quite clear to me that women were caught on the negative side
of the traditional dualisms. We shared that position with minorities, the poor,
the marginalized, and the earth. My involvement with the conference entitled "Women in Future Priesthood Now: A Call to Action" in 1975 did not
stem from any desire on my part to be ordained a priest. I saw the issue as
subsuming all the issues on women that prevailed in my church. I chaired the
group that organized the conference. Prior to it I received a letter from the
president of the Bishops Conference at the time who was not happy about
this whole development. I give him credit, however, for not trying to forbid
it. Somewhere in his letter he said, "The church owes women a debt of gratitude." And that has always stayed with me.

So we had the conference and, after it was over, some bishops decided
that they really ought to pay attention to us. For a while I thought I was involved in a Cuban missile–type crisis because I got a call from Maria Riley,
who, you may know, is very involved globally with women's issues. At the
time she was on a committee in Washington, and she called me one morning
to say "You're going to get a phone call today." She had been called by then
Father Kelly, OP, secretary to the U.S. Catholic Bishops Conference, now
the archbishop of Louisville. He had called Maria to tell me that I was going
to get a phone call. The next day he called me and told me that I was to call
Bishop Malone of Columbus because there was a committee of bishops that
met with nonofficial groups and of which he was the chair. I was to call
Bishop Malone and ask to meet with his group. I did and we met at the airport in Detroit. We from the organizing committee met with these men and
discussed the conference. It was not a very fruitful exchange. On the part of
one bishop in particular there was a good deal of animosity.

I remember at one point saying, "One thing bothers me and that's the
sentence that I received from your current president, who said that 'the
church owes women a debt of gratitude.'" I added, "The church doesn't owe

me a debt of gratitude. I think I'm in the church." One of the bishops, who was very sympathetic to this whole thing, said, "Ah, Sister, you know they talk like that all the time: the church owes the Knights of Columbus a debt of gratitude, the church owes the Holy Name Society a debt of gratitude." I said, "I've never heard anybody say the church owes men, meaning males, a debt of gratitude."

These forms of speech imply that the church is male. Women are adjuncts or helpmates. We are not totally in the church. One of the bishops at the meeting became so upset with the whole conversation that he left and said he had a plane to catch. It was a fast getaway. But within the year he called and asked me to talk on the issues with the priests of his diocese. Eventually I did.

Early on I wrote a paper entitled "The Spirituality of Women: A New Immanence."[4] In speaking of God, the church always preferred the transcendence of God over the immanence, another dualism to be sure. But what I wrote at the time was not the beginning. An insight into a spirituality that is nondualistic, integrative, and mutual had been brewing in me for a long time. Relationship is all-important in such a spirituality, and it extends out from the personal to the social, economic, and political arenas of our life.

In the end I want to say that my religious congregation of women is, as I said earlier on, of tremendous support to me. People here have talked a lot about community. We *have* community. We are not in the hierarchical structure of the church. We have as yet not fully realized just who we are in the church and what we can be in the church. As we go along our way we get into trouble from uncomprehending officials very often. But nonetheless, I think that one of the great challenges that we have within the whole strain of feminism in the church is to realize fully who we are, to put it into practice and achieve what we can. I think we can do a great deal as an authentic ecclesial reality rooted in the church as the people of God and outside the hierarchical structure.

Finally I would like to read the vision statement that comes from our congregation's chapter enactments. We have vision statements on the poor, on women, on the environment, on racism, as we try to address these things that are crucial to the community life in mission that I live with my Adrian Dominican sisters. I experience our shared common life as appreciative, supportive, and inspiring. In all of our general chapters since 1968 we have made a commitment to women. Our current vision statement reads:

We stand in communion with women of the world.

Compelled to confront violence and oppressive systems, we break our silence of complicity.

We claim our freedom to liberate the creative woman-spirit.

We call for the full release of women's energies to bring about balance and harmony with all creation.

Central to my personal search has been my understanding of the role of the Holy Spirit in my own life and in the life of the faith community.

Prior to my entering religious life, a sister friend had given me a lengthy prayer to the Holy Spirit that I began to say then and have continued to use to this very day. It came to me this morning actually. But over time my relationship to the Holy Spirit has changed from just prayers to an understanding of the Holy Spirit as dwelling in me and directive of the mission of the gospel. In that understanding and experience I know the Holy Spirit as the inner source of my better motivations and actions as well as the one who forms and moves our faith community in our mission of compassion to the world.

These realizations were reinforced by my discovery, along with so many others whose writings have inspired me, of the wisdom tradition of the Hebrew scriptures, long neglected in our history. Even in the Christian scriptures Jesus is identified as Wisdom, something for centuries gone unnoticed or ignored. Catherine of Siena, the great spiritual light of the order to which I belong, speaks so often of the Holy Spirit as "mercy." It is interesting too that she identified Jesus as the "wisdom of God." Such ideas encourage me in what I embrace as Christian feminism, religion, and spirituality.

Wisdom (*Sophia*) and mercy (*rahamim*) have reinforced for me the realization that in the long religious tradition to which I belong, feminism and spirituality come together in my life and have enriched my self-understanding as an empowered woman of faith.

NOTES

1. Carol P. Christ and Judith Plaskow, *Womanspirit Rising: A Feminist Reader in Religion* (San Francisco: Harper & Row, 1979).
2. In Vatican Council II (1962–1965), *Vatican Council II: The Conciliar and Post Conciliar Documents*, gen. ed. Austin Flannery (Dublin: Dominican Publications, 1975).
3. In ibid.
4. This is an unpublished work.

SIXTEEN

Blu Greenberg

1973 Spoke at first National Jewish Women's Conference
1981 Author, *On Women and Judaism: A View from Tradition*
1997 Cofounder, Jewish Orthodox Feminist Alliance

IN MANY WAYS, I WAS THE LEAST LIKELY CANDIDATE TO BECOME AN
Orthodox feminist activist. And in a very real sense, I've been on an incredible spiritual and intellectual journey—without ever really leaving home.

To begin with, I was born into an Orthodox Jewish family in Seattle, Washington. These two factors—of birth and geography—would powerfully affect the way I would later integrate feminism into my life.

First and foremost, it was communicated to me as a very young child that being an Orthodox Jew was a great gift. It was not a burden as some would think, but rather a joy and treasure. My earliest experiences were grounded in the rich culture of Sabbath and holiday observance, *kashrut* (dietary laws), the special value of Torah study, and my parents' deep involvement in communal institutions—all of this in a time and place in which Jewish particularity was going upstream against the process of American homogenization.

One example to illustrate how privilege and joy were communicated: On Friday afternoons, an hour or two before the onset of Sabbath, my father would call out to his three young daughters, "Girls, who wants a mitzvah?" A mitzvah is a good deed, the fulfillment of a commandment; in this case, the fifth one, "Honor thy father and mother." My two sisters and I knew this was a call for us to polish father's shoes for the Sabbath, a chore reserved for children in those days. Of course, we immediately jumped to the task, for who would not want a mitzvah? His call was not simply a Tom Sawyer ploy of Orthodox Judaism; it was his way of transmitting to us the deep love he had for Torah and mitzvot. We absorbed this into our bones.

Given this background, when the earliest feminists criticized the rabbis, patriarchy, and tradition, I felt a certain cognitive dissonance. The rabbis were my heroes, not the enemy. As an adult, I wanted to defend them even as I myself was beginning to criticize bits and pieces of the tradition myself.

Second, an Orthodox way of life is strongly family-centered. Family was the defining structure and remains the most important aspect of my life. Early radical feminists, then, could criticize the family as the locus of abuse for women, but I would have none of it. It ran counter to the truths I knew.

Third, Orthodox Jews in Seattle were a minority within a minority, as they are in fact today in most places. Though it was never articulated to me as such, somehow I absorbed an early sense of what it took to bring me into the middle of the twentieth century as an Orthodox Jew. Studying history and social and religious institutions as an adult, I came to understand that it is far easier to destroy systems than to build them up. So when other feminists were speaking of taking down walls and doors, I was cautious about destroying what I knew had taken centuries to create.

One other factor about my upbringing surely influenced my adult feminist activity: the difference in styles between my parents as regards criticism. My father, a peacemaker by nature, could not stand criticism. I never heard him speak ill of anyone all his life. His pattern was to distance himself from negative speech and defend the other under attack. This was also true of his attitude toward his beloved faith. He was a Talmud scholar, and his love for Judaism ran wide and deep. He suffered when he heard someone attack orthodoxy. My mother, on the other hand, loved criticism, not of the tradition, for she too loved her heritage, but simply as part of her total honesty about what is right and wrong, just and unjust in life. She is truly the most penetratingly honest person I have ever met, sometimes too close for comfort for a daughter who preferred a tall tale to owning up. My mother could puncture every balloon and hear every false note. Thus I grew up with this interesting combination of a father who would brook no criticism and a mother who would take no prisoners. When the feminist critique of traditional Judaism intersected my life, it found a reluctant customer. I came to feminism without any sense of oppression at all and, therefore, felt no personal need to criticize. On the other hand, criticism was connected to justice, not anger. So I had to accommodate these two internalized streams—an uncritical love for my community and its traditions and the need for truth and justice. I would shuttle back and forth between these two poles, flinching at the harsh criticism of orthodoxy from without yet offering my own internal critique as I felt appropriate.

Recall of childhood and teenage years turns up very few experiences that can remotely be called feminist, and if someone were to argue that I am confusing "tomboy" with "feminist," I would offer no quarrel. As a young girl in Seattle, I was aware that I could ride my bike down a steep hill with no hands, like any boy in the neighborhood. And during my teen years in Far Rockaway, New York, I took pride in the fact that frequently I was the pitcher and only girl at the ad hoc baseball games on the sandlot near my home. The boys were my friends from the orthodox community; in retrospect, the fact that they raised no gender barriers is an act for which I would now, half a century later, like to thank them. I am not sure why these experiences resonate with echoes of women's liberation, but I do know that given my love of sports, it surely would have been painful for me to be sidelined because I was female.

Two other "prefeminist" experiences occurred when I was nineteen and spending seven months in Israel on a teacher's training program. One of the teachers of our mixed-gender group was a woman by the name of Nechama Lebowitz. Nechama, as she was called by all, recently died, leaving a legacy of many thousands of students, including most of the modern Orthodox rabbis in America today. She was not quite as famous then as she later became, but for me she was pathbreaking, mind-opening. Aside from being a spectacular educator, she was well versed in rabbinic texts and used them freely in her courses on the Bible. This was a totally new model for me because throughout the centuries, rabbinic texts were virtually closed to women.

The second experience took place while on a shopping trip with my roommate, Barbara Edelman. Barbara took me to a bookstore in Mea Shearim, an ultra-Orthodox section of Jerusalem, where she bought for herself several whole sets of sacred books. Though I grew up in a household surrounded by such volumes, it had never occurred to me that a woman herself could own them. Strange as it sounds now, I was then of the impression that only men could possess libraries of religious texts. But without missing a beat, I simply bought whatever Barbara bought. Even today, as I open one of those worn volumes from long ago with my name written inside the flap, I feel a small thrill. Albeit slowly, things are changing in this area: though bat mitzvah girls still get mostly jewelry and bar mitzvah boys mostly books (and one should acknowledge that girls always love the jewelry and thirteen-year-old boys don't always love the books), some girls today do begin to build their sacred libraries from bat mitzvah gifts.

After my tour of study in Israel, I returned to the United States, fell in love with a young rabbi, and married a year later, in 1957. In the early 1960s, we began our family, which would soon include five children, born within six years. I was indeed content and fulfilled. I was not in search of women's liberation. When feminism arrived at my doorstep—in the form of *The Feminine Mystique*, a gift my husband purchased for me at an airport bookshop—I could engage the matter intellectually and at arm's length. I did not come to feminism out of a sense of oppression or deprivation. In fact, the anger of others frightened me. Nevertheless, I understood that the underlying basis was just, and I could not easily let go of the idea.

Still, I did not see that any of the ideas about women's liberation had anything at all to do with Orthodox Judaism. Here was feminism and here was orthodoxy, and never the twain shall meet. Personally, I had it all—a wonderful family, validation in my community, studies in a graduate program, and a part-time career. It is fitting here to acknowledge that in addition to my husband's srong support, the ability to "have it all" was thanks to the help of other women in my household upon whom I could consistently rely. Each housekeeper or baby-sitter made it possible for me to accomplish other things in life beyond raising a family, and to each of these women I am eternally grateful.

Although secular feminism got my attention and religious feminism did not, I wasn't totally brain dead in the latter area. Like everyone else, I experienced a series of click, clicks of which I will here mention only two:

One had to do again with studying with my teacher Nechama. Toward the end of the study tour in Israel, I realized that I wanted to stay, follow her around, and study from her day and night. To earn room and board, I would be her assistant, travel with her, carry her papers, and so on. I had it all worked out. But the universal response from family and friends was that this was a wild idea for a young woman. "Come home," my parents said, which, of course, I did. My cousin, a year younger than I, came to the same conclusion the following year, at the end of his study program in Israel. He, too, wanted to stay on for another year under the tutelage of a beloved teacher. He was given great encouragement and stayed the second year. It gave me pause for thought.

The second experience took place during my mid-twenties in Washington Heights, New York, where my husband and I were then living. We were participating in a social-intellectual evening at the apartment of friends nearby. The group consisted of colleagues and friends who had gathered to hear a talk prepared by one of the group, followed by a discussion. Most of the men were rabbis or professors at Yeshiva University; most of the women, homemakers or teachers. The speaker addressed the topic of interpretation as a means of changing Jewish law. In the question-and-answer period, I raised a two-part question. I remember it well: are there any limits to interpretation, and what are the categories? The speaker, an old friend, totally dismissed my question. As an answer, he repeated what he had said earlier in the lecture, as if I somehow hadn't listened or hadn't understood. Rather than say, "That wasn't my question," I just let it go, feeling self-conscious and quite stupid. Ten minutes later a young rabbi in the group asked the very same question, and the speaker and others in the group fell all over him with his brilliant question. I remember smarting from the incident and feeling baffled by it for some time. I genuinely believed—and still do—that it was not the conscious desire of anyone in the room to put me down or humiliate me, but maybe it was something worse: the subconscious or underlying assumption that women were not capable of participating in such "high-level" discussions or that these ideas were simply not the purview of women. Fortunately, there were not all that many such incidents during that period of my life, but there were enough to retroactively call it the "righteous feminist indignation" period or the "I'm not a feminist, but . . ." period.

In 1973 a watershed experience occurred that was to forever change my life, personal and professional. This was the first National Jewish Women's Conference. By a mere fluke, I was invited to give the keynote address, and if I was a more spiritual person, I would surely say that God called me at that moment to be an Orthodox feminist, for I arrived, all at once.

I learned much from that conference, and from the preparation for my talk. Remarkably, the things I learned then have stayed with me all these years. In systematically researching the sources on women for the first time, I came to realize that a dialectic exists within the tradition regarding women's rights and roles as well as the value statements about women. On one hand, the tradition is filled with benevolence toward women, and while I know that women today are seeking equality, not benevolence, nevertheless it should be recognized that benevolence exists and is one way of looking at the tradition. Yet I also found hierarchy in the sources; contrary to what I had been taught that Jewish women were on a pedestal, I could see for myself pockets of disadvantage, disability, and discrimination. One must call a spade a spade.

Second, as I reflected on sources that span many centuries, countries, and host cultures, I came to realize that a great deal had changed, and this fact stood out in stark relief against fundamental claim of orthodoxy regarding the immutability of the tradition. From this exercise, I was able to extrapolate the principle "Where there is a rabbinic will, there is a halachic way." This principle has held up under scrutiny all these years, and I have stood by it despite continuing criticism. The reason that statement rankles others in my community is that it implies that a great deal of subjectivity is brought to the interpretation of the sources.

In preparing my remarks for the conference, I also came to see that a dialectic also exists between Orthodox Judaism and feminism. Certainly I was not about to throw out the baby with the bathwater, no matter how urgent it was to integrate the new values for women into ancient law and custom. In fact, from my traditional perspective, early feminism deserved as much of a critique from the perspective of ethical Jewish values as did orthodoxy from the perspective of women's equality. This dialectic presented an interesting challenge, and one of my memorable experiences of the conference was that of receiving half of a standing ovation. I remember it clearly. The feminists in the audience loved it when I critiqued Orthodox Judaism, but could not take the critique of feminism, which was a new orthodoxy for many Jewish women.

The experience of the conference taught me many lessons, among them the value of cohorts and the fact that so much had been taking place of which I was unaware. I learned there was a group called Ezrat Nashim (the Women's Gallery) that had been steadily working for half a dozen years to bring change to the Conservative movement. I learned how gracious it was of those who had labored in this area for years to step aside and offer the conference keynote to a virtual newcomer. A dozen pioneer Jewish feminists involved in planning the conference rightly should have come before me. I was most grateful and have tried to keep the model of their generosity before me throughout the years.

I learned something about the real power of women. The conference was truly my first direct, personal encounter with women's initiative and power. It was cutting edge, sophisticated and well organized, with over 500 participants. A handful of young women had put the whole thing together.

I learned that feminism was a way into religious tradition and not a way out, as others were suggesting. I learned that it is possible to engage a critical eye and a loving heart at one and the same moment. I learned that a woman can criticize her own faith tradition and the earth will not swallow her up. I learned that if anyone tries to push you out, you just don't have to go. I learned that there is a difference between doing something yourself and observing someone else doing it, a matter of great significance in a tradition that is highly focused on ritual.

At the conference, I began to realize how much I could learn from non-Orthodox feminists. I have been able to acknowledge that debt over the course of many years, for it has been a continuing learning experience for me. During the past thirty years, I did not become a Conservative, Reform, or Reconstructionist woman, but a great deal of my own ideas about feminism were mediated through the work and understanding of these women in their respective communities.

After the conference, I began increasingly to turn my attention to feminism and orthodoxy, as well as to following the early writings and actions of other religious feminists, Jewish and otherwise. Arlene Agus, Rachel Adler, Paula Hyman, Judith Plaskow, Cynthia Ozick, Judith Romney Wegner, Suzanna Heschel, Letty Pogrebin, Aviva Cantor Zuckoff, Letty Russell,

Rosemary Reuther, Carol Christ, Riffat Hassan, Margaret Ellen Traxler, Jeanne Audrey Powers, Len Swidler, Virginia Mollenkott, Ann Patrick Ware, to name but a few of those who influenced me. These were the pioneering religious feminists in the 1960s and 1970s, and many of them stayed the course and are present today. During the 1970s, several Orthodox rabbis—Eliezer Berkovitz, Zev Falk, Emanuel Rackman, Saul Berman, Avraham Weiss, and my husband, Irving Greenberg—were writing and lecturing on the subject of gender equality in Orthodox Judaism, and it was important to me to hear voices from the religious leadership sector of the community.

Gradually, throughout the 1970s and 1980s, a fledgling Orthodox feminist community began to grow, first around the women's prayer groups and then around the *agunah* problem. (An *agunah* is a woman anchored to a husband who refuses to grant her a Jewish legal writ of divorce that ends the marriage.) This group became a necessary and valued cohort, a new subcommunity with which to chart new paths. Their names are too numerous to mention here, but each and every one is precious to me.

In sum, during these last thirty years, I have continued to explore the dialectic in the tradition, to read, write, and lecture on the subject, participate in and organize conferences, and interface my dialogue work with Orthodox feminism. Five years ago I helped found an organization, the Jewish Orthodox Feminist Alliance (JOFA), to carry out the agenda of Orthodox feminism. Though new and small, JOFA has become a significant resource in the community, having real impact on Orthodox women's and men's lives in a relatively short period of time.

Ideologically, during these past thirty years, I have changed my mind about certain things and have deepened my conviction or ambivalence about others. Basically, however, I've remained close to the core theological beliefs I held in 1973, which is why I commented earlier that I have been on an incredible journey, without ever leaving home. I still affirm that change must be wrought within the parameters of halakha, that halakhic change comes about incrementally and through the process of interpretation of sources—and I still feel a great desire to stay firmly rooted within my community and protective of it.

This summary of the past thirty years has been brief, because I want to focus on a different aspect of the last three decades: those techniques that have enabled me to swim upstream in my own community all these years yet not feel exhausted or feel burned out. Indeed, I am often amazed at the fact that I still feel energized by the Orthodox feminist agenda, not ready to throw in towel, though there is no guarantee that might not change any day now.

Below, then, are the personal techniques I've developed over the years, twelve steps to negotiating the impasses, avoiding burnout, and staying committed.

TWELVE STEPS

1. *Celebrate the gains.* Contrary to the widely held view that nothing ever changes in orthodoxy, there have been incredible gains in orthodoxy. Looking at the last thirty years, I would probably say now that the cup is now more half full than half empty. One example is this is the area of women's study of sacred texts. This is surely the most learned generation of Jewish women in all of Jewish history. At the top of the Orthodox women's learning pyramid, we have Talmud scholars and teachers where we had none thirty years ago. This is truly a source of excitement and exhilaration. Moreover, the gains have come in every area—in ritual, liturgy, leadership, and family law. I believe that ordination for Orthodox women is just around the corner. I believe that a global solution to abuse in divorce law is also just around the corner; and I want to be part of the joy when that happens. So celebrating the gains is an important piece of the staying power.

2. *Recognize the power of women, an awesome aggregate.* Though I believe that women have not yet used their powers sufficiently, every once in a while I step back and look at the matter and realize how much power women have; women united even more so. I was sitting in the lecture hall yesterday thinking about the fact that this wonderful conference simply grew from an idea in Ann Braude's mind. That's how we all got here today. To be sure, there were many others who made this happen along the way, but the sheer power of an idea in a woman's head and the initiative of going forward with it never ceases to amaze me.

3. *Create networks.* Leaning into the networks of support and staying close to them is crucial. For me, those networks have been my family, particularly my husband, who is never afraid of criticism, and my children, who have validated my work on a daily basis; Orthodox Jewish feminists, who have grown in numbers; feminists in other denominations

and of other faiths, many of whom have been friends of many years. I had to make a choice in preparing my remarks, either to name all those who have been supportive and influential in my life or to give a talk about issues, for each would have taken the same amount of time. I chose the latter but hope that all of my friends will understand and know the love I feel for them and the gratitude at having learned so much from them.

4. *Protect oneself by choosing one's battles.* Perhaps more than anything else, the practical decision not to enter into every fray has kept me from burnout. One must be selective of the arenas for debate; one cannot take up every gauntlet thrown down, nor respond to every insult or act of baiting. I came to this decision some twenty-five years ago, on a very cold afternoon in February after Sabbath synagogue service. As I stood on the sidewalk for half an hour in debate with an earnest young man, I began to feel my toes getting frostbitten. Suddenly I realized that I could be spending the next fifty years of my life doing this very thing. Actually, I had a vision at that moment that in thirty years, someone would come around the synagogue corner and see Petrified Blu standing there.

I have chosen writing and public lecture and debate as my primary venue. While I know that I may have lost out on some wonderful one-on-one discussions and ideas and insights, I also know that I could easily have been chewed up long ago had I not learned to protect myself.

5. *Depersonalize criticism.* In the early years, I found it difficult to deal with criticism. I was stung by it. It wasn't crippling, but it was intimidating, for, like most people, I wanted to be loved by everyone. I did not want to be a misfit, but I was one, and misfits do get a certain amount of criticism. Gradually I learned to accept criticism as a form of editing. As a writer, I love the work of a good editor, but I also know that I can take it or leave it. I have learned to do exactly that with criticism: take it or leave it. At times, criticism is significantly integrated into my work; at times, I simply set it aside. In my more magnanimous moods, I will recognize that the critic is coming from the same place as I, with a desire to protect the tradition and to maintain its continuity. This enables me to see the criticism not as misogyny but as faithfulness to the tradition and fear of its erosion. I can

totally identify with these sentiments. (I must admit that such an equanimous attitude toward criticism drives some of my friends mad and evokes their criticism that I have lost the fire in my belly.)

6. *Maintain a sense of humor.* Humor is more than a talent or ability. It is an attitude toward life, an attitude throughout life: the ability to laugh at oneself, to take one's journey seriously, but not take oneself seriously at every given moment. If you lose a sense of humor along the way, you become spent, boring, and unappealing to cohorts. Worse, the joy of the journey dissipates.

7. *Know when to step back from time to time.* Many years ago I learned a valuable lesson from Jean Audrey Powers: though she was nowhere near finished with her organizational and volunteer work, she decided to declare for herself a sabbatical. Her action had great resonance for me because at the time I was beginning to feel exhausted and overextended; yet I did not want to abandon the cause nor cut my ties with organizations and projects I had been intensely involved in for many years. So I followed suit and declared a sabbatical. This gave me the ability to scale down and the time to stand back and see what was important to step back into when the self-imposed sabbatical was over. I was grateful that my friends and colleagues accepted the premise of a sabbatical—that I could reenter whenever I wanted.

   Stepping back is especially important to do before getting to the point of burnout or exhaustion, because by then the temptation is to walk away entirely. It is not surprising that so many of the early feminists are no longer involved in any way with feminism. They simply got worn out. The knowledge that you need not leave when you are tired or not contributing anything, but rather can temporarily step out and then step in again, is a wonderful, restorative feeling.

8. *Make peace with inconsistencies.* The idea that not everything need be taken to its logical conclusion and that it is perfectly all right not to have all the answers is a most liberating thought. At the beginning of my work, I was of the impression that I had to know the answer to the question, "What is your final agenda?" The question was unnerving because, in truth, I did not know what the final landscape of Orthodox feminism would look like. I felt constrained to draw a picture that sounded too radical even to my ears. In time I learned to make peace with the fact that I simply didn't know what the final scenario would

be and that there would likely be many positions that would require midcourse correction. Once I was free enough to say, "I don't know; all of the equality issues will have to be worked out in partnership with rabbinic leadership and community," I could develop a theology of distinctive-but-equal roles for orthodoxy.

9. *Make trade-offs.* As a woman holding on to the tradition while swimming in the modern world, I have come to understand the great value of making trade-offs and not to feel apologetic for them. We are engaged in a process, not a battle. Some advances will happen overnight; others are going to take much longer in a community so heavily vested in tradition and ritual. Trade-offs are part of the ongoing process. Trade-offs are the price, and not a terribly heavy one, to pay for privilege of staying within my own faith community and continuing to be nurtured by its sacred texts, teachings, and cohorts. I feel very fortunate to be an Orthodox Jew and live an Orthodox way of life, and even though I am a gadfly within the community, the fact that I can pass the tradition on to my children has been very important to me.

10. *Reconfigure one's role.* Twenty-five years ago, Letty Russell wrote that there are times when having a sense of pride is the greater merit; a sense of humility, the greater sin. I loved her words but truly didn't understand them until perhaps ten or fifteen years later, as I began to look at Orthodox feminism in a different light. Originally, I saw this enterprise as one in which I and other women were asking for a few handouts, a few crumbs, a few reinterpretations of law, a few dispensations, if I may be permitted that analogy. Suddenly it occurred to me that this was not at all what Orthodox feminism was about. What we were all about was making a contribution to the community; what we were about was squaring our shoulders and saying the following: without integrating the values of gender equality, our own traditions would be like a train standing still in a station. Orthodoxy would become moribund instead of dynamic; out of touch instead of relevant; fossilized instead of full of life. Thus we must feel a sense of pride in what we were calling for; women's new rights and roles were giving a lift to the whole tradition and whole community.

11. *Build in continuity.* Creating an organization is the primary way to do this. Organization came late to me, twenty-five years after I was involved in my first conference. The organization, I know, as many of

you in organizational life know, can also be the greatest source of burnout and frustration. On the other hand, an organization brings new energy and new cohorts, and it creates an address for people who ordinarily would not gather around the issue. An organization is really a covenantal structure: the chain grows, and the agenda passes on to a new generation. That's what I've been experiencing these last few years. Seeing that the work is being taken over by the next generation has been one of the highlights of my life. So all that energy invested in meetings and in details, and in stroking egos, which often has to be done, is really about the continuity of the agenda.

12. *Keep in mind exactly what brought me to this task in the first place.* This is all about a sense of justice. Orthodox feminism is not merely about religious tradition, or rights and responsibilities, or the details of canon law. At its heart, it is about the overarching matters of justice and ethics. One never wants to walk away from that, and one never may.

These then are the twelve steps that have kept burnout from the door, long past time it should have entered. Needless to say, these steps have not a rose garden created. Indeed, disappointments and frustrations have changed over time but have never quite totally dissipated. My disappointments today are different from the ones I felt thirty years ago, and though that should give me some perspective, nevertheless, they are ready to be put behind me. One bugaboo is that "feminism" is still a suspect word, not an honored word, neither in Orthodoxy nor in significant segments of the secular world. Legions of professional women who look out of large glass windows in corner offices see no relationship between their well-earned positions and feminism. More, they dismiss feminists as a fringe, somewhat radical group. The same thing takes place within the Orthodox community: women who have benefited from educational opportunities and the opening up of leadership roles to women distance themselves from feminism. It is quite frustrating.

Second, the frustration is personal: where did thirty years go in terms of my writing? The tension between activism and writing is enormous for me. Activism is so seductive, and writing, so isolating and requiring such discipline. Have I frittered away a God-given gift of letters?

The third disappointment concerns the same passage of thirty years. Every once in a while, I get this nagging feeling that the things we are working on are matters that really could be resolved by sleight of rabbinic hand, by creative interpretation of those who carry the chain of authority and hold the interpretive keys in their hands. In Orthodoxy, the argument is over whether women can be ordained, whether divorce law can be reformulated, whether women can read from the Torah in the synagogue. While we are doing this, Rome is burning. Violence against women, lack of peace—especially in the Middle East—the havoc of AIDS, the ravaged environment: these are the burning issues. Sometimes I wake up and ask myself, "What am I doing in this little, little box?"

Finally, there is disappointment over anti-Zionism and anti-Semitism in the women's movement. Letty Pogrebin spoke of this in detail, and I identify with all of her concerns; the only place where we differ is that she sometimes makes the choice for ethical feminist concerns even when they conflict with her passionate Zionist heart, whereas my choice is always my community, my people. I see much less danger in the potential withdrawal of abortion rights than I do in the continuous undermining of Israel's viability or in the specter of anti-Semitism rising around the world and how it will impact on my children and grandchildren. I identify with the young African American women who have spoken here about the choices they make. Moreover, I believe that a great deal of anti-Semitism and anti-Zionism in the women's movement is based on misinformation and lack of knowledge; that the women in the movement are highly intelligent yet don't want to unlearn their animosities toward Israel makes this phenomenon even more painful.

What are the challenges that lie ahead for Orthodoxy, for feminism? They are too numerous to catalog here, but I shall mention three. One is to wrestle with a new understanding of homosexuality in the context of the tradition. Given what we now know about the biological nature of homosexuality, the questions are more theological than anything else. Why did God create homosexuals and then disallow them in sacred law? It is a mystery to me.

A second challenge is to figure out the ways in which equality and gender role distinction can coexist. I believe there is a place for distinct-but-equal roles for men and women; and my gut tells me that there are places beyond biology where male and female roles suit the human psyche quite well. But what are the limits? What are the categories? The global differentiations in roles and responsibilities no longer work, but what are the fine distinctions and who will be the ones to define them?

The third challenge is a personal one: How will I continue to feel the power of the Commanding Voice in my life as I go through this process? I'm not an authoritarian personality, yet I have always found comfort in the idea of God as the source of authority and commandments as emanations from that source. Observing God's law has always been a way of God speaking to me, and me speaking to God. Reinterpreting the law is one of the ways in which traditional Jews make changes that are seamless with the past yet meet new realities and needs. On the other hand, existentially, I begin to feel in my bones a weakening of the powerful sense of the Commanding Voice in all that I do. I can live with this, and have lived with it. I believe, as my husband has written, that we are part of the generation after the Holocaust that accepts the covenant as a voluntary covenant. Yet perhaps because of my own background and upbringing, I know that too much emphasis on volunteerism won't quite sustain me as *Homo religiosis.* Thus one of the great challenges, as we tinker with the tradition, is to find ways to build in inspiration and awe as we move forward.

Still, in all, I can look at my life these last thirty years and acknowledge that it has been thoroughly exhilarating, a great blessing, with more ups than downs. I cannot imagine how boring my life would have been without all the energy and drama, the incredible gains, the new strengths and new challenges for women. I can wake up every morning, and—bending the sacred liturgy a bit—I can recite as part of my morning blessings these words: "Thank God for creating me a woman."

INDEX